DATE DUE

ISRAEL ON THE SEVENTH DAY

Israel
ON THE SEVENTH DAY

by Ruth Gruber

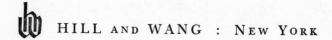 HILL AND WANG : NEW YORK

TO PHIL

Contents

MAPS

Photographs appear between pages 118 and 119.

In Appreciation

This book is a summing up. Except for the history and the battles, it is a record of what I saw, felt, and learned since I first went to Palestine right after World War II.

A list of the people and organizations that helped make this book possible would read like a small telephone directory. I owe them all my deep gratitude. But I want to thank especially the late New York *Herald Tribune*, the newspaper for which I was the correspondent in Israel over many years, *Look, Reader's Digest, Collier's, Survey Graphic, The New Republic, Saturday Review, Hadassah Magazine*, the United Jewish Appeal, the National Broadcasting Company, and the Ford Foundation for permission to use material which I first wrote for them as articles, columns, pamphlets, reports, or dramatic scripts.

I owe special thanks to my friends Cyrilly Abels, Katherine Bregman, Joey Criden, Paul Freeman, Sylvia and Lou Horwitz, Jen Kessler, Dan Levin, Pnina Shallon, and to my editor Frank Brunotts for their tireless editorial help; to my children Celia and David Michaels, who are my best researchers and who help me see Israel fresh through their eyes; and to my husband Phil Michaels, whose book this is.

R.G.

"The Six Day War is over, but the Seventh Day, the day of rest, has not yet been gained."

—YITZHAK RABIN

1

"We Were Like Them That Dream"

T<small>HIS WAS</small> my fifteenth trip to Israel, but in a sense it was my first. I had never known an Israel like this before. The war was over—but soldiers were still dying. There was victory—but peace was unreal. They had fought six days, and on the seventh day they did not rest. Yet there was a Sabbath mood in the whole land.

They had conquered enemies forty times their size on four fronts. Yet they did not look like conquerors. They looked like what they were: high school youngsters who had gone into the infantry, college students who had become air force pilots (along with veteran pilots who had been flying for El Al Airlines), taxicab drivers and scientists, young farmers who became paratroopers, shopkeepers from Casablanca, butchers and bakers from Czernowitz and Budapest, middle-aged reservists called from their desks and farms. They did not look like conquerors at all.

And they weren't. They had not fought for conquest, but for the life of their land. They had fought for wives, children, parents—for preservation. The enemy had vowed, officially, to exterminate them.

What had made the difference that I felt now? Was it what the Israelis had done in six days in June? Or were those climactic hours only one manifestation of what the Israelis had been working toward for twenty years?

The change, I finally decided, lay in a new sense of unity, and of nationhood. Somehow what many of us had feared—a nation divided between Jews from the Western World and Jews from Moslem lands—seemed no longer a danger. After three weeks of tension and the lightning war the two nations had become sealed into one.

The process was not yet complete, to be sure. Israel's old problems had not been magically solved. Poverty and illiteracy and serious unemployment were still present; the differences between the educated and the uneducated remained. But for years the question in many minds had been: How would the Moroccan Jews, the Tunisian Jews, the Algerian and Yemenite and Iraqi Jews react when the guerrilla war the Arabs were waging moved onto the battlefield?

The war in June gave the answer. The Jews from Egypt in the Israeli army stood and fought and, when need be, died. The Arab soldiers in the Egyptian army fought bravely, but many of their officers took off their uniforms and ran away.

This was a war fought by immigrants, new and old. Israel is a land of immigration, and in nineteen years one million four hundred thousand newcomers had been taken in. Nearly six hundred thousand were Jews who had come from Arab lands in a kind of reciprocal though involuntary exchange for the six hundred thousand Arab refugees. The Jews from North Africa and Moslem lands now make up 60 per cent of Israel's population and, in an army composed of civilians and reservists, they make up at least 60 per cent of the army.

With skins ranging from white, to shades of gold, to black, Jews from Yemen and Ethiopia, from Afghanistan and Cochin, India, from Persia and Libya and Iraq fought side by side with European Jews who had blue numbers stenciled on their arms. They fought with men who had fled from communist lands, and with those born in Israel. Together they drove their tanks into the fire of the Gaza Strip and the Sinai desert, confronted the Arab Legion in the narrow passageways of Jerusalem's Old City, stormed the Golan Heights in the north.

Some of these soldiers, barely a decade ago, had come out of the Middle Ages. Some had never seen a fork or a car or an airplane.

Some had lived, illiterate and unskilled, in caves in Libya and in the Atlas Mountains north of the Sahara. Yet now they or their sons had fought the Arabs and defeated them.

A nation is an abstract thing. For nineteen years Israel had taken in Jews from seventy-nine lands; they belonged to one people but they were not one nation. This people became a nation in 1967.

Nor was the change only in Israel. In America, in England and France, in South Africa and Germany and Italy thousands of Jews and non-Jews acted as if their lives would be bereft of meaning if Israel fell. Why? Other small countries had been surrounded and attacked. What was it about this beleaguered land that made Patrick O'Donovan, a famous Irish correspondent writing for the *London Observer* from Israel, cable, "One is almost ashamed of not being a Jew"?

Perhaps, I thought, if one talked to old friends and new ones, walked and drove across the whole land, trudged again through the little development towns where most of the new immigrants from Arab lands had settled, one might unravel some of the latest enigmas in the three-thousand-year mystery of Jewish survival. For almost two decades I had been wrestling with that mystery as I journeyed to Israel almost every year for the New York *Herald Tribune*, witnessing nearly every crisis and every triumph. From the first shock of the concentration camps and the D.P. camps, to the tragic voyage of the ship *Exodus 1947*, to the birth of Israel and the War of Independence, on through the great migrations in which whole countries were emptied of Jews; as I flew with the Yemenites up the Red Sea, sailed with Moroccans out of North Africa, lived with newcomers from Africa and Europe in isolated little frontier towns, trekked through boom towns bursting out of the desert, and watched Israel mature, until she could share with other developing countries what she had learned through trial and error—through all of twenty years I had witnessed nearly every step in this nation's and this people's growth, obsessed by the mystery of Jewish survival even as I sought to record it.

Then came May 1967. Egypt blockaded the Gulf of Aqaba, massed troops and Russian tanks on the Sinai border; Jordan was armed and poised on the east; Syria on the north pointed her guns down from the Golan Heights. All were screaming death to Israel. It was life or death, annihilation or survival. It was the greatest crisis in twenty years. Israel's doom seemed certain.

Then came the breathtaking Six Day War. When the fighting stopped and the results of the battles became clear, the longing to return to Israel, where I had been only a few months before the war, and the desire to participate and understand were over-whelming. So, six weeks after the war, I returned, with my husband and two children, to explore and prowl, to search and comprehend.

We spent our first days and nights in Jerusalem—among the first to move into the Old City—talking, looking, listening, walk-ing, walking endlessly through the labyrinthine passageways. Barbed wire still blocked the roads. Houses were sliced down the front, like stages on which the curtain had been raised, exposing bedrooms and living rooms in pastel colors, stairways that led nowhere, stoves and refrigerators that looked like props. Skinny cats cried and wild dogs howled outside our balcony every night.

Friends from the other side of Jerusalem asked us: "Aren't you afraid? There's still a curfew. There are still snipers . . . mines . . . unexploded shells . . ." Afraid? Of what? The air was shat-tered every day as mines were discovered and detonated, but I had never felt so secure in all my visits to Israel.

For the first time we could pass through the Mandelbaum Gate, a euphemism for the ugly corrugated-iron shed spanning the road where Abraham Mandelbaum, a scholarly merchant, had built a parapeted house for his family. Mandelbaum entered history when the armistice line of 1949, which broke Jerusalem in two, was drawn through his war-wrecked house. Only a few years before, I had stood beneath the shed, waiting to welcome an old friend, the Reverend Edler Hawkins, the first Negro to be elected Moderator of the United Presbyterian Church of the United States, who was coming to Israel from the Arab world less than two city blocks away in Jordan. Carrying his own suitcases in the late August sun, he walked up the lonely no-man's-land road like a tiny figure in a Dali landscape. The broken houses of the War of 1948 lay still untouched on the Jordanian side. Beyond the road and the rubble lay the Old City, barred to us for nineteen years. Now, like liberated people, we went back and forth through the Mandelbaum Gate at all hours, until the shed was taken down and the barrier remained only a memory.

We stayed in the St. George Hotel, on the Old City side of the Mandelbaum Gate, and because most people were still afraid to stay overnight in the Old City we were the hotel's only guests. Three Arab night watchmen, having no one else to watch, sat vigil outside our bedrooms every night. In the huge dining room Arab waiters had only our table to serve. Sayid, a slim, handsome young man of twenty-five with liquid brown eyes and dark hair, hovered over us as we ate Israeli rolls baked on the other side of the Mandelbaum Gate.

"We are Israelis," Sayid said. They were the first words he spoke, as if in salute. "And we are happy. We travel all over Israel just to look—Tel Aviv, Natanya, Haifa. Who would have believed it, a thirty-four-story building in Tel Aviv! We never heard about it. We never saw anything like it in our lives."

Sayid, born in Abu Ghosh, a green and lush mountain village in Israel's Judean hills, had grown up in Jordan, where in 1948 his mother had taken her children to live as refugees while his father stayed in their house in the Israeli village.

"This war brought us together," Sayid said. "We didn't see my father for nineteen years. Now I cannot see him enough. I go every day to see him after work. I take the bus from the Damascus Gate to the Egged Station in Yerushalayim." He pronounced the most beautiful of all of Israel's place names in Hebrew, and it did not seem strange. "Then I take another bus, and in fourteen minutes, I am in Abu Ghosh."

"What do you like best when you travel around Israel?"

"The people. I love the people. Their hearts are white. Not like here. They love. They don't hate."

We knew he might be talking for our benefit, saying what he thought we wanted to hear, but we were willing to believe some of it. For an air of bewilderment and wonder still infiltrated every conversation, whether with Arabs or with Jews, in the weeks right after the war.

In the dimly lit cavernous lobby friends came to visit, almost tiptoeing, like archaeologists on the site of a once lost civilization. They greeted us out of the Psalms:

> When the Lord turned again the captivity of Zion,
> We were like them that dream.
> Then was our mouth filled with laughter,
> And our tongue with singing.

Day and night Hassidic Jews in long black caftans, soldiers with Israeli-made Uzi machine guns slung on leather straps, men and women and little children wearing the clothes of the lands they had come from prowled the streets of the Old City as though they needed to reassure themselves each waking moment that the dream was real.

Inevitably, myth began to overtake reality. Yet one sensed a special air of mystery, a religious awe I had not known in the War of 1948 or the Sinai War of 1956. The word "miracle" was on the lips of everyone—the devout, the orthodox, the agnostic, the atheistic, and the religiously indifferent.

On Mount Zion, near the Tomb of David, an Israeli unit had stood on a rooftop shooting at Jordan's Arab legionnaires less than fifty yards away. "I can't understand it," their commanding officer said later, pointing to the spot where the Arabs had been dug in. "The Jordanians were tough fighters; the toughest in the war. Yet every shot we fired, we saw a man fall. Then they ran. It was as if an unseen hand—an unseen army—was helping us."

Deborah Wigodor, a white-haired Irish-American woman who had converted to Judaism, talked of a boy from North Africa in the tank corps: "He tried to cut himself off from his immigrant father. He broke with religion completely. He was in a tank in Sinai when it was hit. He helped get the two other men out and then found the hatch was somehow closed. He was alone and terrified. Without thinking he began the ancient Jewish prayer 'Shma Israel': 'Hear, O Israel. . . .' Then, 'My God,' he said, 'I don't know the rest.'

"He tormented himself; he shivered in the desert heat, trying to recall his childhood, everything he had rebelled against. Suddenly the words *'Shma Israel, Adonai Elohainu, Adonai Echad'* came back to him. He put his hand up and the hatch opened and he was saved."

A soldier described how his company had fought the Arab Legion at the Mandelbaum Gate. "One of our group, a Hassid with earlocks under his field helmet, was frightened. We all were. He had a sack of hand grenades. He would dig into the sack, as if it were a bag of potatoes. He'd pull out a grenade, cover his eyes with his left hand, mutter the 'Shema,' and toss the grenade. We all fought, but I think he alone drove back the Arabs, and we took the Mandelbaum Gate."

We visited General Ezer Weizman, who built the Israeli air force. "Miracles? Bah!" scoffed the General as he paced up and down the room, reliving the war. "Ridiculous. We had good organization. Good weapons. Hard, damn good training. And above all, dedication and a love of Israel. . . . That's what you can't teach . . . how to love your country. That comes from long history, and being rooted to the Jewish past. That's how we won the war."

But some of the youth had rebelled against their long history, and especially against their Jewish roots. In the early sixties middle-class parents in Israel had been tormented (no less than middle-class parents in America) because their adolescent children were in danger of losing their idealism, their sense of pioneering. Materialism had made them soft. Rebellion against their parents' idealism had turned some into cynics and nihilists, others into delinquents. They were, to be sure, only a small number, but visible enough so that a new label was created, "B'nai Tovim" (literally, "The Sons of the Good")—rebellious teenagers who stole cars and broke windows, though their fathers owned cars and their families lived in elegant suburban homes. Thanks to the Arabs threatening death to Israel, much of the alienation had ended two or three years before the war in June. Rebellion and delinquency evaporate when there is a common enemy outside the borders.

Miriam Eshkol, the young librarian wife of the Prime Minister, recalled a visit she had made with her husband to friends in Haifa: "They had a son interested in absolutely nothing that they cared about. He was almost anti-Israel. All of a sudden he decided to become a frogman—one of the most dangerous jobs in the war.

When the war ended and he came home, he had a breakdown. Finally, when he recovered, we said to him, 'Why did you volunteer—of all things—as a frogman?' He said, 'I think I owe it to the six million.' "

A day before the war Israelis were still worrying about their "discotheque youths," more at home in the nightclubs of Tel Aviv than in the border villages of the Galilee and the Negev. But under fire these untested young people became the backbone of the conscripted army. Of Israel's three wars this was truly the war in which the *sabras* (the native-born) and the new immigrants fought as one. And like the two Israels that moved toward becoming one nation in the war, the once alienated youth came home.

There was no exultation in their victory. On returning from the battlefront some sat alone in their bedrooms for days, unable to talk. When they finally emerged, their families learned of the comrades who had died next to them, or in their arms.

"I strangled an Arab with my own hands," a young soldier blurted out. "But I couldn't help it. He was trying to strangle me. . . ."

The number of Israeli combat casualties, 679 dead and 2,500 wounded, had reached into the whole population. For a people who had known decimation, it was a staggering loss. Proportionately in the United States it would have been 60,000. From the mountain city of Safad in the north, a friend had written us: "Women who were young yesterday have grown old overnight. One of our friends learned yesterday morning that her first-born son, a pilot, was shot down. In the afternoon her second son, also a pilot, was killed in action in the Golan Heights. Today her first-born son was brought home alive. Those boys belong to all of us."

Yet there was little hatred of the enemy. How was it possible, people asked each other, that the soldiers fought without hate? Even the Jews who had lived in Arab lands and been persecuted seemed to fight without hate. There were some, of course, who saw their comrades killed and who fought blindly, furiously. But now, with a war ended that they had not asked for, they spoke of the enemy with neither bitterness nor hate. How could one explain it?

Each day in Jerusalem I walked to the Wailing Wall, in Hebrew the Western Wall, to touch the gnarled and pocked and sun-beaten stones. Deep in the ground, below these stones, was the wall Solomon had touched—Solomon who had asked God for "an understanding heart." And a kind of yearning seemed to come through the stones, a yearning for the wisdom to understand these past twenty years of Israel's existence, and perhaps through them, the mystery of Israel's survival.

2

"Earth, Conceal Not the Blood
Shed on Thee"

I HAD COME to Palestine straight from visiting the Displaced Persons camps of Germany. It was early in 1946. The war in Europe was over. The liberating armies had opened the gates of the gas chambers and found the remains of six million Jews. A handful were still alive, their faces gaunt, their bodies debilitated. They had touched death and survived.

The Allies had set up the D.P. camps to feed and house the victims of the war and nurse them back to health. As the Jews returned to life, they left the camps and went back to the villages and towns of eastern Europe where they had been born. They went searching for their families, but everyone was dead. So the Jews left their old homes and went west again, to Germany, in the hope that from there they could go south across the Mediterranean. A new dream was stirring—Palestine.

But Palestine was barred to them by the British. It is ironical that the British, who had promised to establish the National Homeland in 1917, turned the D.P.'s away. In the failure of the promise, in the waste and the betrayal, the seeds of the war in June 1967 were sown.

For numerous reasons Britain, fighting the Turks in the Middle East in the First World War, had espoused the cause of the Jews. Colonial France and imperial Britain were vying for the spoils of the Ottoman Empire. There were no Arab states then; new nations would be created and Palestine, which had not been a nation for two thousand years, was marked off for "special treatment" by the two powers in their secret and infamous Sykes-Picot Agreement of 1916. France's sphere of influence was to be in the northern Mediterranean—Syria and Lebanon. Britain would get nearly everything else except the Holy Land, whose fate was yet to be determined.

Britain, in spite of the secret agreement, decided Palestine belonged within her colonial orbit. But she needed an excuse. The opportunity came fortuitously in the middle of the war. She had cut down most of her trees from which she derived the acetone used in making gunpowder. Her guns were running dry. She turned to Dr. Chaim Weizmann,* then working in his chemistry laboratory in Manchester, and Dr. Weizmann in a few weeks perfected his own invention, a new fermentation process for making synthetic acetone from starch.

The legend has grown that it was as a wartime reward to Dr. Weizmann that the British issued the famous Balfour Declaration on November 2, 1917, a turning point in Jewish history. This declaration proclaimed to the world that the British government favored "the establishment of a National Home in Palestine." Dr. Weizmann himself disputed the legend. "I almost wish it had been as simple as that," he wrote in his autobiography *Trial and Error*, "and that I had never known the heartbreaks, the drudgery and the uncertainties which preceded the Declaration. But history does not deal in Aladdin's lamps."

The promise of a national homeland was given the Jews, Weizmann believed, because British statesmen, such as Lloyd George, then prime minister, and Lord Arthur Balfour, his foreign secretary, "were genuinely religious. They understood as a reality the concept of the Return. It appealed to their tradition and faith." Lunching with Lloyd George at 10 Downing Street on November 11, 1918, the day the war ended, Weizmann found him reading the Psalms, "moved to the depths of his soul."

But religious faith was strongly buttressed by politics. The

* Dr. Weizmann spelled his name with two n's; his nephew, General Ezer Weizman, spells it with one. English spelling in Israel is still capricious.

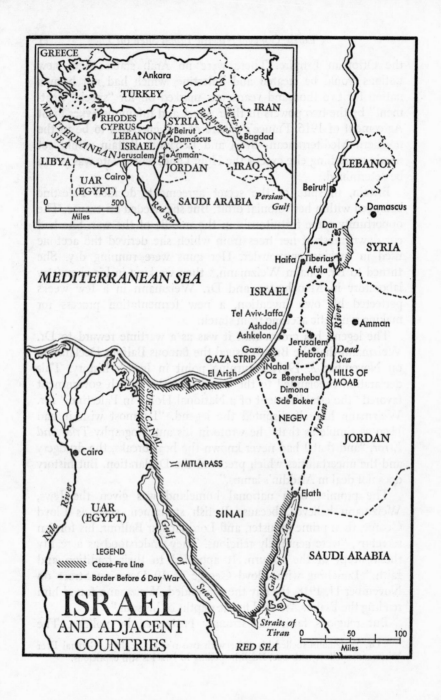

ISRAEL AND ADJACENT COUNTRIES

LEGEND

||||| Cease-Fire Line

- - - - Border Before 6 Day War

geography of the Holy Land, crossroads of Europe, Africa, and Asia, made it a heartland for Britain's thrust into Arabia and India. To the British leaders, Zionist or anti-Zionist, pro-Jewish or pro-Arab, Palestine would have to remain part of the Empire.

To reassure the Arabs, General Edmund Allenby had suggested to Dr. Weizmann that he journey to Amman to talk with the Emir Feisal. It was June 1918. The war was in a critical stage and the Turks were still in the Jordan Valley. But General Allenby, who had entered the Holy City of Jerusalem on December 8, 1917, wanted Weizmann to talk with "the only representative Arab whose influence was of more than local importance."

Weizmann took the long journey through Suez to the Gulf of Aqaba and then overland by car, camel, and foot to the head-quarters of the Arab army, where officers riding camels came out to greet him with gifts of the desert: water and fruit. The Emir was surrounded by his warriors, among whom moved the mysterious Lawrence of Arabia.

Sitting in the Emir's tent, Dr. Weizmann explained his mission to Feisal, assuring him that the Jews wanted to do everything in their power "to allay Arab fears and susceptibilities." The Emir, Dr. Weizmann recorded, "was eager to see the Jews and Arabs working in harmony . . . in his view the destiny of the two people was linked with the Middle East and must depend on the good will of the Great Powers."

The Emir proved to be prophetic. The two people would, from thence on, be linked with the Middle East, their fates determined to a large degree by the Great Powers, then England and France, and, long after the Emir and Dr. Weizmann were dead, the United States and the Soviet Union.

The two leaders became lifelong friends, and at the Versailles Peace Conference Feisal, spokesman of the Arabs, recognized the Balfour Declaration, accepting "the fullest guarantees" for imple-menting it with all "its necessary measures to encourage and stimulate immigration of Jews into Palestine on a large scale." It was a historic moment of Arab-Jewish accord.

Nations, being only human, have the weaknesses of men. Greed outweighs religious faith and self-preservation circumvents the law. Britain, having decided she needed Palestine more than the Jews needed a home, made certain that she would be given the mandate for Palestine.

"We should so order our policy that when the time comes to choose a mandatory power for its [Palestine's] control . . . we shall be the most likely candidate," wrote Sir Mark Sykes, the colorful Foreign Office advisor who was both pro-Zionist and pro-Arab, to Sir Robert Cecil, one of the founders of the League of Nations.

Britain's maneuvers succeeded. At the San Remo Conference in 1920 Britain was given the mandate, and the League of Nations ratified it in 1922. The Jewish Agency for Palestine was created in 1929 to represent the Jews in their relationship with the Mandatory Government. Later, the Jewish Agency became the shadow government of the Jews in the homeland.

In 1921 the British, beginning a long and sordid story of betrayal, unilaterally chopped off four-fifths of Palestine, handing the whole East Bank on a platter to King Abdullah, grandfather of King Hussein. It was called the kingdom of Transjordan, whose very name meant the other side of the Jordan.

The years from 1922 until 1948 were years of turmoil in Palestine. Jews in eastern Europe were carefully selected by representatives of the Jewish Agency or by Zionist leaders in their own countries to create an elite of young men and women, intellectuals and idealists, who would train to become farmers and migrate to Palestine. The Jewish National Fund, set up at the end of the nineteenth century to acquire land-holdings in Palestine, continued to buy land, most of which the Arabs regarded as worthless. Over much of it only Bedouins roamed, their goats nibbling away the last roots of life. The Jewish farmers fought a desperate battle with the swamps and the desert. Many died of malaria. Newcomers from Europe replaced them. The return from the ghettos of Europe was essentially a return to the land. And because these were idealists who were returning, they chose a form of communal life based on their ideals—a unique agricultural community called the *kibbutz*. No one owned anything; profits from farming, and later from industries in the village, were the property of the whole kibbutz. No one was to grow rich from the sweat of another man's face.

The kibbutz was a mirror of the Jewish state long before the state was born. At the turn of the century it was a lonely island in a sea of Bedouins and "Turkmen," who had been brought to Palestine by the ruling Turks to counterbalance the Arabs. With no one to protect them, the Jews learned to protect themselves. In 1907 they organized the Hashomer (the Watchman); they learned to farm with a plow and a gun. Later they evolved a special kibbutz architecture; the first building they put up was the watch-tower with barbed wire and trenches; and even while they lived in tents and in deserted Arab shacks, they built defense walls around their villages—stone walls with holes in them for guns.

The Jews realized quickly that they could not depend on the British to defend them. At a conference in 1920, held in Kinneret, a village on the Sea of Galilee, they decided to dissolve the Hashomer and create a new organization, the Haganah (self-defense). The *Yishuv*, the Jewish community in Palestine, made up essentially of farmers and workers, would now become fighters as well. It was a new chapter in Jewish peoplehood. Jews had always been people of the Book. Now they were in the Land, and they would have to fight to survive. They were learning a lesson that would turn the tide in the war in 1967: to rely only on themselves; to develop the military capability of insuring their existence.

The Mandatory Government soon began to set up schools and health clinics for the Arabs, while they left the Jews to take care of their own needs. It was to be a blessing far beyond any British conjecture. Forced to fend for themselves, the Jews created their own school system, their own hospitals, their own welfare institutions, and their own political administration—all of which became the nucleus for a Jewish state.

In the early and comparatively peaceful years of the twenties, the Arabs saw a new Palestine emerging, with seedling trees planted on barren hills to hold back the soil, and rich fields of wheat and barley and sesame and fodder on the old malarial swamps. The civilization of the Jews spilled over; the Arab standard of living began to rise, their life span lengthened, their babies ceased dying like flies under a D.D.T. barrage. Jewish doctors and nurses, many of them Americans sent by Hadassah, began to cure trachoma, the dread disease of the desert which for generations had left the Arabs' eyes milk-white sockets of blindness. Now their children were healed before the disease could scar them forever.

This was the era of nationalism, and its magnetism attracted Arabs as well as Jews. More Arab children began to go to school— mostly boys, since education was frowned on by most parents for their daughters. Young men attended the American College at Beirut, some went to Oxford and Princeton; and they became increasingly articulate in their desire for nationhood.

But the new civilization which the Jews had brought to the desert land was a threat to the sheiks and the mukhtars, the Arab chiefs who for generations had controlled their extended families. Rejecting the Jews, the chiefs led riots against them; sporadic at first, the riots grew in intensity and number, attracting especially the nationalists who were anti-British as well as anti-Jewish.

Saturday, August 24, 1929, in Motza, a mountain village in the Hills of Judea approaching Jerusalem, a band of thirty Arabs, brandishing curved knives, broke into a small hotel and slaughtered the owner, his two daughters, his twenty-two-year-old son, and the two hotel guests, an old rabbi and a visitor from Tel Aviv. They robbed, then burned the hotel, and continued on to another house where they murdered the Makleff family. One of the children, young Mordecai, hid from the Arabs and escaped. Later he would become one of Israel's chiefs of staff; and Motza, in 1967, would be singled out by the Jordanians in a secret battle order: ". . . carry out a raid on MOTZA colony, to destroy it and kill all its inhabitants."

The same Saturday, August 24, 1929, in Jerusalem, the Arabs attacked thickly populated sections of the Old City and the new quarters the Jews were building up. The Haganah fought back, but the Arabs, far outnumbering them, broke into houses with knives and shrieks, wounding and murdering. The British police did nothing for two hours. Their acquiescence was not lost on the Arabs.

The worst slaughter on that same Sabbath day was in Hebron. The British-appointed Arab governor disarmed the police. No one stopped the butchery. Sixty-five Jews were murdered, while the governor wired the British in Jerusalem: "Hebron all right."

The Jews knew now—if they had not known before—what lay in store for them if they did not arm and protect themselves. Hebron was a turning point in Jewish survival, a blood-stained symbol and a warning.

The crisis grew acute with Hitler's rise to power in 1933. In the first years, Hitler allowed Jews to leave Germany, and in three years seventy thousand emigrated to Palestine. The Arabs went on a new rampage in 1936, led by Haj Amin el-Husseini, the Mufti of Jerusalem, who had captured control of the Arab nationalists, and who later spent the war years with Hitler in Germany.

The Mufti's guerrilla forces attacked the kibbutzim, burning houses and fields. But the Haganah was now better prepared and fought back. The kibbutzim became strongholds which the Arabs could not storm; they turned to murdering travelers on the roads.

The Haganah was concerned only with self-defense. But there were young men and women who felt self-defense was not enough; they left the Haganah and formed the Irgun Zvai Leumi (known as Etzel, a secret underground organization) and later the Stern Group to fight the Arabs, drive the British out, and free Palestine.

Everything has a rhythm. After each riot, the British sent a commission of inquiry to study the problem. Regularly, the commission members trekked to Palestine, talked to the Arabs and the Jews, and filed their reports, with recommendations. The British Foreign Office acted, of course, only on those recommendations that justified its policy.

After the 1936 riots they sent a Royal Commission, composed of distinguished lawyers and scholars and headed by Lord Peel, to study the problem again and find a solution. "If you want us to grow," an Arab suggested, "tear us apart." The Peel Commission Report, issued in 1937, recommended that Palestine be "torn apart"—partitioned into a Jewish state and an Arab state. The members of the commission were not cutting the Solomon baby. They were separating two peoples who were experiencing the growing pains of nationalism.

The report of the Peel Commission was never implemented. But in its essence it was to turn up again at the United Nations in November 1947.

The British, following the hallowed colonial doctrine of "divide and rule," had long befriended the Arabs; now, as the Arab guerrilla fighters, led by the Mufti, threatened to grow out of control, the British allowed Captain Orde Wingate to help the Jews master their art of self-defense.

Wingate was a maverick Scot. Like Lloyd George and Arthur Balfour, he believed in the Biblical prophecy of the Return. He chose bright men in their early twenties and taught them the strategy of surprise and the concept of mobility. "Get out into the open," he schooled them. "Fight in the enemy's territory." He was a hard taskmaster whose pupils adored him. He drilled them in a motto they would never forget: "Know the enemy."

They began to know the enemy. They studied the Arabs—their psychology, their emotions, their dreams. The Arabs were frightened of the darkness; Wingate's youngsters, known as Wingate's Night Squads, learned to fight at night. Two of his disciples were unknown teenagers named Moshe Dayan and Yigal Allon. Dayan would become the hero of the war in Sinai in 1956 and the war in June 1967; and Allon would become the head of the Palmach (the striking force of the Haganah), which surrounded a young Egyptian officer named Gamal Abdel Nasser in the Negev in the War of Independence and would later become Minister of Labor. Had Wingate lived (he was killed in Burma in 1944), he would have seen his lesson—know the enemy—carried out almost flawlessly exactly thirty years later.

In 1939, just as Hitler shut the gates completely, trapping most of the Jews of Europe, Britain decided to end the whole pretext of a Jewish homeland. A "White Paper" was issued, and this time Britain began to implement it. Jewish immigration would be restricted to fifteen hundred a month for five years, after which no more Jews could enter. The sale of land to Jews was limited to 5 per cent of the country. Palestine would become an Arab state.

On September 1, 1939, the Germans marched into Poland, and Britain declared war on Germany two days later. The Jews of Palestine pleaded with the British to let them join the fight against Hitler. David Ben-Gurion, then Chairman of the Jewish Agency Executive in Jerusalem, issued his famous edict: "We shall fight the White Paper as if there were no war; we shall fight the war as if there were no White Paper."

Their backs to the wall, the British finally agreed to allow the Jews to fight Hitler; they dropped young Haganah men and women behind the enemy lines in Hungary, Yugoslavia, and Romania. Some were captured, tortured, and killed. In 1941 the Jews created the Palmach; trained by the British, they fought against Rommel in the desert and the Vichy French in Syria. Dayan lost an eye fighting for the British; Ezer Weizman became a pilot in the Royal Air Force; and the Jewish Brigade, made up entirely of Palestinian Jews, fought part of the war in Italy.

Throughout the Middle East, the Arabs spent most of the war as "neutrals," or openly allied with the Axis. The Arabs of Iraq attempted a Nazi coup, and several of the Arab leaders of Palestine joined the Mufti in Germany, perfecting genocide.

Though grateful to the Jews who were fighting the Axis in Europe and the Middle East, and fully aware of Hitler's murders, the British still locked the Jews out of Palestine. Just as the Germans fought two simultaneous wars—a war against the Allies and a war against the Jews—so the British fought two wars, a war against the Axis and a war against the Jews who were trying to escape Hitler and enter Palestine. In Germany, the Wehrmacht fought the Allies, and the S.S. fought the Jews. In Britain, the army fought the Axis, and the Foreign Office fought the Jews. Ships carrying refugees who had managed to escape the Nazi ovens were sent back by the British or sunk. A few thousand Jews were brought to Palestine illegally both by the Haganah and the Irgun in the midst of the war, but one-third of the Jews of the world had no escape route and were shot or gassed or burned in crematoria.

Working in Washington during the war as Special Assistant to the Secretary of the Interior, I learned of the slaughter. We knew the report "Acquiescence of this Government in the Murder of the Jews" that was given to President Roosevelt by Henry Morgenthau, Jr., the Secretary of the Treasury. Cables were being sent from Switzerland to the State Department describing the gas chambers and the murder of the Jews.

It was 1944. Millions were already dead. But now the Germans were losing; Eichmann was in Hungary, and it was possible to negotiate for the lives of one million Hungarian Jews. "One million Jews for ten thousand trucks," Eichmann had proposed to

Joel Brand, a Hungarian member of the underground. "Whom do you want to save? Men capable of procreation? Women who can bear children? Old people? Children?"

Rabbi Stephen Wise and Dr. Nahum Goldmann, whom President Roosevelt regarded as Jewish spokesmen, traveled back and forth to Washington to plead with the President and the State Department for the lives of the Hungarian Jews. I would see them, frustrated, yet somehow always hopeful. Surely the United States, with its great traditions of compassion and refuge, would save a million Jews from the furnaces. Years later Goldmann would confess that the great crime of his life was his silence; his guilt was that he had not cried out the truth, that hundreds of thousands of people had not stormed the White House and the State Department to alert the conscience of the American people. But would the United States have taken in the Jews from Hungary? "The plain fact," Eichmann wrote later in his own story, "was that there was no place on earth that would have been ready to accept the Jews, not even this one million."

We learned afterward that the Jews in Europe themselves could not believe the atrocities. Elie Wiesel, the poet of the holocaust, tells of a man who had escaped from Auschwitz and returned to his village in Romania on the Russian border. He described the tortures and the ovens. He begged the people to flee across the border while there was still time. Nobody believed him. In the end he sat insanely on the street, muttering that the people must leave. Nobody listened.

By January 1944, when some of the facts could no longer be denied, President Franklin D. Roosevelt created the War Refugee Board to help rescue "the victims of enemy oppression." One thousand refugees would be brought to the United States and housed in a former army camp at Oswego, New York, to be administered by Secretary of the Interior Ickes. Ickes sent me to Italy in August 1944 to accompany the refugees to America.

The people, all Hitler's victims, were mostly Jews, but there were also Protestants and Roman and Greek Orthodox Catholics among them. They had escaped to southern Italy from eighteen countries that Hitler had overrun. While Nazi planes flew near, they waited for several days aboard ship in Naples—part of a convoy of thirty-two ships that would steam across the Atlantic—not knowing why they were waiting. Suddenly the cause of their delay climbed up the Jacob's ladder, wearing a big straw hat, a bright blouse, and sailor's pants. A naval officer had given me the pants, knowing there would be thousands of eyes watching me swing up the side of the ship. "Why it's Mrs. Roosevelt," someone shouted as I was lifted aboard. (Surely a convoy would wait only for Eleanor.)

Each day and night as the ship steamed across the Atlantic I learned something of what it meant to be a Jew in Hitler's Europe. I had been born a Jew; but on this voyage, I *became* a Jew. Suddenly every life was sacred. Every face was the face of survival. Many of the refugees had tried to get to Palestine. Some told of having left the Balkans on an unseaworthy ship named the *Pentcho* that had sailed down the Danube bound for Palestine. No country along the river would let them in; no port would give them water. They painted the word "Hunger" on the ship. No one cared. The captain and his wife were drug addicts, growing fat on money from fleeing Jews. They were shipwrecked in the Aegean Sea; they were rescued and interned in Italian concentration camps until American G.I.'s liberated them.

For the next eighteen months I was to commute between Washington and Oswego, New York, as Ickes' liaison with the refugees, until President Harry S. Truman allowed them to cross into Canada in December 1945 and then re-enter the United States and become citizens.

The one thousand Jews saved by Roosevelt now had a home, but the thousands who were being saved by the Allies in Europe had no home. They were put in D.P. camps.

When the war ended and the magnitude of the holocaust became known, President Truman asked the British Labour Government to do what the Conservative Government had refused to do: open the doors of Palestine for one hundred thousand D.P.'s. Prime Minister Clement Attlee, unable flatly to refuse the request of the President, suggested that a commission of inquiry should look into the problem. It was the eighteenth commission on Palestine.

The *New York Post* asked me to take a leave of absence from

Washington to cover the story of the Anglo-American Committee of Inquiry on Palestine as its members traveled from Washington to London, Germany, and Austria, into eastern Europe, then to Cairo, Palestine, Lebanon, Syria, Iraq, and Saudi Arabia.

For four months I grew to know and respect the integrity of men like the American chairman, Judge Joseph C. Hutcheson, a crusty Texan who had broken the Ku Klux Klan in Houston and who described himself as an "Old Testament Christian"; Dr. James G. McDonald, who had been League of Nations High Commissioner for German Refugees and later became the first United States Ambassador to Israel; Bartley C. Crum, a liberal Catholic and crusading Republican lawyer; Frank W. Buxton, a Pulitzer Prize winner and editor of the *Boston Herald*; Dr. Frank Aydelotte, Director of the Institute for Advanced Study at Princeton; and William Phillips, former Ambassador to Italy.

The British were carefully selected men who were earnestly searching for a humane solution to the problem of the D.P.'s and of Palestine. The British chairman, Hutcheson's counterpart, was Sir John Singleton, Judge of the King's Bench, who had tried and sentenced a number of nationalist Irishmen to be hanged; there were several members of Parliament, including Richard H. S. Crossman, the Labour M.P., and Sir Frederick Leggett, a labor conciliator and close friend of Foreign Minister Ernest Bevin. To head up the British staff, Bevin had sent Harold Beeley, his chief expert on the Arabs, a well-known Arabphile who later became Ambassador to Egypt.

In Europe the commission split up into subcommittees, each traveling to different countries to talk to survivors. I traveled to Germany and Austria with Bartley Crum and Sir Frederick Leggett and their aides, with Gerold Frank, representing the Overseas News Agency, and Judge Simon H. Rifkind, advisor on Jewish Affairs to General Joseph T. McNarney.

The whole ghastly horror of the holocaust came home to us. We were face to face with the survivors. They showed us pictures of their wives, their husbands, their children—all burned, all dead. They told us of atrocities and obscenities until we could not sleep at night. The committee questioned them on the nightmare of their lives, their beliefs, what they dreamed they could make of what was left of their lives. Their answer was: "We want to go to Palestine."

Dachau, Buchenwald, Treblinka—the roster of death camps gave way to a new roster of D.P. camps. In every camp we were greeted with Jewish flags and huge banners: "We all want Palestine as our country."

"Why do you want to go to Palestine?" the committee asked the people. "Why do you wish a Jewish state?"

A man in Zeilsheim, outside Frankfurt, answered the question by asking another one: "What kind of question is that? We are Jews. The Americans have America. The English have England. We want a Jewish state. Palestine is the only state in which we can order our own existence. If you tell me that we are not Jews, but Germans or Poles or Austrians, I give you the testimony of six million dead."

The education of the committee continued. In the British zone of Austria, a boy of sixteen turned on the committee: "Why did you come here to ask us questions, questions! Am I on trial? What have I done to the world to lose my parents and my entire family? What have I done except to be born a Jew?"

The committee was silent.

"Don't ask *me* questions," he said. "Ask the world!"

Each day the committee learned a new lesson in the mathematics of survival. We spent a rainy afternoon outside Munich on the model farm of the late Julius Streicher, editor of the vitriolically anti-Semitic *Der Stuermer*, watching young Jewish boys and girls who had survived Hitler as they prepared to become farmers in Palestine. As naturally as if this were a kibbutz in the Hills of Judea they formed a circle, and Englishmen and Americans, who had never seen the *hora*, locked arms with the youngsters and hopped on Streicher's floor.

"Where were we during the war?" we asked each other, riddled with guilt, as we drove out of Germany. "Why didn't we do something? Why didn't we bomb a single gas chamber? How could we have let six million die?"

The education of the committee continued as they heard Arabs testifying in Cairo and Jews testifying in Jerusalem, until, in a unanimous report, the British members joined with the Americans and voted to allow the one hundred thousand D.P. survivors to enter the so-long-promised home.

But overnight the joy in the D.P. camps turned to bitterness. British Foreign Minister Ernest Bevin, furious that his own appointees had betrayed him, scuttled the report. In Palestine Jews responded with acts of terror and sabotage. Some of the infamous Black and Tan policemen, who had once suppressed the Irish, were sent to Palestine to keep order. The Holy Land was a police state.

"Palestine today is the Ireland of 1921," I cabled my paper from Jerusalem. The fierce hatred of the British, the concentration camp atmosphere, the destruction of civil liberties, the growth of a people's army—the same social and political explosives which had made Ireland the tinderbox of 1921 were making Palestine the time bomb of 1946.

The Jews were waking up to the facts of colonial life. On their island home the English were as valiant and admirable as they had been during the war when they held the Nazis at bay. But the Foreign Office was run, for the most part, by men who had never broken with the tradition of the old British imperialists, men who, knowing the days of grabbing and expansion were over and only the days of clutching and hoarding were left, had become imperialists by habit.

Early on Saturday, June 29, 1946—a day that would become famous as Black Saturday—British trucks and tanks drove through the streets of Jerusalem announcing a curfew. The streets were emptied of people. Troops shot and dynamited their way into the offices of the Jewish Agency (which had become the shadow government of the Jews), rounded up thousands of people, and tossed the leaders into the British prison in Latrun, between Jerusalem and Tel Aviv.

Ben-Gurion, the leader of the Jews of Palestine, escaped the dragnet. In Paris he set up a government-in-exile, and then flew on to New York. Working now in the New York office, I suggested to my editors that we do a profile on Ben-Gurion, still largely unknown to the American people.

In the Hotel 14 on New York's upper East Side Ben-Gurion sat in a modest suite talking of the future. Knowing the danger he was in, I offered to let him see a draft of the article to make sure nothing I wrote would jeopardize his safety, and the next morning brought the manuscript to him. He read the first line: "There is a man in our town tonight who is to the little people of Palestine what Abraham Lincoln was to the people of America in his day."

Ben-Gurion jumped up from the sofa. His high-pitched voice hit the ceiling. "Lincoln! How can you compare me with Lincoln?"

"But you really . . ."

He shook his massive head and sank back on the sofa. "When I think of a great man, I think of Abraham Lincoln. Who am I? Just a little Jew."

After five months the British released the prisoners of Latrun, and Ben-Gurion and the government-in-exile returned home. But Jewish survivors were still barred from Palestine. The illegal ships that continued to sail across the Mediterranean out of secret ports in France and Italy were captured by the British and their passengers deported to prison camps in Cyprus. In Palestine house-to-house searches went on and there were thousands of arrests. The Irgun, now a paramilitary organization, bombed the prison at Acre to free their comrades. Two hundred Jewish and Arab prisoners escaped.

Foreign Minister Bevin, impotent and more desperate than ever, asked the United Nations to send still another commission to study the problem. A session of the General Assembly was called, and in May 15, 1947, it established the United Nations Special Committee on Palestine (UNSCOP), made up of representatives from eleven small nations. During the debate, the Soviet Union, watching the sun begin to set on the British Empire, openly declared its interest in the Middle East. Andrei Gromyko announced at Lake Success that his government favored a solution that would "compensate for what the Jews had suffered in Europe." Gromyko's statement was accepted at face value. The Russian people had suffered tragic losses in the war; Russia had compelling reasons to sympathize with the Jews. At the same time Russia was putting a toe in the Mediterranean, in the hope that she might boot Britain out and fill her place in the Middle East.

For the first time Britain was not a member of a commission investigating her role in Palestine; this set UNSCOP apart from all the commissions that had preceded it.

When UNSCOP left for Europe and the Middle East the *Herald Tribune* asked me to cover the story. The shadow of the six million haunted the commission. We flew to the former German concentration camp at Bergen Belsen. There a small man with piercing blue eyes, Josef Rosensaft, held the commission riveted to their seats as, like a Jewish "ancient mariner," he described the destruction of Europe's Jews.

At last he released us, and in silence we walked through the cemetery where German children were playing while their fathers burned the striped pajamas the Jews had been forced to wear under the Nazis. One of the members of the commission asked a child, "Do you know what your father is burning?"

"*Ya*," the child answered. "*Dreck* [filth]."

The cemetery was filled with little hills in which the bodies of the Jews were buried. On the mounds were simple wooden sticks with the stark legends: "Here lie 5,000 dead" or "Here lie 10,000 dead."

In the center of the cemetery stood a wooden monument which said in simple English:

"Israel and the world shall remember the 30,000 Jews exterminated in the concentration camp of Bergen Belsen at the hands of the murderous Nazis. EARTH, CONCEAL NOT THE BLOOD SHED ON THEE."

Then, in Jerusalem, in the auditorium of the handsome Y.M.C.A., the committee listened to the testimony of the leaders of the shadow government: Ben-Gurion; Moshe Sharett, who was in effect the foreign minister; Golda Meir from Milwaukee, the leader of the Histadrut (General Federation of Labor) and the most powerful woman labor leader in Palestine.

Almost blind, Dr. Weizmann was hardly able to read his prepared speech. But, sitting at the foot of the horseshoe table on the lighted stage of the "Y," he fascinated the committee with his whimsical wit and wisdom. "What is a Jew?" he asked them, and answered: "He is a man who has to offer an explanation of his existence. As soon as you have to offer an explanation, you are under suspicion."

He went on: "I am old enough to warn you. For us the question is of survival, and it brooks no delay. All that you have seen here constitutes national progress. All of it we did with our own hands. Here in Palestine there were marshes and we drained them. There were no houses and we have built them. All that has been done here, from the modest cottage of the settler to the university on Mount Scopus, is the work of Jewish planning, Jewish genius, and of Jewish hands and muscles—not only of money and initiative.

"The White Paper released certain phenomena in Jewish life, which are un-Jewish, contrary to Jewish tradition. 'You must not kill,' was one of the Ten Commandments on Mount Sinai. Today they are killing. I hide my head in shame before you gentlemen when I must speak of them. I hope international action will clear up this disease. Do not let it drag out. Do not prolong our agony. It has lasted long enough, and has caused a great deal of blood and sorrow. God has chosen the small countries as a vessel through which He sends His best message to the world. And now that the old wanderer is coming back to his old home, perhaps once more a message of peace will come out of this country to a world which stands sorely in need of such a message."

But even as the commission listened, a ship was breaking its way through the blockade. It was an old American river boat, renamed *Exodus 1947*, carrying forty-five hundred Jewish survivors to Haifa. The captain was a slim young Palestinian, Ike Aronowicz. Most of the crew were boys from America, ex-G.I.'s and sailors who had never been interested in Jews until Hitler murdered six million in Europe.

At 2:00 A.M. on Friday, July 18, the *Exodus 1947* was attacked. Two British destroyers came alongside and crushed the refugee ship between them. The British boarded the damaged ship with pistols and clubs. The *Exodus* passengers and crew were armed with potatoes and kosher beef. The British killed two D.P.'s and an American—Bill Bernstein, of San Francisco—who were buried in Haifa.

I left UNSCOP to cover the story of the *Exodus*. At four

o'clock on Friday afternoon the battered ship sailed into Haifa, escorted by British tugs and destroyers. On the pier at Haifa was a pile of savage-looking Sten guns, laid on top of each other on hospital stretchers as though cause and effect had already been confused.

The ship looked like a huge splintered box. Through one tear, a hole as big as an open barn, could be seen a muddle of bedding, personal possessions, plumbing, broken pipes, overflowing toilets, half-naked men, women looking for children. Cabins were bashed in; railings were ripped off; the lifesaving rafts dangled at crazy angles.

The British got the people off the ship by telling them they were being sent, like all the other illegals, to the prison colony of Cyprus. Families were separated. There were screams (in Auschwitz and Dachau and Treblinka separation had always meant death), but they were separated anyway, gently for the most part. They were searched, sprayed with the flourlike powder of D.D.T., and then put on three prison ships.

I flew to Cyprus to wait for the people of the *Exodus*. You had to smell Cyprus to believe it. You had to smell the latrines used by thirty-two thousand people to believe it, and even then you didn't. There was no water in the barbed-wire camps. Each day the thousands of adults and the two thousand orphans waited for a squat water truck to materialize out of the dust. When it appeared they ran down the streets, shouting "*Wasser! Wasser!*" and collected water in little tin cups.

There was no privacy in the hot tents and quonset huts; yet, in one year five hundred babies were born. I asked one of the pregnant women how she could bring a child into this twentieth-century purgatory. "Don't you know," she said to me, "don't you know that, under Hitler, as soon as a Jewish woman was pregnant, she was burned? Today, every woman who can have a child is determined to have one. This is our answer to Hitler. That we can have a child and live."

Even Cyprus was declared too good for the people of the *Exodus*. They were taken back in prison ships to Port de Bouc in southern France, whence they had embarked for Palestine. By that time UNSCOP was in Switzerland, writing its report. I left the commission again to fly to Marseilles, from there to drive to Port de Bouc.

The French disagreed with Bevin's policy ("We know the enemy," they told me. "Jews are not the enemy.") and they helped smuggle me aboard one of the prison ships. Forty-five hundred Jews were squeezed into cages; yet they refused to come off the ships. They hung hand-printed signs on the decks: "We will come down only in Palestine."

Each day on the ships, schools were held. Older people took turns teaching the orphaned children who had come aboard with Youth Aliyah (the Children's Immigration). Mostly they taught the children the Hebrew language and literature and the Bible stories of the Exodus.

Of all the things that were done to the people, nothing seemed so grim as when the British burned the books brought in on the food launches. Afraid of books as propaganda, the officer in command of troops aboard the *Empire Rival* ordered the burning of all books in Hebrew and Yiddish. Among them was the Bible. These were the people of the Bible; it was the book which they had given to the world; it was the book which had kept them alive and integrated as a people. Now their book was burned on the prison ship. Each evening in the prison cage, they sat silently, mourning the Book as if a person had died. They were the People of the Book and the Land, and on this prison ship both had been taken from them.

After four blistering weeks, the British announced they were sending the Jews of the *Exodus* back to Germany. By now hundreds of newspapermen had arrived in Port de Bouc to cover the action. The British declared they would allow one representative each of the British, French, and American press to board the ships. They selected me to represent the American press.

I climbed the Jacob's ladder onto the deck of the *Runnymede Park*, named for the park where the Magna Carta was signed. As we watched, the people unfurled a huge black banner; the Union Jack was painted in the top left center and a red swastika was in the lower right.

Down below, in the cage, the bodies of the people crushed up against us. It was like a charcoal drawing of the Inferno. A woman held up her baby. "Take a picture of my baby," she said. Without aiming, I took a picture.

"My life is over," she said. (She was twenty-four.) "But I'm going to live for this baby. I'm going to stay alive so my child won't be killed in a gas chamber. There are no frontiers to Jewish hope."

As the ships pulled away from the harbor, sailing for Germany, a young Haganah girl standing near me said, "Now you will see the birth of a Jewish state."

The Jews of the prison ships later slipped out of the barbed-wire camps in Germany, found their way across the face of Europe to new secret ports in France and Italy, climbed on other illegal ships, and broke their way through the British blockade again.

On the first of September UNSCOP voted to recommend the partition of Palestine into a Jewish state and an Arab state, and on November 29, 1947, exactly thirty years after the Balfour Declaration, the United Nations voted approval of the partition plan. Britain was ordered to leave Palestine within eight months. The delegates of the Arab states marched out of the Assembly hall. The undeclared war began.

Outside of Palestine, volunteers and guerrilla fighters were recruited into the "Palestine Liberation Army," commanded by Fawzi el-Kaukji, who had led some of the Arab riots in Palestine and, like the Mufti, had joined Hitler in Berlin during the war.

Arabs sat on the Hills of Judea gunning down and burning the trucks which sought to bring food and supplies up the mountain passes to Jerusalem. In April, scarcely a month before the Mandate would end, they murdered 77 doctors and nurses riding in a convoy to the Hadassah Hospital on Mount Scopus. In May they surrounded four orthodox kibbutzim in Gush Etzion on the road from Jerusalem to Hebron and mutilated 160 young men and women settlers. Twenty women who had hidden in a cellar were massacred by Arabs with hand grenades.

Some of the English in Palestine hated the policy of their government, but they could do little except watch as Britain, in the death throes of the Mandate, armed the Arabs and disarmed the Jews. The Mandatory Government gave the Arabs 50 of its 124 giant police stations. The Haganah would have to fight desperately against these fortresses, and against Sarafand, the huge British army camp that was turned over lock, stock, and barrel to the Arabs.

On the other side of the Atlantic, a serious cleavage had developed between the State Department and the White House over Palestine. President Truman in his *Years of Trial and Hope, 1946–1952* describes the fissure in his government at that time.

> The Department of State specialists on the Near East were almost without exception unfriendly to the idea of a Jewish state. Their thinking went along this line: Great Britain had maintained her position in the area by cultivating the Arabs; now that she no longer seemed able to hold this position, the United States must take over, and it must be done by exactly the same formula.

"I was never convinced by these arguments of the diplomats," Truman avers. In any differences of opinion between the State Department and the White House, "there was never any question as to who made the decisions and whose policy would be followed."

As word of the cleavage spread, delegations of Jewish leaders descended on Washington. At length, Truman decided to see no more Zionist spokesmen, not even the ailing and nearly blind Dr. Weizmann, who had come from Europe hoping to talk to him.

There was one visitor, however, to whom the White House door was always open. He was Eddie Jacobson of Kansas City. Eddie, whose orthodox Jewish parents had fled Russian oppression in the early 1880's, had served under Captain Truman as a sergeant in France in the First World War. In 1919 the two ex-soldiers had gone into business together, opening Truman & Jacobson, Haberdasher's, on West 12th Street in Kansas City. Hit by the postwar recession of 1922, their business was liquidated, and the two men struggled until they repaid every one of their creditors.

On Saturday, March 13, 1948, Eddie entered the White House. "I was sitting there, trying to figure out how I was going to persuade the President to take back his order and see Chaim Weizmann," Eddie told me a few days later. "I talked and talked. I couldn't think of any arguments to give him. His turndown of my request, firmly and in anger, left me completely crushed. Then

I happened to rest my eyes on a beautiful model of a statue of Andrew Jackson mounted on a horse. I found myself saying to the President: 'All your life you have had a hero. You are probably the best read man in America on the life of Andrew Jackson. I remember when we had our store together and you were always reading books and papers and pamphlets on this great American. When you built the new Jackson County Court House in Kansas City, you put this very statue, life-size, on the lawn right in front of the new court house, where it still stands.' "

The haberdasher looked at the President, who said nothing. He went on. "Well, I too have a hero, a man I never met but who is, I think, the greatest Jew who ever lived. I too have studied his past and I agree with you, as you have often told me, that he is a gentleman and a great statesman as well. I am talking about Chaim Weizmann. He is a very sick man, almost broken in health, but he traveled thousands and thousands of miles just to see you and plead the cause of my people.

"Just as I was finishing I noticed that the President began drumming on his desk with his fingers, and as I stopped talking he abruptly turned around while still sitting in his swivel chair and started looking out the window into what in the summer is a beautiful rose garden—gazing out the window just over the pictures of his mother, his wife, and his daughter. I knew the sign. I knew that he was changing his mind. I don't know how many seconds passed in silence but they seemed like centuries. All of a sudden he swiveled himself around again, facing his desk, looked me straight in the eyes, and then said the most endearing words I had ever heard from his lips.

" 'You win, you baldheaded S.O.B. I will see him.' "

The appointment was made for Thursday, March 18, 1948. Weizmann was brought incognito through the East Gate. The meeting was to be kept completely off the record; the press was not to see Weizmann enter, and the British Ambassador who had an appointment just before his would be leaving by the Northwest Gate.

Weizmann had requested twenty-five minutes for the interview; the President extended it to forty-five, as Dr. Weizmann talked of the role Palestine could play in the Mediterranean; how, with science and brain power, Palestine would become another Switzerland; how vital the Negev desert was to the future Jewish state.

"When he left my office," Truman wrote, "I felt that he had reached a full understanding of my policy and that I knew what it was he wanted."

That night Eddie was informed that the President stood firm on partition. The next morning Truman left on a vacation. In the afternoon United States Ambassador Warren Austin mounted the rostrum in the United Nations to announce that America now favored, instead of partition, a trusteeship for Palestine.

Eddie Jacobson sat dazed and unbelieving in his office in the haberdashery store in Kansas City. "I don't believe this," he told everyone who telephoned questioning this sudden switch in American policy. "I have explicit faith in my friend and that faith will remain unshaken until he himself tells me differently with his own lips."

On Monday Dr. Weizmann too telephoned Eddie. "Don't be disappointed and do not feel badly," the wise old statesman comforted him. "I do not believe that President Truman knew what was going to happen in the United Nations on Friday when he talked to me the day before." (Events were to prove he was right.) "I am seventy-two years old, and all my life I have had one disappointment after another. This is just another letdown for me. Don't forget for a single moment that Harry Truman is the most powerful single man in the world. You have a job to do, so keep the White House doors open."

But in the Middle East the rush of history made the maneuverings at the United Nations seem almost irrelevant. The Jewish community was faced with complete chaos. The British, preparing to depart on the fifteenth of May, cut off all telephones. International communications ceased to exist. In April, a month and a half before they were to leave, the British ended the postal services. Letters were dropped into post boxes that were never emptied. The Jews opened their own post office, and on May 9 began to issue stamps of their own.

Ben-Gurion announced that Israel would become a state on the fifteenth of May. Arab armies surrounding Israel began to mass at the borders. Moshe Sharett flew in from Washington with word that Secretary of State George C. Marshall strongly urged Israel to delay the proclamation.

Golda Meir, disguised as an Arab woman, heavily veiled, drove to Shuneh on a dangerous secret mission to talk with the Jews' old friend, King Abdullah of Transjordan. Still assuring her of his friendship, the Bedouin king asked: "Why are you Jews in such a hurry to proclaim a state?"

Golda replied, "Would you call waiting two thousand years hasty?"

Abdullah told her he opposed partition. He was ready to use his British-trained and British-armed Arab Legion to get all of Palestine.

Some of the Jewish leaders cautioned delay, but Ben-Gurion was unswerving. The name for the new state—Israel—had already been selected. The problem was the Sabbath: the Mandate was to end at midnight on Friday, and among the leaders were religiously observant Jews who could not travel on the Sabbath. It was decided the state would be born before the Sabbath sun would set.

Friday the fourteenth of May arrived. On the Hill of Evil Counsel in Jerusalem, Sir Alan Cunningham, British High Commissioner for Palestine, closed the door of Government House behind him. He looked for the last time at Jerusalem as the early morning sun rose over the city he had grown to love.

In Tel Aviv, by mid-afternoon, hundreds of people were assembled outside the little Tel Aviv museum. Silently they watched the leaders of the Jewish people of Palestine enter the hall that had been hastily converted into a historic meeting room. Paintings had been taken down and on the wall, behind a long table, hung a portrait of Theodor Herzl, the brooding, black-bearded journalist who in dreaming of this day had said, "If you will it, it is no dream."

At four o'clock David Ben-Gurion rose, and from a piece of paper in his hand read the Proclamation of Independence:

The land of Israel was the birthplace of the Jewish people. Here their spiritual, religious, and national identity was formed. Here they achieved independence and created a culture of national and universal significance. Here they wrote and gave the Bible to the world. . . . We hereby proclaim the establishment of the Jewish State of Israel to be called *Medinath Israel*, the State of Israel.

The leaders of the new nation sang "Hatikvah." It had been their symbolic "Song of Hope"; now it became the anthem of the first Jewish state in nearly two thousand years. On the streets the people cheered wildly, but Ben-Gurion spoke solemnly to his wife Paula: "I feel like the mourner at the festival." Arab armies were encircling the new nation. Jerusalem lay under siege.

In Washington eleven minutes later, President Truman took the State Department by surprise. I was at the United Nations, covering the debate on Palestine, when I saw a newspaperman rush in and hand a ticker-tape message to Warren Austin. Austin looked stunned. We sped to telephones as rumors raced around the hall. Finally, there was silence. One of the American delegates, who had called Washington, stood up to announce the birth of Israel and reveal what President Truman had done: "This Government has been informed that a Jewish State has been proclaimed in Palestine, and recognition has been requested by the Provisional Government thereof. The United States Government recognizes the Provisional Government as the *de facto* authority of the new State of Israel."

During the night Ben-Gurion was awakened by a radio operator pounding on his door. The news that President Truman had recognized Israel had just come over Haganah Radio. Still in his pajamas, with a coat flung over them, Ben-Gurion drove to the radio station to broadcast his people's gratitude to the President and the people of America. It was 5:20 on Saturday morning in Israel; in New York it was 10:20 Friday night. Many Americans, listening to the new prime minister, sensed this to be one of those events in history, like the Passover, that parents would forever recount to their children.

Suddenly the Americans heard an explosion over the radio. Ben-Gurion halted for a moment. Then, quietly, he went on: "Bombs have just been dropped on the city by enemy aircraft which are flying over our heads."

Sabbath descended on the infant nation with Egyptian bombs.

Five Arab states—Egypt, Jordan, Syria, Lebanon, and Iraq—with additional troops from Saudi Arabia and Yemen, attacked. The armies of forty million Arabs hurled themselves against Israel's six hundred and fifty thousand Jews. The "War of Liberation" had begun.

In the middle of the war a cable was delivered to me in the little Armon Hotel, the unofficial press camp in Tel Aviv. The *Herald Tribune* wanted a story on Ben-Gurion.

When I entered his study, his desk was piled high with newspapers and magazines in Hebrew and English. In front of him was the copy book in which he wrote, in small neat Hebrew script, his daily diary. Behind him were rows of books in Hebrew, English, and Greek—the language he was studying so that he could read Plato in the original. "To read Greek in translation," he once told me, "is like kissing a woman through a veil."

I reached across his desk and placed the cable in front of him. "I'm not going to ask you a thing about the war," I said. "I know you're going to win it. I'm not going to ask you about politics. I just want you to shut your eyes and tell me what Israel will look like when the blood has stopped flowing and the Jews have come home."

He shut his eyes, and for a few moments one could almost forget that the war was being fought a few miles away.

"There will be no more desert. There will be trees on every hill. The sky will be full of planes. The sea will be full of ships. There will be cottages all over the country. We'll have towns and villages filled with flowers and trees and lots of children. Children are our future."

"And what," I asked, "will be your philosophy of life? What will be your Bill of Rights?"

"It takes many words in English," he said. "In Hebrew it takes only three, V*eahavta re-ekh'a kamoh'a.* They mean 'Love your fellow human as yourself.' "

3

The Twenty-Year War

THE YOUNG NATION defeated the seven Arab states, and the
War of Liberation was over. Almost overnight Jewish animosity
for the British ended. Israelis began to talk nostalgically of the
good old days of the Balfour Declaration and of the common
cause when they fought against the Germans in the Second World
War.

Early in 1949 on the island of Rhodes, Dr. Ralph Bunche,
working as the mediator of the United Nations, persuaded each
Arab state to meet informally with Israel and hammer out an
agreement. Egypt, Jordan, Syria, and Lebanon signed armistice
agreements with Israel as "an indispensable step toward the
liquidation of armed conflict and the restoration of peace." But
these agreements were broken by the Arabs and the armed conflict
developed into guerrilla war. Israel became obsessed with survival.

One aspect of survival was defense against attack; another was
to rescue thousands of Jews living in Arab lands. On Israel's borders
some six hundred thousand Arab refugees who had fled from Israel
were living in camps supported by the United Nations. During the
next few years some six hundred thousand Jewish refugees would
flee to Israel from Arab lands.

In 1949 fifty thousand Jews began an exodus out of Yemen.
Silver-winged American Skymasters, piloted by Americans who
wore Texan cowboy boots, flew the Yemenites along the Red Sea
Bible route to the Bible land. In one of the planes flying out of

Aden I asked a bearded patriarch if he was frightened. He shook his head and quoted the beautiful passage from Isaiah:

> But they that wait upon the Lord shall renew
> their strength; they shall mount up with
> wings as eagles; they shall run, and not be
> weary; and they shall walk, and not faint.

"They are the Lord's words to Moses," he said, holding his prayer shawl around his shoulders. " 'Ye have seen what I did unto the Egyptians, and how I bore you on eagles' wings, and brought you unto myself.' "

After the Yemenites came the Iraqis, a Jewish community of one hundred and twenty thousand, their roots embedded in Iraq since the exile to Babylon twenty-five hundred years ago, when their ancestors had sung: "By the rivers of Babylon, there we sat down, yea, we wept, when we remembered Zion." Hundreds of thousands more fled from other Arab lands—from Morocco and Tunisia and Algeria, from Syria and Lebanon, from Libya and Egypt.

The first law passed by the Knesset (Parliament) was the Law of the Return. Any Jew from any country in the world was free to come to Israel to live—whether he was blind or sighted, strong or maimed, rich or poor. The young country, its economy shaky, with scarcely enough food to feed its people, turned back no one. From Bulgaria, Yugoslavia, Czechoslovakia, and Poland, nearly all that had survived the holocaust emigrated to Israel. Ana Pauker, dictator of Romania, whose father lived in Tel Aviv, allowed thousands of old and sick to leave.

Overwhelmed by the floodtide, Israel made grievous mistakes. She opened huge refugee camps—tent cities—to house the people until she could decide where to send them and what they could do. (The United Nations fed the Arab refugees; Israel alone fed the Jews, with help from the United Jewish Appeal.) The tents were boiling hot in summer; in the winter, heavy rain and even snow made them unbearable. The tents gave way to quonset huts, and they to little wooden shacks. Gradually Israel awoke to the fact that no human being should be asked to live in a camp. Even in the best of camps human beings deteriorate. For European

Jews, the memories of Dachau, Bergen Belsen, the D.P. camps, and Cyprus were still raw.

The Jewish refugee camps were converted into transit villages, called *mabaroth*. But these villages were little more than glorified camps with wooden houses. Like the Arab refugees a few miles away, the Jewish refugees had free rent, free food, free medical care—and mass deterioration.

Israel decided to end the deterioration. From the ships at Haifa the refugees were taken directly to new little development towns in the Negev and the Galilee. The people were moved out of the *mabaroth* to the new towns. The men worked, they built their own homes, and they were paid. They began to live, not as refugees, but as citizens.

Industries were encouraged to open in the little frontier towns. Bonds were floated in America and Europe to establish new plants. Money from German reparations helped speed the industrialization. The United Jewish Appeal helped pay for the housing and social welfare. And even while Israel struggled to give the newcomers a sense of dignity, she built up her army and air force.

For outside her borders, the danger to survival grew. "Israel, to the Arab world, is like a cancer to the human body," the king of Saudi Arabia proclaimed in 1953. "The only way of remedy is to uproot it, just like a cancer. . . . why don't we sacrifice ten million of our number to live in pride and self-respect?"

The Arabs were not yet ready to sacrifice ten million. Preoccupied with their own troubles, they were split into republics and dictatorships and kingdoms, oil-rich states and poor states, united only in their hatred for Israel. They differed even in their alignments with world powers. Britain kept its presence in the Mediterranean by financing Jordan; it continued its old associations with Egypt and Iraq. Saudi Arabia tied itself openly to the United States. Israel, although politically aligned with the United States and Great Britain, found that only France would sell her planes to deter the Arabs. Franco-Israeli friendship grew.

In the early fifties the Soviet Union had few friends in the Middle East. She had backed Israel in the vote for partition, but because of Israel's alignment with the democracies later wrote Israel off and turned to the Arabs. She began with Egypt, the most populous and strategically the most important nation in the Arab world. In 1952 Egypt's corrupt potentate, King Farouk, was overthrown by a military coup under Mohammed Naguib and the "Free Officers," with Nasser in the background. In 1954 Nasser seized power, first as premier and in 1956 as president and premier.

More astutely than any other politician in the world, Nasser played the East against the West. In 1955 he made the first of his deals with the Soviet Union and Czechoslovakia: he bartered Egyptian cotton for Russian guns, tanks, and MIG's. At the same time he persuaded the United States and Britain to finance the Aswan Dam, through which he genuinely hoped to alleviate some of the poverty of his *fellahin* (peasants) who live along the Nile. To reassure the democracies, he arrested the local Communists inside Egypt.

But he overreached himself. In May 1956 he recognized Red China. Secretary of State John Foster Dulles announced abruptly that the United States was no longer interested in financing the Dam.

Nasser retaliated. He hit back through Britain and France. He nationalized their lifeline—the Suez Canal. Now he could dictate how much coffee a Frenchman could drink, and how much gasoline an Englishman could get for his car.

Meanwhile, he waged a three-pronged attack against Israel: he continued an economic boycott; he blockaded the Straits of Tiran to cut off Israel's southern port, Elath; and he created the Fedayeen—terrorist gangs schooled in infiltration and murder.

Secretly, England and France decided to regain the Canal. At the same time Israel decided to end the three-pronged attack, free the Straits of Tiran, and halt the terrorism of the Fedayeen who were tossing bombs into children's homes in the border villages and penetrating even to Tel Aviv.

On Monday, the twenty-ninth of October 1956, the Israel Defense Forces, under General Moshe Dayan, marched into the Sinai peninsula. Their speed took even the Israelis by surprise. In one hundred hours they knocked out one-third of Nasser's Sinai army, wiped out the Fedayeen nests, captured all the Soviet hardware in Sinai and the Gaza Strip, reached the Suez Canal, and opened the Straits of Tiran.

England and France bombed the Egyptian air bases. But they dragged their feet on an invasion, and by the time they began landing their troops, the war was already over.

Under threats of Soviet intervention and pressure from President Dwight D. Eisenhower and Secretary of State Dulles, Israel withdrew her troops from the Gaza Strip. Troops of the United Nations Emergency Force (UNEF) were moved into Sinai and Sharm el Sheikh to serve as a peace-keeping buffer between Israel and Egypt.

A new era began in the Middle East. Britain and France lost their place in the Mediterranean sun. The United States, now a major presence in the region, was aligned with both the Arab states and Israel. The Soviet Union emerged, committing itself to the Arabs. Nasser, defeated as a soldier, was triumphant as a politician. Throughout the Arab world Nasserism became the new nationalism, and Nasser was its god. The Suez Canal was his. Former Prime Minister Harold Macmillan, looking back on these events during a television interview in New York in January 1968, rued the nationalization of the Canal: "Eisenhower and Dulles forced England and France to give the Canal to Nasser. Once you allow a corruption of international law you have anarchy."

By February 1958 Nasser's political stock rose so high that the Syrians joined him to form the United Arab Republic. Soon Yemen entered, and Iraq, which had overthrown its king, seemed about to join. Nasser would be over-all president.

It looked as though peace might break out among the Arabs—but not for long. Iraq refused to join. The Syrian officers resented the Egyptianization of the Syrian army. The industrialists resented socialization, and the bankers, nationalization.

After a swift revolution in September 1961, Syria broke up the marriage and resumed her maiden name. Yemen soon followed suit. Egypt continued to call itself the United Arab Republic, although it was a tight military dictatorship united only with itself.

In the revolving door of Syrian politics, the Syrian army overthrew the civilian government on March 28, 1963. It was the eighth revolution in fourteen years. President Nazem el-Kodsi was imprisoned in a military hospital; a military junta took over under the dictatorship of Lieutenant General Amin el-Hafez. All politi-

cal parties were outlawed except for the Ba'ath party, a mixture of
Marxist socialism (though not communism), nationalism modeled
on Hitler's Germany, and Pan-Arabism.

Nasserism was waning; only hatred for Israel kept the Arab
rulers, vying for leadership in the disunity of the Arab world, from
tearing at each other's throats. But inside their countries their
political careers often rose or fell by the intensity of their passion
against Israel and the bloodthirstiness of their oratory.

The Soviet Union continued to arm Egypt, then Syria, and then
Iraq. Reacting to that move, the United States ended its total
embargo on arms to Israel and on September 27, 1962, announced
that Israel could purchase Hawk ground-to-air missiles for defense.
France sold Mystère jets to Israel. In the escalating arms race in
the Middle East, the Arabs far outdistanced Israel.

In Palm Springs, Israel's Foreign Minister Golda Meir visited
President John F. Kennedy. "Mrs. Meir," he assured her, "nothing
will happen to you. We are committed to you." He reminded her
that America was determined to support the integrity of Israel and
all its neighbors.

"Mr. President," she answered, "I believe you one hundred per
cent. I just want to be sure we're still there by the time you come
to honor your commitment."

For Nasser was now building his own missiles. German scientists
were working in the Cairo suburb of Heliopolis building rockets
that could penetrate Israel within minutes. "It is we," Nasser
boasted in February 1964, "who will dictate the time. It is we who
will dictate the place."

Not to be outdone, young King Hussein of Jordan offered his
country as the launching pad for the invasion. On April 12, 1964,
he declared: "Jordan with its Left and Right Bank is the ideal
jumping ground to liberate the usurped homeland."

On the Syrian front, General Abdullah Ziada, that month's
defense minister, used the mountains from which Syrian guns
were pointing at Israel in an ominous metaphor: "The Syrian
army stands as a mountain to crush Israel and demolish her. This
army knows how to crush its enemies."

Syrian governments continued to rise and fall, but each new

administration outdid the last in blowing the hot trumpets of war. In December 1965, the leftist prime minister, Youssef Zayyin, was overthrown by the more moderate Salah al-Din Bitar, but in a new revolt two months later Zayyin returned and arrested the government in power. Syria's relations with Russia grew so cordial that the head of Syria's Communist party, Khalid Baqdash, was brought home from exile.

On the twenty-second of May 1966, the new president, Nureddin al-Atassi, addressed the Syrian soldiers as they stood above the Golan Heights concrete fortresses overlooking Israel: "We raise the slogan of the People's Liberation War. We want total war, with no limits, a war that will destroy the Zionist base."

Meanwhile, the new Syrian government intensified guerrilla warfare, sending infiltrators into Israel through the easily accessible West Bank of the Jordanian frontier.

Israel had evolved a technique of retaliation. She would allow a number of incidents to occur (from January 3, 1965 to June 3, 1967 there were 121 acts of sabotage: pipelines were blown up, railroads dynamited, people killed at least once every three days) while her Intelligence determined where the infiltrators were harbored; then, with tanks and heavy guns, she would punch back.

On November 14, 1966, Israel punched back at the Jordanian village of Es Samu on the West Bank, where the infiltrators from Syria were harbored. The United Nations censured Israel, but the infiltration from Es Samu ceased.

The infiltrators moved to other villages, the saboteurs to other borders. Hit-and-run Syrian sappers planted Israeli fields with Soviet and Red Chinese mines. Men driving tractors in their fields were blown into the air. Fishermen were shot as they fished for St. Peter's fish in the Sea of Galilee.

Each night, in Israel's border regions, men trudged cautiously around the perimeters of their settlements, Uzi submachine guns pressed against their sides, their eyes sharpened for infiltrators, their ears attuned for stealthy footsteps.

The kibbutzim in the Galilee are among the most beautiful in Israel, with pomegranates and apple blossoms, with tropical flowers, with fish ponds stocked with carp, and landlocked seas of cotton. They have historic and proud names: Dan, famous as the northern frontier in the Bible; Kfar Hanassi, the village called "The President"; Kfar Blum, named for Leon Blum, the Jewish leader who had been premier of France in the mid-1930's; Ein Gev on the Sea of Galilee, where a music festival is held each year, attracting musicians like Isaac Stern and Alexander Schneider.

By day and night, the people in these villages could see and hear and feel signs of warlike activity in the cliffs above them. At dusk, sitting on the shores of the Sea of Galilee, as the hills turned pink and mauve and then purple-black, they could see strings of lights where thousands of Syrian soldiers had dug themselves in. During the day they could see men building fortifications and hear the rumble of tanks and bulldozers.

The Israeli air force had sharp reconnaissance photographs, but no photographs could pinpoint the incredible number or define the almost indestructible bunkers which Soviet instructors helped the Syrians build. They were made of concrete or of earth and stone, with walls four and five feet thick, sunk deep into the cliffs. No photographs could penetrate the underground labyrinths of apartments—with officers' quarters and dormitories large enough to hold a hundred and twenty-five soldiers—interlaced with well-hidden trenches. No X ray could reveal the sensitive communications equipment, the underground supply rooms for ammunition, or the cunningly carved slits through which the Syrians kept the Israelis under constant surveillance without being seen. The villages lay below the Syrians like lines in the palm of the hand.

The record books will tell you that the 1967 war began on the fifth of June. This is not so. For Gadot, a small kibbutz in the north, the war began two months earlier.

It was a Friday afternoon when, their work done, most kibbutz-niks had showered in their little two-room apartments, and now were either playing with their children or grandchildren or relaxing on canvas beach chairs, reading newspapers and magazines in the sun. Suddenly, shells landed in their midst; within thirty-five minutes the Syrians had lobbed in some 350 shells at the rate of 10 a minute. They were using a powerful Soviet cannon that could send its shells twenty miles away.

With the first sound of fire, the people jumped into the trenches and raced down the steps to the shelters. Only one person in Gadot was injured, a Christian tourist from Switzerland who received a minor injury in his foot.

The Syrians began to shell two other kibbutzim on the Sea of Galilee, Ein Gev and Tel Katzir. Within minutes, the Israeli air force wheeled its planes out and silenced the Syrian guns. The air thundered with the roar of Russian MIG's as the Syrian air force attacked. The Israelis shot down six MIG's, and the Syrians retreated. This was on April 7, 1967.

Gadot is a small kibbutz, with eighty adults and eighty children, and there was a moment when people wondered if Gadot was too badly crippled to survive. The Syrians had succeeded in burning the crops, destroying four homes, demolishing the kindergarten and two of the children's nurseries, and weakening the structure of almost every house. But volunteers moved into Gadot, helped the people rebuild their homes, and the tiny kibbutz was kept alive.

Israel's nineteenth birthday was celebrated on May 15, 1967. The annual Independence Day parade was held in Jerusalem. Soldiers marched in the streets; the leaders of the government took the salute. Because of the armistice agreement with Jordan, and because Israel was not eager to create new furor in the Arab capitals, there were no planes or tanks.

As dusk fell, Prime Minister Levi Eshkol was attending the International Bible Competition for Youth. The Bible contest in Israel is the national sport; the Bible champion is the national hero. The prime minister welcomes him, the president kisses him; the first winner (in 1958), Amos Hacham, a cripple, was given a free apartment by the Histadrut and was greeted, wherever he went, like a movie star.

While the judges were quizzing the young international contestants with tough interpretations of the Bible, Eshkol was called to the telephone. Egyptian troops in vast numbers, he was told, were moving through the streets of Cairo. Some had already reached the Sinai peninsula.

Eshkol immediately called his advisors. The next day he ordered a limited mobilization. Later, at the Overseas Press Club in New

York, Eshkol admitted, "We were caught completely by surprise.
. . . Our national estimate," he explained, "had foreseen the
possibility of renewed Egyptian aggression not before 1970."

Nasser had said at the Arab summit conferences in 1964 and
1965 that he would not be ready for all-out war for several years.
To the Israelis his caution seemed justified. He was facing defeat
in Yemen and starvation at home. His rocket program was still not
off the ground. His population was exploding. His charisma was
wearing thin. What then made him choose Israel's Independence
Day to flaunt his troop movements?

Military experts in Israel point to Moscow. The Soviet Union
early in May had warned a parliamentary delegation from Egypt
that Israel was planning to attack Syria. The Soviet Ambassador
asked to see Eshkol who promptly offered to call his car and drive
with him anywhere he selected in the north to prove the absurdity
of the charges. They would leave immediately so that there would
be no time to withdraw any troops. The Russian refused.

U.N. Secretary General U Thant sent United Nations Truce
Supervision observers to the Galilee and the Syrian border. On
May 19 he reported to the Security Council that the story of
Israel's massing of troops was a complete fabrication: "UNTSO
observers have confirmed the absence of troop concentrations
. . ."

Whether Nasser believed the Russians or not is irrelevant. He
had become convinced the time was now.

Wars may be set off by a single act, but the strength of the
enemy's army, the mood and morale of the enemy's people, the
determination of the political leaders to fight or their willingness
to negotiate for peace at any price—all must be weighed before an
attack. Nasser, surrounded by Soviet advisors, felt the constellation
was right. Heavily fortified with Soviet arms, he had swifter planes,
deadlier tanks, and more troops than Israel. In early May Israel
seemed listless and vulnerable. She was deep in an economic
depression, which was euphemistically called "a slowdown."
Morale was low. Unemployment was mounting. Eshkol and Ben-
Gurion were bitter enemies. The leadership was split into political
factions and personal feuds. For Nasser this was the moment to
strike.

On May 18 he informed U Thant that he wanted part of the United Nations Emergency Force troops removed from Egypt. He sent Egyptian troops to reoccupy Sharm el Sheikh even before the UNEF could be withdrawn. Here he obviously miscalculated—he thought the United Nations would surely indulge in a long debate while he maneuvered for time. But U Thant, on May 19, announced that either the whole of UNEF would be removed or none. Nasser could not back down now and lose face, even if he had wanted to. The world was watching.

In the Middle East the Arabs cheered Nasser's ultimatum to the United Nations. Once again his picture appeared in shops and on newsstands. Nasser had defied the imperialists.

On May 22 he closed the Gulf of Aqaba. He announced that no Israeli ships or vessels of any nation carrying strategic materials to Israel would be allowed to sail through the Gulf to Elath. It was an overt act of war. The U.N. Security Council was called into session. The Soviet Union announced its unequivocal support for Nasser.

Eshkol sent his foreign minister, Abba Eban, to London, Paris, and Washington. Eban sought to persuade the three nations to honor their commitments to guarantee Israel's integrity. Everyone recommended patience and restraint.

On May 26 Nasser blockaded the Straits of Tiran, flew more troops out of Yemen, and marched them across Sinai until eighty thousand soldiers and nearly a thousand tanks stood on Israel's borders. "We are ready," he wrote in *Al-Ahram*, "to undertake total war with Israel."

The ring was tightening. Eager Arab nations offered their troops. On May 30 King Hussein journeyed to Cairo and signed a defense pact with Nasser, who only a few months before had called Hussein "the adulterer of the Hashemite family," the Hashemite harlot.

While Hussein listened, Nasser proclaimed: "The armies of Egypt, Jordan, Syria, and Lebanon are stationed on the borders of Israel in order to face the challenge. Behind them stand the armies of Iraq, Algeria, Kuwait, Sudan, and the whole of the Arab nation.

"This deed will astound the world. Today they will know that the Arabs are ready for the fray. The hour of decision has arrived."

Overt acts of war were building up like a chain reaction. Egypt's General Riadh was made commander of Hussein's Arab Legion. This meant Egyptians were in command of Jordan's army. Jordan's integrity as a nation was compromised first by Egypt, then by Iraq. Pilots of the Iraqi air force and Iraqi troops were dispatched to Jordan; from there they could attack Israel within minutes.

"My sons," said President Aref of Iraq, giving his farewell blessings to his pilots at the Habbaniya airport base on the first of June, "this is the day of the battle and of revenge. . . . We will meet in Tel Aviv and Haifa."

Inside Israel tension mounted. Time seemed to be running out while Eshkol and Eban explored the possibilities for negotiation. Cabinet meetings were stormy. Eshkol was exhausted. These had been sleepless nights. The weeks of negotiation, Eban's journeys to world capitals had won Israel the sympathy of most of the free nations. As a public relations feat, the negotiations were incomparable; but they had confirmed the suspicions of the populace: no one would come to their aid if they needed help. Once again, as in Dachau and Bergen Belsen, they stood alone.

The people clamored for the hero of the Sinai Campaign, Major General Moshe Dayan. Dayan's political enemies delayed his return to the Cabinet; their choice was another war hero, Yigal Allon, Minister of Labor. Allon was in Moscow attending a conference. He hurried home, but he was too late.

On Sunday, May 28, Eshkol had been prevailed upon to make a radio address to the nation. The people were glued to their radio sets—the soldiers mobilized in the Negev, the parents of the soldiers, old-timers, new immigrants, many who wondered if they had fled to Israel only to be killed.

Ordinarily Eshkol's speeches were taped; any errors or slips of the tongue could be wiped out. But this speech was live. The people who had known him in the early days, as a shrewd negotiator with a fund of Jewish folk tales, were shocked. He kept questioning the speech as he read it. He seemed to forget he was on the air. His voice was querulous. He hesitated; he fluffed words. At one point, he even asked one of his aides, "Mah zeh?" ("What is this?").

The speech was a turning point. His followers wrote it off as one of his poor ones, but for the populace the speech was a disaster. The clamor to bring back Dayan grew. Eshkol bowed to it and on the first of June invited Dayan to become Minister of Defense. "It took eighty thousand Egyptian soldiers," Dayan said later, "to get me into the Israeli Cabinet."

Instantly morale soared. The Cabinet was enlarged until the national government represented every party except the Communist.

Nasser watched closely. Did Dayan's return change the constellation? Would Israel now stop negotiating for peace at any price?

Hundreds of newspapermen, T.V. and radio commentators, authors, and photographers descended on Israel to cover the story. Could this little country in the Mediterranean break out of the iron collar of Soviet armor and Arab troops? Could it strike back before it was strangled? Had the weeks of tension wrecked its most vital strategy—surprise?

Dayan held a press conference on Saturday afternoon, the third of June, to answer some of the questions. He knew his remarks would be covered by the Sunday papers in America and Europe; he also knew the Arabs would monitor each word and search its meaning.

Q. Do you believe Israel lost any major military element by agreeing to this long drawn-out diplomatic action to try to solve this crisis?

A. I accept the situation as it is. I know it is always easy to say last week we were in a better position. This is not the point. The point, I should think just now, is that it is more or less a situation of being too late and too early—too late to react regarding our chances in the military field, on the blockading of the Straits of Tiran, and too early to draw conclusions as to the diplomatic way of handling the matter.

Q. Has the government asked for guarantees on the other two conditions your government has given for bringing about peace in the Middle East; that is, drawing back of the Egyptian troops from the borders and the ending of sabotage on your borders?

A. I do not know whether we got such promises or not, but let me say that I, personally, do not expect and do not want anyone else to fight for us. Whatever can be done in the diplomatic way I would welcome and encourage, but if somehow it comes to real fighting I would not like American or British boys to get killed here, and I do not think we need them.

In England and the United States, the Sunday headlines carried comforting news. Israel wanted no American or British boys to die for her.

It was too late for military action and too early for diplomacy. Dayan told the press he was planning to spend the weekend at an archeological dig. Chief of Staff Yitzhak Rabin was going swimming. The beaches of Tel Aviv filled up. Correspondents flew home. The National Broadcasting Company television representative cabled New York not to send an extra television crew. There would be no war.

4

The Call-Up

IN THE LAST WEEKS of May, bells began ringing in people's homes. Messengers scurried through the country, bringing sealed envelopes. Notices were slipped under doors or handed to people in factories, in universities, in hospitals, and in the fields. The country was mobilized.

Some dashed home for their uniforms; others telephoned their homes or offices—"This is it!"—and rushed to join their groups. Red-lettered notices were posted on doors, and copies slipped under doorways. It was total mobilization.

Every able-bodied man—teacher, taxicab driver, doctor, hotel bartender, banker, street cleaner—up to the age of forty-nine was called up. They had been practicing for years; the whole army could be mobilized within twenty-four hours and placed in the field twenty-four hours later. Enlisted men, long after their regular stint in the army, had been serving a month each year, and officers five or six weeks. To many the practice had been a "bloody nuisance."

"I used to laugh at all this kid stuff," a senior El Al pilot told me afterward. "I would see these intellectuals get together in little groups—all hush-hush. But when the mobilization came, every man knew exactly where he had to go and what he had to do."

Israel discovered a new kind of desertion: men went AWOL, not out of but into the army. Before May some of the reservists would report sick or busy or were abroad. Now those who were

51

abroad hounded the airlines and slept in airports to catch the first flight home. In a unit in the Galilee, 280 were called and 410 appeared. Their commanding officer was bewildered: "I don't have enough jobs for you."

"You do your job, we'll do ours," they answered. "We don't ask you for food, for uniforms, nothing. But we're staying."

Normally, married women with children are not expected to be called up; but some of the married women with certain essential skills—such as doctors, nurses, computer and radio operators, and intelligence officers—were mobilized before their husbands, and the telephone wires in Colonel Stella Levy's office at the headquarters of Chen (the Women's Army) were hot with angry husbands demanding to know why they weren't called up first. Why should their wives be given this privilege? What kind of reverse sex discrimination was this?

Occasionally couples were called up together, and then there was a problem of what to do with the children. Kindergartens were arranged inside some of the army camps; such arrangements were part of the flexibility and civilian climate of this army, of its relaxed discipline in everything except in fighting. Led by eighteen-year-old girl soldiers, the children sang and danced happily. They played games with army equipment; at times they answered telephone calls from astonished commanders. They gave the camps a playschool atmosphere that would have scandalized commandants in any army except Israel's.

Of the highest priority throughout Israel was survival. Survival was the imperative commitment—survival against the Arabs, as once it had been against the Germans. This time there was a land in which to fight, and an army to do the fighting. This time there were planes and armor and men superbly skilled in mobility and flexibility. The people turned to the army to save them, and in this army of reservists—who made up 80 per cent of the total forces—the army was the people.

"Even in the darkest days of the tension, it was as though a huge smile had spread across the land," said Rahel Katinka, wife of the army poet and educator Ze'ev. "There was such a love, a love you could feel in the air, a love you could touch with your fingers."

Israel had neither money nor time to give the mobilized reservists proper uniforms. They wore a wild assortment of flowered shirts over paratroop trousers. They covered their heads with helmets, Australian profile hats with cords that tied under their chins, and blue kibbutz hats called *tembels*. Some of the girls wore ballet slippers. No one minded. It was "a love you could touch with your fingers."

Every soldier who came to the mountain city of Safad in the Galilee got free underwear and a free bath. There, Mrs. Sarah Perl, the owner of the Herzlia Hotel who in 1947 had hidden Irgunists from the British police, headed up a committee of volunteer women. When the Herzlia Hotel ran out of blankets for the soldiers sleeping in the cold woods, the women brought blankets from their homes. When the hotel ran out of towels, the women pulled towels out of their closets and shopkeepers donated towels from their shelves. The women brought the soldiers shoes and socks and sweaters; the men of Safad went to their closets and found them stripped bare. It was a love you could touch . . .

As the trucks and tanks drove through the towns, carrying the mobilized soldiers, women rushed into the streets and onto the roads, shoving bottles of orange juice into the soldiers' hands and into the very turrets of the tanks. The soldiers handed the women little slips of paper with telephone numbers: "Call my mother. Tell her I'm O.K. Tell her I'm alive."

A soldier telephoned his father from his army outpost dug in behind a kibbutz. "*Abba* [Papa], you know what kind of a crazy army this is? At night the women sneak out of the kibbutz and take us to their homes."

"What?" his father exploded.

"You know what they do? They make us take showers and telephone home."

Surely food is related to love; and even while the women fixed chicken soup for their beloved soldiers, they kept up a running catechism of Jewish motherly concern:

"Did you phone your mother today? Did you reach your wife? How are your children? Eat."

Tons of cakes and cookies were sent to the boys in the fields, until some of them decided if the Arabs didn't kill them the cakes would.

Far off the main road in the north lie three tiny villages inhabited by a group of former Catholics who had converted to Judaism and migrated to Israel from San Nicandro, Italy, in the early fifties. Few people visit the villages. An army officer, seeking outposts where he could leave spare parts for the army, entered one of them, Alma, in a jeep with two other soldiers.

"I barely got out of there alive," he told me. "Those women had been baking cakes for two weeks, just praying a soldier would come through. They wanted us to eat all the cakes at once. We took two showers in every house. They loaded our jeep with so much cake, tobacco, candies, soda pop, we could barely take off."

In the cities, the schools were closed. Teen-aged boys and girls filled the sandbags for the populace; they ran the post office and delivered the mail. Women drove the milk trucks, and bakers worked around the clock; at least there would be milk and bread—if war came.

There were varying estimates on how many casualties Israel would suffer. Some of the men when called up gave their wives final instructions, and enough poison tablets for each member of the family. The army prepared coffins which could hold bodies for a year in case there was no time for burial. Hassidim in silk caftans joined bare-legged teenagers digging graves in the parks. Tel Aviv was prepared for forty thousand deaths.

Intelligence had warned that the Egyptians, who had already used poison gas in Yemen, were planning to use gas in Tel Aviv. Israel shopped Europe and America frantically for gas masks; Germany agreed to sell them forty thousand masks. But the new and old Nazis in the right-wing parties tried to sabotage the sale. "We can't sell instruments of war to Israel; we can't take sides," they argued.

The Bonn Government outwitted them. "We won't sell khaki gas masks. Those are for war; and you're right, we can't take sides. We'll sell only white gas masks. Those are for civil defense."

The men of Haga (the Civil Defense) patrolled the city streets and shelters carrying white gas masks made, of all places, in Germany.

The city women blacked out their windows. Israel's radio station, Kol Israel (the Voice of Israel), told them how to prepare for the enemy bombers:

—Tape your windows, to prevent them from splintering.
—Get black-out material. Black out at least one room, so you can have a light in one room in your apartment.
—Fill your sandbags, and pile them at the entrances of your house.
—Inside your apartment, put sandbags around the butane gas metal tanks near your stoves. If tanks get a direct hit, they will ignite.
—Get first aid materials. Every pharmacy has kits already made up.
—Disconnect electrical appliances whenever possible.
—Keep a small bag of clothing ready to take into an air raid shelter.
—Prepare water in cans and in the bathtub, so you have enough water for each member of the household.
—Stock up with a week's supply of food.

In the little frontier towns where the Jewish immigrants from Arab lands had put down roots, fear—like love—was something you could touch. Women were bewildered. Their sons and husbands were somewhere in the desert or the mountains. The government sent them money; at least there was food in the house to feed the children. But they had lived through so. much—fleeing the Arabs back home, the flight to Israel, the strange land, the new tongue, the children going to school, learning all these strange new ways—and now this: *tape your windows!* How does a woman do it all?

The schools in these little immigrant towns stayed open, but many of the teachers and even the principals were mobilized. Army girls took over. Awaking each morning with the sun, the girls left their army barracks and walked down the lonely roads to teach the children. In the afternoon they went into the little two-room homes or back to the schoolrooms to teach the illiterate and the semiliterate parents who came from exotic cultures and strange lands. And the teachers became the taught.

In the border kibbutzim, women and children moved underground. Trenches leading to bomb-proof shelters were gouged through the lovely green lawns, like scars in a man's face. Little children were taught to jump into a trench or walk into a shelter calmly, without panic, the moment an air raid alarm went off.

In the kibbutzim under the Syrian Heights, death stalked the homes. Any possible safety lay only underground. Newborn infants were rushed from the hospital to spend their first hours on earth in bunkers. Some young women who were born in air raid shelters in 1948 gave birth to their babies in air raid shelters in 1967.

The bunkers were camouflaged against air attacks. Some had entrances made of concrete slabs; others looked like archaeological digs, with mounds of earth piled on them. The architecture was simple: they were long and narrow, with curved concrete ceilings covered with rocks, to explode a shell, and with earth, to bury shrapnel. They were defenseless against direct hits.

Below, the shelters were like bunks in a submarine. Tiny beds with skinny mattresses were stacked on top of each other against the arched walls. Some shelters had tunnels of underground rooms that held sixty or eighty people; some had small, single bunkers. Each was lit by naked electric bulbs, and had a telephone and a supply of water. These were the essentials. After that, the bunkers varied. Some had refrigerators, primus stoves, stocks of canned food, chemical latrines. Some had piles of diapers; and some even raised little plants that needed water but no sunlight.

Near the entrance of one shelter was a list of instructions:

1. Remove the rat poison.
2. Check the water.
3. Check the telephone.

Safety, food, communications—these were the historical imperatives of living underground.

Israel is child-oriented; the kibbutzim are child-oriented; and even the shelters were child-oriented. It was the children who slept on the ledges and the mattresses, not their mothers. "We sleep," one mother told me, "on shelves, on floors, on nails, on hooks— even standing up."

The underground world was a world of women and children; men were absent. The teenagers who were not standing with guns at the perimeter defenses helped the women keep their children sane. They held classes, read books, sang songs, dreamed up new games, made cutouts and pictures showing the peaceful, idyllic life in a kibbutz. In the wet and damp shelters some of the children caught cold and some were seriously ill with flu. The women ran from shelter to shelter doctoring the children, for the doctors were away at the defense positions. Not one woman or child was evacuated from the kibbutzim. It was different in 1948. Then there was no air force to come to their aid.

A whole strategy of defending the kibbutzim and the border villages had developed in the twenty years of war. Each kibbutz was a self-contained stronghold with its own built-in defenses. Members of each kibbutz were officers and enlisted men on reserve, trained to protect their homes and, if need be, their country. The border settlements were the front line of Israel's system of static defense. Behind them were the mobile troops of the three Regional Commands of the army, the Northern, Central, and Southern.

Now the kibbutzim prepared for the onslaught. They stockpiled food, stored fodder for their cattle, put aside reserves of fuel and oil. Every day there were drills and alerts. Watchers scanned the skies looking for enemy planes and enemy missiles.

Yet life went on. Three couples were scheduled to be married in Kfar Blum in the Galilee on the evening of the agricultural festival Lag b'Omer, which fell on Sunday, May 28. In Sinai, eighty thousand troops were massing against Israel; from the Syrian Heights, sixty-five thousand troops looked down on the Galilee and Kfar Blum. But the weddings would go on.

The guests were Kfar Blum's women, children, old people, and a handful of security men who watched anxiously as the rabbi married the young couples in the dining room. "One small bomb on the roof, and Kfar Blum would have been finished," one of them told me.

At eleven at night the weddings were over. The children ran through the darkened village to sleep in their underground shelters. The security men, prowling the defense perimeters of the kibbutz, sighed with relief.

Encamped outdoors in the mountains of the Galilee, in the central plains, and in the southern desert, troops of the three Regional Commands were dug in, waiting.

There was little question that if war came, it would begin in the south—with Egypt—in the Gaza Strip and the Sinai desert. Here, with its men and armor and planes, the enemy was the strongest.

In Beersheba, Brigadier General Yeshayahu Gavish (nicknamed "Shaikie"), the tall quiet-voiced Chief of the Southern Command, sat at his headquarters command post studying Intelligence reports and aerial photos of the enemy. On opposite sides of the long Sinai border, marked by boulders with white U.N. letters painted on them, Egyptians and Israelis were dug into the sand dunes, watching each other. Gavish sent tanks and vehicles to maneuver near the border, letting the Egyptians know the Israeli army had dug in there. Some of the tanks moved in circles, with plows behind them raking up a whirlpool of sand. Let the Egyptians believe there were hordes of armor assembling east of Sinai.

Camouflaged in the yellow rolling dunes and barren hills, Gavish's army was spread out across the Negev. Shalom, whose name means "peace" and who had come from Yemen, walked and talked and laughed with Rachamin from Persia and Chaim from Poland. The so-called Oriental Jews from Arab lands had dubbed the Polish Jews "Vus Vus" (meaning "What? What?") because it seemed to them the Polish Jews were forever asking, "Vus? Vus?" Jews from seventy-nine lands maneuvered together, built fortifications together, wrote post cards home in Hungarian and Bulgarian, Romanian and French, Yiddish and Hebrew—and waited.

The commanders kept them busy during the day, but afternoons and evenings, and especially on the Sabbath, the men grew exhausted killing time. Psychiatrists, part of the regular army teams, talked and counseled and tried to help them.

Many who had been oppressed in Arab lands now offered to undertake any mission, no matter how dangerous. They knew the Arabs; they spoke Arabic; they could easily slip by as Arabs.

At night, lying in the desert, a heartbeat away from the Arabs, the soldiers talked of Elie Cohen, an Egyptian-born Jew who had come to Israel in the 1950's and was one of Israel's heroes. He had made his way to Damascus, posed as a wealthy Arab bachelor, and become the intimate friend of the Syrian president, cabinet ministers, and army generals. In 1965 the Syrians arrested him, just as he was transmitting information to Tel Aviv, and he was condemned to hang. People in Syria, and in Israel—among them, Elie's wife and children—watched on television as the Syrians put a rope around his neck and carried out the sentence. For hours his body dangled in Damascus' Martyr's Square.

Gavish knew that the greatest danger among his men was not hatred of the Arabs. The danger was contempt—contempt for the Arabs' illiteracy, their feudalism, the corruption of their officers. He understood, as all the officers who had trained under Wingate understood, that Israel must know its enemy.

He was aware of the enemy plans: to break through the border at the Gaza Strip and Sinai, slice off Elath, cut the Negev desert in half, join up with Hussein's Arab Legion near Mount Hebron; then mass slaughter.

On the third of June, the soldiers listening to the Arab broadcasts they understood only too well heard Field Marshal Abdel Hakim Amer, Nasser's closest friend, issue "Egyptian Command No. 2" to his troops: "I call on each and every one of you to fight with the maximum of violence."

The soldiers listened to broadcasts coming to them direct from the United Nations. It seemed to them the United Nations was set for another Munich. The nations of the world were apparently preparing to sell them down the river. Would the United States stand by? Every few years the United States and Britain had reaffirmed the integrity of Israel's borders. Were these empty words?

Apparently the Egyptians were asking the same questions. Field Marshal Amer gave them the answer: "It is now clear that the United States will under no circumstances embark on the adventure of direct action on Israel's side, because of the Soviet Union's firm stand."

Time had no meaning, save that it was running out. Death and annihilation hung in the air. The Arabs were marching. Arab states thousands of miles away—Kuwait, Saudi Arabia, Sudan—had smelled blood and were running to join in the slaughter. On the twenty-seventh of May, Algeria called up her troops. On the twenty-ninth, Morocco promised Nasser and Hussein "effective support." On the thirty-first of May, the Arabs announced, "Iraqi troops have landed in Jordan."

June 1st. Ahmed Shukairy, head of the Palestine Liberation Army, prepared his troops for the Holy War: "We will allow the Jews who survive to return to their countries of origin," the Associated Press reported his generous peroration. "As for those born in Palestine, they can remain—whatever is left of them. But I doubt that even a single one will survive."

The word "survival" swept out of Israel. From Germany a few young students, sick with the guilt of their fathers, flew to Israel to help fight the enemy of the Jews. In Munich, birthplace of Nazism, thousands of Christians marched with signs, proclaiming their support for the Jewish state. In Geneva, where there are scarcely seven thousand Jews, over thirty thousand people assembled in an outdoor mass demonstration for Israel in a night of driving rain. In France the French people, defying de Gaulle, who had halted the shipment of planes to Israel, marched through the streets in giant protest rallies. In England and South Africa, in Canada and South America, tens of thousands of people pledged their solidarity with Israel, while in America, Christian as well as Jewish young men and women stormed the offices of the Israeli Consulate and the Jewish Agency. They could not fight for Israel—Dayan had said Israel wanted no American boys to die for her—but perhaps they could drive cars or trucks or ambulances, or pick fruit in the kibbutzim. They could relieve the men who were mobilized in the call-up and sent to the front. People emptied their pockets and withdrew life savings, until half a billion dollars was raised around the world.

Would this be a new holocaust? Had Israel been born in 1948 only to be destroyed in 1967? Had the great "ingathering of all the peoples" brought them into one tiny land, the more easily to be slaughtered?

These were the darkest days the people had known since Auschwitz.

5

The First Twenty-Four Hours

TEL AVIV, Monday, June 5, 7:00 A.M. Chaim Balicki, an official in the Ministry of Labor, tiptoed into the bedroom to make sure his wife Gabriella, who had not slept well that night, was comfortable. Good. She had fallen asleep at last. He shut the door of their apartment on La Guardia Street and went to work.

At a quarter to eight the air of Tel Aviv was shattered. Air raid sirens screamed through the city into the bedroom. Gabriella jumped up. Another nightmare? The recurrent dream? Poland? She ran to the terrace. People were racing into sandbagged hallways. A plane flew overhead. Theirs? Or ours?

She flung on a cotton housedress and sped down the stairs to the improvised air raid shelter in the basement. "What does it mean?" she asked neighbors who had already assembled.

"Who knows?" Her downstairs neighbor had her own problems. Her children had gone off to school. Would they be trapped? Should she flaunt the alarm, run through the streets and bring them home?

Someone had brought a transistor radio. "This is Kol Israel," they heard, "broadcasting from Jerusalem. The military spokesman announces the Egyptians this morning launched a land and air attack. At daybreak Egyptian armored forces started advancing toward the Negev desert. Israel's forces went into action to repel them."

There was no more news. Kol Israel played music, and told the people to be calm. Gabriella huddled against the shelter walls, braced for the bombs that might fall on La Guardia Street.

At 9:00 A.M. the music stopped. Once again the announcer delivered his cryptic broadcast. "Battles in the southern sector . . . still going on. The next newscast will be at 10:00 A.M. Be calm."

The owner of the radio began switching his dial. To Gabriella the radio was like a symbol of the world they lived in. In the very center of the dial was Kol Israel; on both ends were the Arab stations. At 9:20 they tuned in Cairo Radio: "Arise!" the voice implored in Arabic. "Go forth into battle! The hour of glory is here."

A twist of the dial. Now it was Damascus Radio: "The time has come! Silence the enemy! Destroy him! Liberate Palestine!"

Back to the center of the world, Kol Israel: music, and still no news. Had the war begun?

Gabriella was frantic. "Why don't they tell us what's happening? Action in the south—hm-m. There's action in the south all the time." What did it mean? Had they sighted Egyptian bombers heading for Tel Aviv? Tel Aviv would have to be the first target. It was the biggest city in Israel. Were the Egyptians pressing buttons somewhere? They had missiles—everybody knew that. Did they have the bomb? She put her hands to her ears. She could almost hear the whine, see the explosion she had seen so often in the movies.

Ten A.M.: "This is Kol Israel, broadcasting from Jerusalem . . . Egyptian land and air attack . . . no more news . . . be calm. . . ."

"What kind of country is this?" she shouted. "Why don't they tell us the truth?"

"Sh-h," her downstairs neighbor calmed her. "Listen, there's more."

The quiet voice of General Chaim Herzog, the military commentator for Kol Israel, entered the improvised shelter. "A new chapter in the wars of Israel has been opened." Gabriella put her hand over her mouth. "As reported, the Egyptians have launched an attack on our forces and have commenced shelling our settle-

ments along the Gaza Strip border." Herzog promised a counterattack by the "armored fist" of the Israel Defense Forces. Then,
quietly, he explained: "The fact that no announcements are being
made does not necessarily indicate that there is nothing to announce. . . . It is not always advisable to report on battles, for at
times the enemy is interested to learn the facts of the situation no
less than we are. Under the circumstances of unprecedented
hysteria on the part of the Arabs, their false reporting and utter
instability, it is advisable that they continue to believe their own
false stories, up to a point. . . . The fog of war hinders the
enemy, and so let us leave him with it rather than dispel it."

The fog of war. Gabriella did not know that the decision to
black out all news had come from a hard lesson learned in the
Sinai Campaign. Egyptian officers captured in 1956 had told the
Israelis that, even while Cairo Radio was broadcasting Egypt's
glorious victories against Israel, Egypt's leaders were tuned into
Kol Israel to learn the truth. In 1967 Nasser would know only the
fog of war.

The neighbors drew closer together in the basement shelter.

"We think of war in general and abstract terms," Herzog said,
"but each and every one of us has a personal interest, and deep in
the heart a feeling of anxiety for the husband, father, brothers,
and sons now in danger."

Gabriella looked at the women. Everyone in the shelter had
someone in the war. Some had husbands *and* sons *and* brothers.

The broadcast went on: "The young people who have abandoned the cafés of Dizengoff Street and the discotheques, the farm
boys, the Yeshiva students, the members of the youth movements,
the boys of the immigrant townships, all are at this moment
shoulder to shoulder fighting in the air, on the land, and on the
sea for our right simply to live."

Our right simply to live—that was all we've ever asked, Gabriella thought. Moving pictures, frayed and yellowed, seemed to race
like shadows on the shelter wall—Warsaw . . . the Ghetto . . .
her father dead . . . the cattle train . . . Auschwitz . . . the
soldiers . . . freedom . . . Cyprus . . . Tel Aviv—*our right simply to live.*

Herzog's voice, rich and musical, sounded now as if he were smiling, as if he were permitting himself a little levity in a morning that had begun in terror. "The Hatikvah Quarter [a low-income neighborhood in Tel Aviv] is silent and the boys are not creating an uproar there. They are busy preparing one elsewhere."

The neighbors nodded. Gabriella touched the hand of a woman whose husband had fought in each of the wars—1939, 1948, 1956—and who was somewhere in the desert now.

"A new page has been opened in the history of our people's battles and of the courage of Israel. And deep in the heart of each and every one of us at this moment when we think of those engaged in the struggle, there is, irrespective of whether we normally pray or not, a prayer that the 'Guardian of Israel shall neither slumber nor sleep.' "

Jerusalem, 10:00 A.M.: The streets were filled with people. There had been no air raid alarm.

Sylvia Horwitz, a New Yorker living in Jerusalem, drove her little Peugeot to the Supersol (Israel's supermarket) near the Kings' Hotel. For days she had meant to follow Kol Israel's instructions and stock up with tape, black-out material, and food supplies for a week. She finally decided she would buy it all on Monday morning.

Survival rations, she thought, as she moved down the aisles tossing food into the shopping cart—cans of tuna fish, giant-sized boxes of matzo, assortments of crackers, the biggest salami they had, a box of Kleenex. She stopped in front of the bins of fresh fruit. These round little green melons they raise here, she thought, are just about the sweetest in the world. She dropped four into the cart.

The check-out line moved fast. She was second now, right behind a young Moroccan mother with a pink-cheeked baby. Suddenly there was a jolting explosion. Sirens screamed. The young mother grabbed her baby and squeezed it in terror. Sylvia froze.

A man's voice came over the loudspeaker: "Please go down to the shelter at once. Don't panic."

Sylvia followed the women down to the cellar. No one talked. Even the children were painfully quiet. Shells blasted around Jerusalem.

None of the shoppers had a radio. Soon the florist from the kiosk on the corner appeared in the shelter with his radio glued to his ear. He turned up the sound. The Prime Minister was speaking. "We shall repulse the enemy and vanquish his forces. United and strong, we shall stand fast in the struggle that has been forced upon us."

In a corner a concentration camp graduate whose job upstairs was collecting soda bottles quietly wept and prayed. A family of Africans in tribal gowns held their toddlers. They had known tribal wars, colonial wars, but no wars like this, with shells and ack-ack fire that grew louder and closer, until the whole supermarket shook.

"I told you," a man said to his frightened wife, "we should have gone home last week."

The Moroccan woman and a Yemenite friend sat quietly, whispering reassurances to their children. It had seemed to Sylvia that in the weeks of tension some of the Oriental Jews had panicked, expecting annihilation. Her own beloved Esther, who came to clean three times a week, had almost gone to pieces when her husband was called up. Now the Oriental Jews were the calmest and the strongest in the shelter. Was it, she wondered, because they had already had so much trouble in their lives? Was that why they could take this ear-splitting noise in stride? Or was it relief? The tension at last was broken.

At twelve o'clock noon Kol Israel announced, "Battles continuing in the south. . . . no more news." Sylvia decided to go home. The all-clear had not sounded. The shelter was packed. If I'm going to die, she thought, I'd rather die in my own apartment. She ran upstairs, found her cart where she had left it, grabbed the two top bags—whatever food was in those bags would have to last—paid swiftly, jumped into the Peugeot and drove through deserted streets that heaved and quaked with each explosion.

Parking her car on the empty street in front of her house, she dashed up the stairs and unpacked the two bags of groceries. They held the Kleenex and the four melons—a week's survival rations.

She switched on the radio, and began taping her windows. In its regular broadcasts in Hebrew, English, and Arabic, and in its "Immigrants' Hour" in Yiddish, Romanian, simple Hebrew, Ladino for the Jews from Spanish-speaking lands, and Mograbi for the Jews from North Africa, Kol Israel still reported no news.

In the valley below her terrace, turned swiftly into an artillery base, she could hear the Israeli soldiers giving their orders— "*echad, shtaim, shalosh, ESH!*"—one, two, three, FIRE! The whining and whistling and banging encircled her, as though she sat smack in the center of a drum.

The telephone rang. "We just heard Jerusalem is being shelled" —it was a friend calling from Tel Aviv. Sylvia held the receiver toward the window. The shelling shook the house and the phone in her hand. Her friend in Tel Aviv caught her breath. "Oh my God. I wish I hadn't called you."

In the afternoon the largest daily newspaper, *Maariv*, came on the streets with a Reuters dispatch from Paris reporting that Israel had destroyed 117 Egyptian aircraft. Even though this news was undoubtedly received in Cairo and the other Arab capitals, the Israeli army, taking no chances on lifting the fog, announced that the stories were "premature, unverified, and highly unreliable."

Night came and still no news. Only the people directly in the range of the enemy's guns and planes knew what was happening in their sector. In Haifa the people knew their bay area had been attacked by Syrian planes at noon. Natanya, named for the American Nathan Straus, a coastal city north of Tel Aviv, was bombed by Iraqi war planes. In Kfar Saba, northeast of Tel Aviv, right on the border of the West Bank, bombs killed four people and wounded fifteen. Only Kfar Saba knew it. At 9:15 at night Tel Aviv itself was hit; the long-range guns of the Arab Legion on the West Bank shelled Masaryk Square.

Meanwhile, Nasser's commanders at the front reported fantastic victories. Nasser shared his exultation with the king of Jordan and the presidents of Syria and Lebanon. He informed the Soviet Ambassador in Cairo, who duly informed Moscow, that the Arabs were winning. At the United Nations an emergency session called at 10:20 P.M. New York time was adjourned at 10:25 P.M. The Soviet Union was silent. No one pressed for a cease-fire.

Tel Aviv, 9:00 P.M.: A press conference was called in Beit Sokolow, the House of the Journalists. Hundreds of press, radio, and television men assembled; but no one appeared from the army to brief them. Nasser too was waiting for word from the press conference. Utterly confused by this time, and wary of his own officers' reports, Nasser had alerted his monitors to copy the news from Tel Aviv.

The reporters waited for hours, and still no one came. Some stretched out to sleep on the warm lawn in front of the House of the Journalists. Some gave up and returned to their hotels.

One thirty A.M.: General Rabin, and General Mordecai Hod, commander of the air force, arrived, and at last the press conference began. Within minutes the cables flew out to an astonished world.

The Israeli air force had destroyed 374 enemy planes and had lost only 19 of its own. In eighty minutes the Israelis had destroyed Egypt's air force in broad daylight.

Israel's armor and troops had captured Khan Yunis in the Gaza Strip; El Arish and Rafiah along the Mediterranean had fallen. Gaza Town was encircled. Israel had taken many prisoners, and a number of Soviet tanks and artillery pieces.

"A few days ago," General Herzog had mused in his nightly broadcast on Kol Israel, "Nasser said that Israel today is different from what it was ten days ago. I would say that tonight Nasser is a very different person from what he was when he started work this morning."

The fog of battle was lifted.

6

Sinai—The War of Fire

BEFORE DAWN on Monday morning, June 5, General Yeshayahu Gavish moved out of his headquarters in Beersheba, and a
convoy of three vehicles started out on the desert road. Farmers in
the kibbutzim and workers in the little development towns hurried
to their jobs, not knowing that the two half-tracks and the jeep
going by were to be the new headquarters of the Southern
Command. Nor did they know that the waiting was over.

At a quarter of eight, four hundred Israeli planes—slim, sleek
Mirages, Mystères, and Super Mystères—shot into the sky. French
Vautours and Ouragons and the little, light Fouga-Magisters—
trainers made in Israel—took off from airfields all over Israel.

Simultaneously Gavish sent his armor hurtling across Sinai in
three columns. In extreme northern Sinai and in the Gaza Strip,
Brigadier General Israel Tal rushed his troops and vehicles toward
Khan Yunis and El Arish. Below Tal's column, Brigadier General
Avraham Yoffe, the stout reservist general who describes himself
as "looking like a tank," sped his tanks through the almost im-
passible sand dunes south of the Gaza Strip along the Rafiah-El
Arish lines. And farther south, Brigadier General Ariel ("Arik")
Sharon dashed across the border to capture the Egyptian strongholds Um Katef and Abu Ageila. All of them, disciples of Wingate,
were taking the battle outside of Israel, fighting on the enemy's
territory.

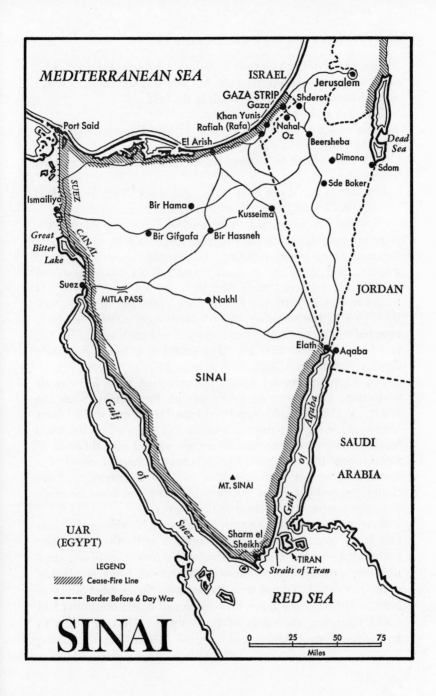

Inside his half-track General Gavish sat on a swivel chair with his maps spread out before him. At his side was his radio, through which he gave orders to his generals in the field.

"Don't run," he cautioned Sharon.

"Slow down a little; if you need planes, I'll send them," he called to Tal.

"We can't afford to lose any lives," he talked quietly to Yoffe, who agreed.

But Gavish could not hold his generals back. They had waited so long; they leaped like race horses from the starting gate.

Overhead, in disciplined formations, the planes zoomed, pinpointing Egyptian airfields, dropping their bombs with deadly accuracy, flying home, refueling and rearming in seven or eight minutes, and returning to their targets. Pilots twenty-two and twenty-three years old made five, six, even ten sorties, flying, in their own jargon, "with the aircraft stuck to the seat of our pants." By eleven in the morning, "Moti" Hod, chief of the air force, reported to Dayan, "I am certain there is not another bomber left in Egypt." By lunch time his pilots were free to bomb and strafe the Egyptian armor in Sinai.

The Egyptian ground forces, unaware that they had no air protection, were emptying their guns on the Israelis. Soon the desert was ablaze. Tanks, napalmed from the air and shelled from the ground, were blistering. The battle had whipped up the sand, turning it into a blinding sea. The air was pierced with the noise of ammunition trucks, exploding. Helicopters chugged above the desert, landing just long enough to pick up the wounded. Parachutes dropped out of the sky, bringing water and more ammunition. The temperature climbed to 105 degrees.

Standing in the half-track with Gavish were his aides and liaison officers in constant radio communication with the units they represented—air force, armor, infantry, paratroops, artillery, engineer corps, medical corps, communications—all flying or plowing across the desert. Troops were moved into the combat zones in buses—old buses, new buses, air-conditioned buses, buses that had ached their way thousands of times up the Hills of Judea to Jerusalem, Egged buses and United Tours buses—trekking through the desert, followed by private cars, taxis, station wagons, milk wagons, and delivery wagons. There was no time to paint them army colors. Children had been given the job of splashing them with mud, "not for camouflage," General Sharon explained, "but to make them look a little military." It was just as well the mud didn't stick. Looking down, the Israeli pilots could tell which were their troops when they saw ice cream trucks, hot dog vans, and laundry wagons navigating the desert.

In the northern sector of Sinai the first objective was the Gaza Strip. There were three cities in the Strip: Gaza Town, Khan Yunis, and Rafiah. Gaza was the capital, but it was too heavily fortified to risk a frontal attack. General Tal decided to bypass it and fight in the southern end of the Strip between Khan Yunis and Rafiah, then attack Gaza from the rear.

Tal, a typical sabra (the word "sabra" means cactus, a plant that is thorny outside, juicy and sweet within), was a short whirlwind called affectionately "Tallek," Little Tal. A farm boy from Be'er Tuvia near Ashdod, Tal was the fiercely loved builder of Israel's armored corps.

Now he talked to his men: "If we are to win the war, we must win the first battle. The battle must be fought with no retreats. Every objective must be taken—no matter the cost in casualties. We must succeed or die."

"My men knew," Tal subsequently said, "that on this battle depended the outcome of the war—possibly the fate of Israel. More than ten years had passed since we had last clashed with the Egyptians. We could not tell what effect the Russian training, the modern Russian equipment, and the new morale of the Egyptian army would have on their fighting capacity. We knew that we would be fighting forces whose equipment was superior both in quality and quantity to our own. For its size the Egyptian army is probably the richest in the world, after the U.S. army."

Tal sent his northern brigade under Colonel Shmuel to attack Khan Yunis. Shmuel is his first name; in the Israeli army only the generals and top commanders are known by their family names; most other officers are called by their first names to protect them from Arab atrocities, should they be taken prisoner.

Shmuel's men broke into Khan Yunis. They lost thirty-five tank commanders, including a battalion commander. "Our reconnaissance units," Colonel Shmuel said afterward, "carried in jeeps and half-tracks, suffered heavy casualties."

His men captured Khan Yunis and without waiting to clear the area rushed on. Two battalions of Tal's men rolled toward Sheikh Zuev and El Arish; Colonel Shmuel's men pushed on to Rafiah at the end of the Strip. There they faced strong anti-tank defense positions, dug-in tanks, and tens of anti-tank guns.

Shmuel described the battle; the Egyptians and Palestinians had concealed themselves behind bushes in the Rafiah sand dunes: "They fired ten rounds at a time, and with each volley one of our tanks went up in flames. . . . Tanks continued to fight though they were aflame. . . . A tank struck a mine; it was fired upon but did not receive a direct hit. Next to it another tank was blown up by a mine, and was on fire. A recovery team moved under fire to help the first tank out of the mine field. The entire team was killed. Despite this, the other recovery teams continued their work, and one realized the men showed a complete disregard for death."

In the tanks, disregarding death, were the Jews from Egypt, the Jews from Yemen and Syria, the Jews from Europe and Israel. In one of the lead tanks an Israeli officer heard Egyptians talking on his radio channel. He turned to one of his Arab-speaking crew: "What is the Egyptian saying?"

"He says, 'They come. They are upon us. Two great columns of dust. What can we do? What can we do?' "

And the Israelis were upon them, moving into Rafiah. The fighting was bloody, and even while they were fighting in the desert, the Egyptians kept shelling the kibbutzim along the Gaza Strip. Gavish called for air cover. In came the Israeli Fouga-Magisters and knocked out two-thirds of the enemy's field pieces. The tanks and infantry swept on; and Tal sent word to Gavish: "I've taken Rafiah."

At three o'clock on Monday afternoon Gavish left his half-track and climbed aboard a helicopter with a few senior aides. They flew over the troops and tanks in the blazing desert. They saw the desert strewn with mines. Egyptians with machine guns shot at the helicopter and missed. They did not know they had come close to killing the General of the Southern Command.

The helicopter landed at Rafiah. Gavish and Tal embraced. The dust-spattered soldiers watched their generals and understood.

The battle for Gaza Town lay ahead. Gaza was the fortified bastion of Shukairy's Palestinian army of refugees; it would be the bloodiest battle in the south. The generals planned their strategy in the field; then Gavish helicoptered back to his half-track in the forward command post.

The next morning Lieutenant Colonel Yehuda moved into Gaza Town from the rear. He led an infantry brigade, reinforced with a battalion of paratroopers and tanks. They were immobilized by the 20th Division of the Palestine Liberation Army, heavily armed and schooled for twenty years in hatred.

Within seconds, Gavish's radio net knew Yehuda was in serious trouble. Gavish called in the air force and rushed reinforcements. Lieutenant Colonel Uri, mopping up in Rafiah, heard that his friend Yehuda needed help. He took a company of tanks and paratroopers to Gaza. "We're not going to save the state of Israel only," Uri told his paratroopers. "We're going to save the Jewish nation."

Street by street they fought for Gaza Town. Snipers shot from windows and doors. Tanks met and battled on the outskirts of Gaza and even inside the town square. The Arabs hit a troop carrier, and set it afire. Israel Zolberg of Beersheba, a twenty-one-year-old paratrooper in charge of the medical outfit, pulled nine wounded men off the burning carrier. Soldiers yelled to the young medic to come away, but he raced back to the truck to pull off another boy. A mortar shell hit both of them, killing the soldier he had tried to save. Zolberg knew he too was dying. He heard a faint moan and saw still another wounded soldier. He handed his morphine syringe to someone to inject the man. Then Zolberg died.

In the heart of Gaza Town where two tanks stood burning—an Israeli Centurion and a Soviet T-54—a statue of a Palestinian refugee stood pointing victoriously toward Israel. It was crumbled by a shot from an Israeli tank. By noon on Tuesday, Yehuda's and

Uri's men had fastened Gaza down. The Egyptians and the Palestine Liberation Army surrendered.

Hiding in the basement of a hospital was Major General Abdul Mun'im Husseini, Military Governor of Gaza and commander of all the Arab forces in the area. As he signed his surrender he told the Israelis this was his third defeat. He had fought first with Kaukji's army in 1948. He had been an officer in the Sinai War in 1956. Now this . . .

On that Tuesday morning, Nasser and Hussein concocted a story for Arab consumption. Israel alone could not be inflicting such deadly damage; the United States and Britain were sending planes from aircraft carriers to attack the Arabs. The Israelis monitored a telephone call between the two rulers, a call both Hussein and Nasser later admitted they had made.

Nasser: How are you? The brother wants to know if the fighting is going on all along the front.

Nasser: Will His Majesty make an announcement on the participation of the Americans and British?

Hussein: (answer not clear)

Nasser: Hello, will we say the U.S. and England or just the U.S.?

Hussein: The U.S. and England.

Nasser: Does Britain have aircraft carriers?

Hussein: (answer not clear)

Nasser: Good. King Hussein will make an announcement and I will make an announcement.

Nasser: We are fighting with all strength and we have battles going on on every front all night and if we had any trouble in the fighting it does not matter, we will overcome despite this. God is with us. Will His Majesty make an announcement on the participation of the Americans and the British?

Hussein: (answer not clear)

Nasser: By God, I say that I will make an announcement and you will make an announcement and we will see to it that the Syrians make an announcement that American and British airplanes are taking part against us from aircraft carriers. We will issue an announcement. We will stress the matter and we will drive the point home.

Hussein: Good. All right.

Nasser: A thousand thanks. Do not give up. We are with you with all our heart and we are flying our planes over Israel today; our planes are striking at Israel's airfields since morning.

An American oilman visiting Kuwait months later told me the Arab populace still believed this story of U.S. and British participation. But the government officials no longer believed it; they had created another myth to take its place—that the U.S. air force had released every Jewish pilot in America to fly Israel's planes against the Arabs.

Meanwhile the Israeli air force flew a cover over the three brigades, reversing the course Moses had taken to lead the children of Israel out of Egypt. Their goal was the Suez Canal. On Wednesday, in northern Sinai, Tal's troops took Bir Hama and advanced toward Bir Gifgafa. In the center, Yoffe's troops moved across the sand dunes toward the vital Mitla Pass, the strategic gateway through the desert to the Canal. In the south, Arik Sharon's troops were fighting their way toward Nakhl, from where they too would try to wedge through the Pass.

On the sea, the tiny Israeli navy harassed the Egyptian navy with frogmen and motor torpedo boats. Early Wednesday morning a small Israeli naval assault force with helicopter cover sailed from Elath to capture the Straits of Tiran. To their complete disgust, they found the Straits empty—the Egyptians had fled two hours earlier. At 11:00 A.M. Israeli sailors raised the flag of Israel over the Straits, and an Israeli torpedo boat sailed through the Straits for the first time since Nasser had closed it on the twenty-second of May.

On Thursday morning the Israelis continued their drive through the sand dunes. Sharon and his men, who had caught two hours of sleep from two to four in the morning, pushed their tanks toward Nakhl on the way to the Mitla Pass. In the desert ahead of them they saw a brigade of Stalin tanks. Sharon opened fire. The tanks did not answer. Sharon attacked. The tanks did not move. The Israeli general investigated. The tanks were empty. The Egyptians had run away.

The Egyptian commander of the abandoned tanks, Brigadier General Ahmed Abd el-Naby, was captured three days later walking, without water, toward Cairo with a lieutenant colonel and a major.

"I was picked up," el-Naby told a reporter, "by a very nice Israeli major and a patrol. They were so kind to me. They got an ambulance and let me sleep in it. I was in very bad shape and they were so kind."

At Bir Gifgafa, he presented his calling card to Sharon. Why had he left his tanks intact, undestroyed, a correspondent asked him.

"I had orders to withdraw," he said. "My orders did not say to destroy my tanks." As his troops fled back to the Mitla Pass, the Egyptian general explained, they left their weapons, even their clothes, in the desert. "I lost all my order at the Mitla. Everyone wanted to flee for his own skin. All vehicles were abandoned and the men set off on foot to cross the mountains to the west."

Later, Sharon discussed the question of morale with el-Naby. Sharon, who looks like a handsome golden boy growing paunchy, is a formidable educator, though his language would shock most academicians. Sharon wanted to know what kind of discussions el-Naby had held with his men in the Sinai desert in the weeks of waiting. El-Naby said he never talked to his men.

"That is the difference between us," Sharon told him. "I had long talks with my men about the war and the fighting that was to come. I have great respect for my men, whereas the Egyptian commanders despise their own troops. I think the Egyptian soldiers are very good. They are simple and ignorant but they are strong and they are disciplined. They are good gunners, good diggers, and good shooters—but their officers are shit; they can fight only according to what they planned before. Once we had broken through, except for the mine field between Bir Hassneh and Nakhl, which was probably there before the war, the Egyptian officers placed no mines and laid no ambushes to block our line of advance. But some of the soldiers, particularly at the Mitla where we had blocked their line of retreat, fought to the death in an attempt to break westward to the Canal—just as they did at Faluja in 1948, where, incidentally, Nasser was fighting as a junior officer."

Sharon went on. "Even at Kusseima [near the Israel border] the Egyptian officers gave the order 'every man for himself,' jumping into the first jeep or transport that was available and abandoning their men. We came across one Egyptian soldier by the roadside crying, 'They left me, they left me.'

"No Israeli officer would ever behave like that. Our officers don't ever use the command 'Forward!' It is always 'Follow me!' That is why officers form more than twenty per cent of our casualties.

"Egyptian prisoners I have talked to said that they had been told that when they reached Israel they would kill the men and rape the women. This might be all right as a philosophy while you are advancing but it is not so good when you are in retreat. Then you're inclined to abandon your rape intentions for another day and wish you were back with your own wife on the banks of the Nile."

Before ten on Thursday morning, Sharon reached Nakhl and prepared an ambush for the Egyptians outside the town. "Our tanks," he said, "lying in ambush, waited until the Egyptians were only two hundred yards from us before opening fire, almost immediately destroying nine T-54 tanks. I reached the road with my mechanized infantry and ran into six Egyptian Centurion tanks which opened fire on us.

"In the battle for Nakhl, we advanced upon the Egyptians from the rear. Between 10:00 A.M. and two thirty in the afternoon we destroyed fifty enemy tanks—T-54's and Centurions—two regiments of artillery, anti-tank and anti-aircraft batteries, and more than three hundred vehicles. The enemy suffered more than a thousand casualties.

"This was a Valley of Death. I came out of it like an old man. Hundreds were killed; there were burning tanks everywhere. One had the feeling that man was nothing. A sandstorm had been churned up by the tanks. The noise was tremendous. Above the din of the guns and the tanks there was the roar of our heavy transport aircraft—Stratocruisers—dropping supplies of fuel, water, and ammunition by parachute, and of helicopters evacuating the wounded.

"Meanwhile the shooting and fighting continued and vehicles loaded with fuel and ammunition were exploding all along the line. The dead lay all around."

I was told by one of his comrades that Sharon had been

wounded in the Battle for Latrun in the War of 1948, and left to die. After hours in the field, under fire and faint with pain and loss of blood, he dragged himself to safety. Now every soldier knew that if he were wounded his comrades would rescue him, no matter what the cost. The Israeli army made certain no Israeli soldier would repeat Sharon's agony.

In one unit, a truck with a driver, a medic, and a Yemenite soldier named Shmuel who came from Hatikvah, a Yemenite quarter of Tel Aviv, were sent by their commander to pick up a wounded officer. Under blistering cross fire, the truck drove to the spot where the officer lay; the medic and Shmuel lifted him onto a stretcher and placed him gently in the truck. The shelling suddenly grew more intense; the driver, thinking everyone was aboard, gunned his car and drove off. Shmuel was left behind.

He fell to the ground and then crawled to an almond tree. He hid beneath the tree for about fifteen minutes, was wounded by gunfire, and realized that if he stayed there, he would never get out alive.

He undressed down to his white underwear, buried his uniform in the sand, and made his way to the Egyptian camp. There, pretending to be hysterical, he demanded to see the captain in charge, shouting in Arabic, as if he were a madman, "They're shooting! They're shooting!"

The Egyptian captain turned to an aide. "He's obviously a Sudanese. He doesn't speak Arabic the way we do. Take him next door and have his wounds bandaged."

Shmuel, dark-skinned and slim, was taken to a woman medic who began washing and dressing his wounds. But the fire became more intense, and now a unit of the Israeli army approached the Egyptian camp. The Egyptians fled, leaving Shmuel again alone. He ran out of the camp and raced toward the Israeli troops who were speeding down the road in tanks, trucks, and jeeps in hot pursuit of the Egyptians.

"Stop," he shouted, in Hebrew this time, "I'm an Israeli."

Nobody stopped. Even if they thought he was an Egyptian, they were too busy to take him prisoner. He kept shouting in Hebrew, "I'm a Jew! I'm a Jew!"

Finally someone in a truck saw him and shouted to his driver, "Stop! That's Shmuel. That's my neighbor Shmuel from Hatikvah."

The truck stopped, and Shmuel was en route to the hospital.

On Thursday at 3:00 A.M. General Yoffe, learning that Colonel Iska and his troops were surrounded by thousands of Egyptians who were rushing back toward the Mitla Pass, sent a second brigade to help. In the dark the Israeli brigade encountered still more Egyptian tanks speeding toward the Pass. There was danger that the Israelis might shoot each other in the darkness. In Hebrew the Israeli commanding officer talked to his men in the tanks: "Move forward with the enemy." His tanks moved forward. "Now, move sharply to the right." The Israelis swung off the road. "Now shoot at anything that remains on the road."

The Egyptians understood not a word. The Israelis, all safely off the road by now, shot at all the Egyptian tanks, which were still moving.

Meanwhile thousands of Egyptians were plunging backward toward the Pass with no way of knowing it was closed. The Israeli air force had effectively sealed the western exit of the Pass by bombing and napalming hundreds of Egyptian vehicles.

Yoffe kept his men at the Pass. "We were there," he told the press later, "for a day and a night and another day, in a defensive position, trying to take all the armor and all the columns rushing desperately toward the Canal area and finding the way blocked. Just imagine, the same brigade [Iska's] that started on Monday went all the way through and blocked the Pass. By Thursday morning they were at the end of their power; they had been fighting for seventy-two hours or more nonstop.

"So I had to do something in the middle of a battle, something which is not usually done. I put in a brigade to take over the job of the other brigade, while keeping the tanks firing. It was a very complicated business, but the boys did it, and did not fire on each other. The initiative and imagination, not only of the commanders but of the tank crews themselves, helped ensure that we did not have any mishaps."

The Israelis had to maneuver their way around the Egyptian tanks blocking the Pass. The Suez Canal was still their goal.

One of Tal's forces had reached the northern part of the Canal from El Arish early Wednesday morning. But Dayan pulled them back, fearing repercussions at the United Nations before his forces had really secured the Canal's East Bank.

"One of the commanders telephoned for my permission to wash his feet in the Canal," Yoffe revealed. "This was the first I knew that he was near there. I said, 'No,' and his feet are still unwashed."

By 2:00 A.M. on Friday (still 7:00 P.M. Thursday at the United Nations in New York), Yoffe's forces reached the Canal. "In just less than four days," General Yoffe said, "this division finished something like one hundred and fifty-seven tanks—counted—and reached three points on the Canal.

"We had quite a lot of prisoners, generals and colonels, who talked quite freely, too. We helped a lot of the prisoners by giving them water and showing them the way to the Canal. By the way, some of our troops saw refugees being mowed down by machine gun by the Egyptians when they came to the Canal. Why they did this, we don't know."

Yoffe pointed out that his whole division, from the commander down, "are civilians and were civilians up to three weeks ago." Yoffe had retired from the regular army in 1965 to become Director of National Parks. "I myself was a civilian for two years after the army, and from my job in nature conservation I had to go and start protecting not nature but the country. This is the common thing in Israel, where today you are a soldier and the next day something else. I got the job of penetrating, which with my weight is something to do, but apparently in the dark the Egyptians can't see even little me."

Scarcely four days after the Egyptian threat to fight a holy war had exploded in the Gaza Strip, the Egyptian army was in flight across the desert. The great Soviet fleet of tanks lay burned or captured.

In New York, Mohamed Awad el Kony, Egypt's suave ambassador to the United Nations, handed a message to U Thant. It was apparent that el Kony found the message too agonizing to read himself. U Thant read it to the Security Council. The Egyptian government had agreed to the cease-fire. The war in Sinai and the Gaza Strip was over. It was not yet over in Israel.

7

Jerusalem

O_F ALL the battles in the Six Day War, Jerusalem was the surprise—Jerusalem, the Holy City of cities, "beautiful in elevation," the psalmist sang, "and the joy of the whole world."

Who would believe that war might come to the Holy City, sitting isolated and lonely on its hills? Not the political leaders. Eshkol and his advisors were convinced King Hussein was too shrewd to fight for Jerusalem and risk losing his army and his throne.

Strategically, Jerusalem had little value. Israeli Intelligence had discovered that Tel Aviv with its dense population was slated for a holocaust. Elath, the southernmost port on the tip of the Gulf of Aqaba, was to be amputated by Nasser's army. But Jerusalem was to be quiet. In the tense weeks of May, Jerusalemites sent urgent messages to their friends in Tel Aviv and Elath pleading that they come to Jerusalem for safety.

For two people war in the Holy City was not unexpected. They were Albert and Pauline Rose—he, eighty-five and ramrod-straight, she, some years his junior, with a regal crown of white hair. The couple lived in the most exposed part of Jewish Jerusalem, a few yards from the Jordanian border from where they could see an outpost of the Arab Legion. Coming from England in 1959, they waited until 1964 and finally persuaded the Israeli authorities to let them live where no one else lived—on Mount Zion. The houses there were rubble and broken stone, inhabited

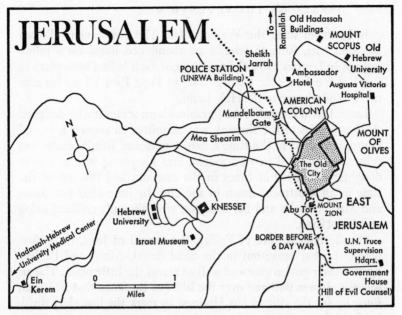

JERUSALEM

To Ramallah

Old Hadassah Buildings

MOUNT SCOPUS

Old Hebrew University

Sheikh Jarrah

POLICE STATION (UNRWA Building)

Ambassador Hotel

Augusta Victoria Hospital

AMERICAN COLONY

Mandelbaum Gate

Mea Shearim

MOUNT OF OLIVES

The Old City

KNESSET

Hebrew University

Israel Museum

Abu Tor

MOUNT ZION

EAST JERUSALEM

BORDER BEFORE 6 DAY WAR

U.N. Truce Supervision Hdqrs.

Hadassah-Hebrew University Medical Center

Ein Kerem

Government House (Hill of Evil Counsel)

N

0   1
Miles

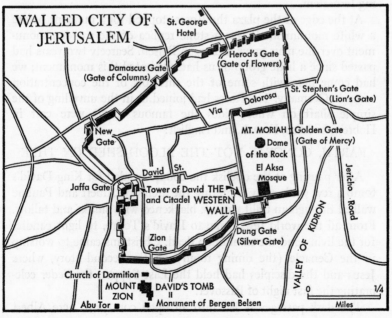

WALLED CITY OF JERUSALEM

St. George Hotel

Herod's Gate (Gate of Flowers)

Damascus Gate (Gate of Columns)

St. Stephen's Gate (Lion's Gate)

Via Dolorosa

New Gate

MT. MORIAH

Dome of the Rock

Golden Gate (Gate of Mercy)

David St.

El Aksa Mosque

Jaffa Gate

Tower of David and Citadel

THE WESTERN WALL

Dung Gate (Silver Gate)

Zion Gate

Church of Dormition

MOUNT ZION

DAVID'S TOMB

Abu Tor

Monument of Bergen Belsen

VALLEY OF KIDRON

Jericho Road

0   1/4
Miles

only by doves since the War of 1948. The government allowed Mr. and Mrs. Rose to rebuild an abandoned house on a promontory. In January 1964, the government itself built a little plaza in front of the house for the welcome to Pope Paul VI on his ecumenical pilgrimage to the Holy Land.

Later, David Palombo, the Jerusalem-born sculptor who designed the black gates of the Knesset, was permitted to convert a second house, next door to the Rose's, into a museum. But Palombo was subsequently killed in an accident, and his young wife and baby daughter now lived at times in the museum and the rest of the time in an apartment down in the city. In June 1967 the Roses and Mrs. Palombo and her daughter were the only civilians living on Mount Zion.

On the Sabbath eve of Friday, the second of June, three days before the war broke out in the Sinai desert, Albert and Pauline opened their garden gate and walked across the little plaza. The air was still. Doves fluttered over the hideous tin fence that had been flung up for the visit of His Holiness to mark the boundary dividing Jerusalem.

At the edge of the plaza the Roses stopped for a moment before a white monument. It was a stone replica of the wooden monument over the mass grave in Bergen Belsen. Scarcely two years had passed since a little group of us had dedicated this monument; we had come here with some of the survivors of the concentration camp in Germany. The Roses had joined us in the unveiling of the simple shaft on whose sides the famous words were cast in Hebrew, Yiddish, French, and English:

EARTH, CONCEAL NOT THE BLOOD SHED ON THEE

After pausing at the obelisk the couple headed for King David's tomb a few yards away. Entering the archway, Albert and Pauline walked through an unlit passage blackened with smoke and tallow. From all the world Jews came to David's Tomb, to light candles for the living and the six million dead. Christians came to worship in the Cenacle (the dining room) on the second story, where Jesus and the disciples had held the Last Supper, the *Seder* celebrating the first night of Passover.

The dark passageway led into an open courtyard; here Albert

and Pauline climbed several flights of stairs, the stones worn down
by generations of pilgrims, until they came to the roof. They stood
for a few moments resting near the old stone parapet that circled
the building unevenly, as if a child had drawn it. They watched
the mysterious light of Jerusalem, as the sun seemed to set *inside*
the stones, suffusing them with gold. The white and yellow
Church of the Dormition, the old mosques and ancient synagogues, the Hills of Judea and Hills of Moab were radiant and
enveloped in gold.

In a corner on the roof was a tiny, one-room stone structure.
Albert and Pauline had discovered it themselves and spent months
cleaning it up. They had filled it with purple and crimson pillows,
oriental couches and chairs, and converted it into a unique synagogue, where the Eternal Flame was kindled.

Together now they recited the Psalms there and chanted the
love song to the Sabbath, "Lechoh Dodi," the poem that Jews all
over the world, in skyscrapers or tents, sang as dusk fell on the
Sabbath eve:

> O come, my friend, to meet the bride,
> O come and welcome the Sabbath queen.

Their service over, the Roses walked home for the weekly
kiddush to usher in the Sabbath. "Next Friday," Albert Rose
prophesied as they crossed the plaza, "next Friday we'll welcome
the Sabbath queen at the Wall."

Three days later the war began in the Sinai desert. To make
sure that Hussein would not fall victim to pressure from Nasser,
Prime Minister Levi Eshkol sent the young king a message
through United Nations' General Odd Bull. "We shall not initiate any action whatsoever against Jordan. However, should Jordan
open hostilities we shall react with all our might. And he [Hus-
sein] will have to bear the full responsibilites for all the conse-
quences."

General Bull delivered the message. Jordan answered by shelling
the area around the Hadassah-Hebrew University Medical Center.

The hospital was prepared. At 8:30 A.M. Dr. Jack Karpas,
Deputy Director, had issued orders to his staff: "Send home all

civilian patients who can possibly be evacuated." At nine o'clock Dr. Kalman Mann, Director General, ordered that patients not yet evacuated be taken down to shelters. An additional fifteen hundred beds were placed in hallways and wards to receive any casualties that might come in.

At eleven o'clock Dr. Karpas, standing at the window of his office, saw shells exploding in the valley. They were coming from Nebi Samuel, east of the hospital. The shells came closer and closer. The hospital was hit but only slightly damaged; a few holes were punctured in the famous Chagall windows. ("Don't worry," Chagall sent word from France later. "I will make you lovelier ones.") It was the beginning of the war in Jerusalem.

Brigadier General Uzi Narkiss, G.O.C., General Officer commanding the Central Command, studied the reports from the Jerusalem border. On May 31, Dayan had told him, "Don't bother the General Staff with requests for reinforcements. Grit your teeth and ask for nothing."

Narkiss was inclined to believe Hussein's shells against the Medical Center were only a kind of obeisance to Nasser. "First move," he said later, "was to hold fast, bite our lips, and not answer fire when the Jordanians opened up." Jordan's continued shelling surprised him.

Hussein's first dangerous act was the invasion of Government House, the headquarters of the U.N. Truce Supervision Organization under General Odd Bull. The Arab Legion wrested control of the House, which was situated on the strategic Hill of Evil Counsel guarding the southern entrance to Jerusalem.

Before noon on Monday, Jordan began a full-scale offensive along the length of Jerusalem and against Israeli settlements on the whole West Bank with 25-pounders, 120 mm. mortars, and 155 mm. "Long Toms." The Jordanians brought the war out of Jordan onto Israel. They too had been trained by the British to fight on the enemy's soil.

Chief of Staff Rabin decided to give Narkiss reinforcements. Narkiss could quit gritting his teeth. The Holy City was to be joined in battle.

At two o'clock on Monday afternoon, Colonel Mordecai ("Motta") Gur sat at a military airport near Tel Aviv awaiting orders to lead his paratroopers—nearly all reservists—to jump near El Arish in Sinai. Suddenly everything changed. A new order came: "Go to Jerusalem with a battalion." Five minutes later another order reached him: "Send a second battalion to Jerusalem."

Motta Gur drove over to the Central Command Headquarters to talk with General Narkiss. Narkiss is short, slight, and unmilitary-looking. In Poland in the nineteenth century, he would have been a *yeshiva bocher*, a Talmudic student who smiled with joy each time he discovered a new meaning in the Talmud. When Gur reached him he was not pouring over the Talmud but over military maps.

"Get right up to Jerusalem," he told Gur. The war in Sinai was going well; Gur's skilled paratroopers were needed more in Jerusalem than in the desert.

Gur, thirty-seven years old, was born in Jerusalem and he was one officer who had studied Jordan's fortifications around the city. "No other mission could have persuaded me to give up the jump in Sinai," Gur said later, "nothing but Jerusalem. For each officer Jerusalem was the big dream."

Narkiss and Gur realized even as they spoke that Gur would need an entire brigade. They would have to change everything: prepare new battle plans, draw new maps, issue new orders, set up communications, tell each officer and soldier what he would have to do.

Ordinarily it takes half an hour to change the battle plans for a section—a unit of ten men. It takes about an hour to change the battle plans for a platoon of thirty men, half a day for a company of three platoons, a day or a day and a half for a battalion of three or four companies, and at least two days for a brigade. Motta Gur's battle plans were changed in one hour.

At 2:25 Narkiss was ordered to counterattack in the Jerusalem area to liberate Government House. He flashed the order to his commanders in the city.

"We broke into the U.N. with armor," an officer said later, "and the Legion began retreating into the garden and then further to the rear. We met General Bull inside the Palace. There were polite exchanges of 'good morning' and the U.N. force agreed not to move. The situation was most delicate since the place had to be flushed. Women and children were in their rooms. Orders were given to evacuate them. They behaved calmly even under fire. General Bull was the last to leave. 'You were quicker than they were,' he told the Israeli soldiers."

Meanwhile Motta Gur's paratroopers were driving up to Jerusalem in old Egged and United Tour buses. The soldiers sat silently, staring at the Hills of Judea as the buses inched their way upward. They had trained hard for the jump in the desert, but they had had no training for this. Most of them had never seen the Old City. The mystery of Jerusalem filled the buses. It was the city of dreams and of law, and of the word of the Lord. "For out of Zion shall go forth the law, and the word of the Lord from Jerusalem"—they had sung these words from their earliest childhood.

At sunset on Monday the paratroopers reached Jerusalem, and at seven o'clock Gur set up his first temporary headquarters in an apartment near the forward line.

While neighbors in the apartment building were coming to the door to offer Gur tea and supper, he took stock of the situation. He realized that his own knowledge of his native city, after nineteen years of separation, was faulty. His junior officers, barred from the Old City, knew absolutely nothing of the terrain or of the Arab fortifications. Officers at headquarters had to create their own maps. Short instruction sheets had to be drawn up and distributed to all the units.

At two in the morning, by the light of lanterns, Motta Gur and his paratroopers moved out of Jewish Jerusalem toward Jordan Jerusalem. Five minutes after they left, a Jordanian shell hit their headquarters. Jordanian mortars zeroed in on the Israelis with such accuracy that many of the paratroopers became casualties before they had a chance to fight. Gur's first operation was neither offensive nor defensive; it was to evacuate the wounded.

"The fighting was of a sort I had never experienced both as to intensity and duration," Motta Gur said later. "We had to penetrate fortifications of nineteen years. We had to break through five fences of barbed wire, kilometers of underground tunnels, kilometers of trenches, hundreds of bunkers."

Gur knew his men. No Jewish soldiers had ever abandoned their armor, their tanks, or their positions until they had used up their last bullet.

"Does that mean that the Jewish soldier, unlike the Arab, does not know fear?" the poet Elie Wiesel asked him afterward.

"Maybe. There's something to it."

"Have you never been afraid? Have you never told yourself that victory would come—and you would not be there?"

"It happened—and how! It happened many times."

"In Jerusalem also?"

"Also in Jerusalem. The shell that hit my command post, the bullets that whistled in the air, the snipers—there was that to fear. Everyone fears—that's human."

"Didn't you want to be free of this fear?"

"No."

"Isn't it easier not to be afraid?"

"No. Fear is a price you have to pay—that I *want* to pay. It is much harder to remain in a trench behind front lines and to send men under fire. It is even harder when the men you send are your friends. And it is even harder when you're radioed that they are wounded, killed. I would have given a lot to be with them, in their place.

"In the attack of the first night I sent six tanks on a special mission. They made a mistake and fell into an ambush of Jordanian armor. The first tank was set aflame with its crew inside. The others realized what happened, but were confused and paralyzed. I sent my staff officers to free them, to return them in force. My military brain—for my good luck and theirs—was ticking. But I could not erase the picture from my mind—my friends were lying dead. At that moment I envied the men in the front line, envied their fear."

For nearly eight hours Gur's paratroopers fought without rest to capture two objectives north of the Old City: the Police School, a building of UNRWA (United Nations Relief and Works Agency for Palestine Refugees in the Near East) on Ammunition Hill and the Sheikh Jarrah quarter, dominated by the Mandelbaum Gate.

They fought everywhere—in the trenches, in the rooms, on the roofs, in the cellars. Officers and men ran back and forth, dropping hand grenades into the bunkers, carrying ammunition, setting off explosives, and encouraging each other. Whenever Gur asked his junior officers how things were going, their answer was "It's O.K. Everything is going according to plan. We just want to get our wounded evacuated as fast as possible so we can go forward." A regimental commander asked two company commanders, Dodi and Dodik, how they were doing. They answered, "Pretty soon it will be O.K." They asked for no reinforcements. They finished the fighting with four soldiers alive in each company.

At one point in the fighting, Nir, a deputy battalion commander, saw that a machine gunner had been hit. The two men were running together. "What's the matter with me?" the gunner asked Nir. Nir put his finger in the man's hip to stop the blood from flowing. He called for a medical orderly who took the soldier back of the lines while Nir ran ahead with the men under his command. Soon the medic returned. He raced back and forth with wounded during the whole attack, until he was the only one in the unit not hit.

A blonde girl riding an ambulance for the civil defense came up to an evacuation point and refused to leave until the battle was over. A mother and a trained nurse, she had left her two children with neighbors and gone off to the war. Walking with paratroopers in the line of fire, she saw an Arab woman standing in front of a house holding a baby. The baby was bleeding. The nurse tried to take the child from the mother, but the mother squeezed him tightly to her body. The blonde girl finally succeeded in releasing the child; then she wiped his wounds clean (they were minor head wounds), bandaged his head, and returned him to his mother. She walked on with the paratroopers while the bullets whizzed over their heads. In a few minutes an old man rushed after her and, with Arab graciousness, handed her a box of candy. She was bewildered. What had she done? The old man was thanking her in Arabic.

"What will I do with it?" she asked.

"Take it," he said.

She decided she would take it for the soldiers. She took a roll of bandage, tied a sling around the box of candy, slung it over her back like a knapsack, and continued on with the paratroopers. She tied up so many wounds that in the midst of the battle the paratroopers began to talk of her as the "Blonde Angel."

At Abu Tor, near Mount Zion, Jonathan Yahiel, a twenty-two-year-old architectural student and a lieutenant in the infantry, was ordered to take his platoon and attempt to break through to the Old City. He assembled his group in the area called the Greek Colony, less than a mile from his home. In front of a Jewish home, he stopped to ask a woman if his boys (who had had little food and no sleep) could get some water.

"Please come in," the woman pleaded. "Let me give you and your soldiers something to eat."

Jonathan thanked her. "We have no time. But if you have water . . ."

"Of course, of course. Perhaps you would like to telephone your families?"

There was no time for food, but the telephone—that was different. The boys rushed into the house to call their parents. Jonathan dialed his number. There was no answer. He did not know that the line had been hit. He gave his name and telephone number to the woman, who promised she would keep trying to call his parents.

The soldiers returned to their jeeps and half-tracks. As Jonathan climbed into his jeep, the woman asked if she could take his picture. He smiled into her camera, waved good-by, drove to Abu Tor, and was killed by a Jordanian shell.

Before dawn Tuesday morning Gur's paratroopers began their advance toward the Old City walls to open the gates . . . To some of the men Isaiah seemed to have prophesied the war for Jerusalem:

> We have a strong city;
> he sets up salvation
> as walls and bulwarks.
> Open the gates,
> that the righteous nation which keeps faith
> may enter in.

"Our two regiments continued to advance," said Gur. "The Ambassador Hotel fell into our hands. The whole of the American Colony fell to us a little later. Some of the Jordanians retreating from the front line took cover inside the buildings, and so there was house-to-house fighting. Sometimes it was necessary to deal with the same house twice. Here we suffered casualties in the streets. The Jordanians continued to fire from those houses which had not yet been dealt with. Some of our men were shot from behind. As dawn broke a little after 0400 hours (June 7), we engaged our tank battalion. We distributed the tanks between the regiments. Fighting went on in the inner courts while we went on mopping up along our main lines of advance up to the Rockefeller Museum. We now threw in our third regiment, the one that had been fighting in the Mandelbaum Gate area. Its orders were to reach Herod's Gate—a very important point, since it was through this gate that we planned to pour our infantry into the Old City . . ."

Meanwhile, at 4:00 A.M. on Tuesday, Colonel Uri Ben-Ari, a forty-two-year-old publisher in the reserves captured the strategic Jordanian road between Ramallah and northern Jerusalem. Ben-Ari, Berlin-born, still smarted from the defeat in the Old City in 1948. Now he was fighting again in the hills of Jerusalem, this time with reservists long past military age, many of them grandfathers. In tanks and half-tracks they captured Radar Hill near Nebi Samuel, a prominent and beautiful hilltop where the Prophet Samuel is believed to be buried.

They stopped on a mountain top between Ramallah and Jerusalem to rest in the cool air. They watched the sun rise over the Valley of Ayalon where three thousand years ago Joshua, the son of Nun, had told the moon to stand still. " 'Sun, stand thou still upon Gibeon; and thou, Moon, in the Valley of Ayalon.' And the sun stood still, and the moon stayed, until the people had avenged themselves upon their enemies." Birds began to sing as Ben-Ari's tanks moved into battle against the enemy. They were on their way to Latrun.

Latrun was a British prison—a Trappist monastery, an Arab fortress—a bitter nineteen-year memory of bloodshed and defeat. It was into the Latrun prison that the British had tossed the Jewish leaders on Black Saturday, June 29, 1946. It was on the hills near Latrun in 1947 after the U.N. vote to partition Palestine that Arabs had shot and burned the convoys bringing food to Jerusalem. In 1948 the Israeli army had tried in four separate assaults to capture Latrun from the Arab Legion, only to be driven back each time. "Latrun drank more Israeli blood than any other battlefield," a correspondent wrote.

"We found our soldiers mutilated, their clothes ripped off, their limbs cut from their bodies," General Amos Horev, Deputy Chief Scientist to the Ministry of Defense, told me. "Of all the wars we fought, 1948 was the bloodiest—especially the battles for the hills leading to Jerusalem. In proportion to the total population, for each soldier killed in 1967, twenty-five were killed in 1948. A population of six hundred fifty thousand Jews in 1948 lost six thousand boys and girls; in 1967, a population of two and a half million Jews lost seven hundred and ninety-nine soldiers—tragic enough. In 1948 we didn't have enough weapons. We knew the meaning of retreat."

Badly beaten and driven back from Latrun in 1948, Israel had built the "Burma Road" to bring supplies to Jerusalem, thirsting and starving and heavily bombarded. The road through Latrun to Jerusalem became no man's land, traversed by convoys only during the intermittent truces.

During one of the first truces, Major Memi de Shalit, liaison officer with the U.N., drove me from Jerusalem to Tel Aviv to file a story. We were in the lead car in a convoy of trucks and buses. At the entrance to Latrun, where a U.N. officer was to escort us through no man's land, a message was brought to de Shalit: "The Father Superior wants to see you."

Major de Shalit invited me to the famous Trappist monastery, where only the Father Superior and one monk, Brother Marcel, could speak. The others had taken vows of silence. We walked the long path through a bare pavilion to the porch. Brother Marcel, a sharp-nosed, blue-eyed Frenchman, brought me a glass of the wine for which Latrun was famous, and he and de Shalit went inside to talk to the Father Superior.

Suddenly six Arab legionnaires in red-checkered headdress appeared in the pavilion at the foot of the stairs. Each of them carried a shotgun. One man, blind in one eye, glared sinisterly at me. While I watched, the sawed-off shotguns seemed to turn into cannons.

The Arab legionnaires shouted. What was a woman doing in the monastery? It made little difference to them that the monastery was neutral, housing the U.N.; that this was a period of truce; and that the Arab Legion had no jurisdiction here.

Brother Marcel heard the commotion, rushed out to the terrace and tried to shoo them away. It was useless. They continued swearing and shouting, demanding an explanation for my presence. Major de Shalit ran out. Now he was included in the range of their guns. The Arabs began to mount the stairs and Brother Marcel lit out across the fields. They were within a foot of us when a jeep with a tall blond Englishman seemed to fly across the fields toward us. He was Lieutenant Burden, one of the young officers who led the Arab Legion. He pulled out his gun, waved it before the Arabs, and talked rapidly. Burden was their boss. Slowly, reluctantly, without turning their backs on us, they descended the porch stairs and stood in the pavilion as the young Englishman bundled Major de Shalit and me into his jeep. Burden waved a white flag as he drove us down the road to our convoy; then he himself conducted the convoy to the end of no man's land, from where we drove in safety to Tel Aviv.

A few days later another convoy traveled through Latrun, led by a U.N. officer. This time the Arabs murdered a woman, an unarmed soldier, and a Christian railroad expert who stood up in the ditch on the side of the road waving his green passport, shouting, "I am an American."

In Latrun and the Old City Israel suffered the two greatest defeats of 1948. The armistice agreement signed by Jordan gave Israel the right of free passage through Latrun; but Jordan never allowed it. For nineteen years Latrun remained one of the most heavily fortified bastions of the Arab Legion, a military salient bulging like a tumor into Israel and blocking the road to Jerusalem.

At eleven o'clock on the morning of the second day of the Six Day War, a mechanized unit of paratroopers attached to Colonel Ben-Ari encircled Latrun, fought the Legion, and captured Fortress Latrun.

"Suddenly, this tough nut has been cracked and shown to be

hollow inside," Menachem Talmi, a reporter from the army magazine *Bemahane*, wrote.

The dream of nearly 20 years is realized in a moment. Suddenly you stand inside Latrun, trying to convince yourself it's not a dream. The deadly bottleneck where so many convoys to Jerusalem were crushed to powder and blood in 1948 has surrendered.

The fields round about are still burning. The big police fortress spattered with the marks of shell hits is silent. The monastery, where the monks have taken a vow of silence, is all closed in on itself, covering up for the fear it seems to conceal. Behind, you can see Mishmar Ayalon in Israel, a front line position which in the course of things has suddenly been pushed to the rear. The old road to Jerusalem is open once again.

Latrun: 20 miles from Tel Aviv, three from Sha'ar Hagai, and 15 miles from Jerusalem the Capital . . . this place, which became synonymous with a lost goal, a dream that you were never sure would ever be realized, which drank thirstily of the blood of so many valiant fighters, the most strategic position between the plain and mountains inland, standing guard over the east-west and north-south axes, was finally ours.

Breathless with joy, you stand at the crossroads at the foot of the monastery. The armor going by is all moving forward, deeper into enemy territory. For them, Latrun is already history and they are on their way to other objectives. The armor moves on and you remain standing, looking out over the burning fields, the death traps of 1948 and fields of victory of 1967.

While Ben-Ari's forces were liberating Latrun, shortening the road from Tel Aviv to Jerusalem, Jewish Jerusalem itself was blanketed by Jordanian fire. Arab legionnaires, in strongly fortified positions on the Old City wall, lay siege to Jerusalem with mortars and machine guns. For the religious Jews in Mea Shearim, an orthodox quarter on the frontier of the Old City, the heavens were trembling, and the earth was shaken out of its place. And the majestic voice of the Lord was heard in furious anger and a flame of devouring fire, with a cloudburst and tempest and hailstorm. Isaiah had foretold it all.

All through Monday and Tuesday Jordanian guns shelled Jewish Jerusalem. Civilians, crouching along the walls of buildings to buy food or get to their offices, were mowed down. Over five hundred wounded and dying men, women, and children were rushed to Hadassah and other hospitals. Nine hundred apartments were damaged. There were few fires only because Jerusalem is built of stone. A shell fell in the children's ward of the Shaare Zedek Hospital in the heart of Jerusalem, and miraculously did not explode. The Israel Museum, the Hebrew University, and many public buildings were hit. The Knesset, isolated and exposed, was somehow undamaged; in spite of the shelling, the Parliament held a regular session in its customary chamber.

The Israel High Command gave orders to the troops nearing the Old City not to damage any of the buildings or sites holy to the three religions. They knew that in the world outside Israel churches and mosques would be considered holier than human beings; many Jewish soldiers lost their lives that buildings might live.

Midmorning on Tuesday, while part of Narkiss' force was circling the hills around Jerusalem, another part was mopping up in the wide and abandoned streets of East Jerusalem that look like streets in Paris or Beirut. Racing through avenues whose shop windows held Damascus cloth and fancy shoes and carcasses of meat, the soldiers looked up at the magnificent stone wall that the Turkish sultan Suleiman the Magnificent had built in 1538 to fortify Jerusalem.

Most of the paratroopers, sabras as well as new immigrants, had never seen the crenelated wall of Jerusalem or the labyrinthine streets and bazaars of the Old City or its architectural wonders. Yet they knew the Old City. They knew it from their books and their parents' stories and their Bible memories. They knew the seven gates carved into the ramparts through which people and camels and donkeys could enter the Old City: the Golden Gate, Zion Gate, Herod's Gate, the Jaffa Gate, Damascus Gate, St. Stephen's Gate (the Lion's Gate), the Dung Gate (the Silver Gate). They knew how the Tower and Citadel of David would look on the wall near Jaffa Gate—like a medieval woodcut in the old Haggadoth they read each Passover. They knew the Golden Gate (sometimes called the Gate of Mercy) was stoned-over and shut, to be opened only when the Messiah came, and they knew the legend of the two bridges that would lead, when the Messiah came, from the Valley of Kidron to the Golden Gate. One bridge would be of iron, and the people who walked on this bridge would fall down. The other bridge would be of paper, and on the paper bridge the people would reach the Golden Gate.

Beyond the Golden Gate lay the Mount of the Temple, Har Ha Moriah. The Sages believed that the word "Moriah" was derived either from "Ora," which in Hebrew means "Light," or "Mora," which means "Awe." Here was the holiest of holies; here Abraham had taken his son Isaac to sacrifice him to the Lord. Here King Solomon had built the first Temple three thousand years ago. Here was the story of Jewish survival and defeat and survival again. Nebuchadnezzar had destroyed the Temple; Herold rebuilt it in 20 B.C., and the Romans destroyed it again, in the holocaust of A.D. 70. All that was left of Solomon's Temple was the site. But on the site of the outer western wall that had protected Solomon's Temple was the Wailing Wall—the Wall of Jewish history.

For generations, Jewish boys had sung the beautiful words of Isaiah:

> "Comfort ye, comfort ye My people,"
> Saith your God.
> "Bid Jerusalem take heart,
> And proclaim unto her
> That her time of service is accomplished,
> That her guilt is paid off:
> That she has received of the Lord's hand
> Double for all her sins."

The paratroopers knew it all. Now they would see it.

In fiction they would have stormed the ramparts in moments, burst through the gates and stood upon the Temple Mount, shouting "We are at the Wall!" But now, something happened. They could not fight as they had been fighting. They were held down, and not only by the Arabs shooting from the parapets; something within them—or perhaps outside of them—seemed to hold them back. They must not enter the Old City too easily or too fast. Gur noted the strange phenomenon: "The impetus of our attack declined. The Arabs held the wall, and it was impossible for us to move."

At noon, Dayan helicoptered to Jerusalem and drove with Uzi Narkiss in a half-track to Mount Scopus. Of all the views of Jerusalem, this is the most breath-taking. The two generals stared in silence at the sight that spread before them in the sun: the gold cupola of the Dome of the Rock, the silver cupola of the El Aksa mosque, the olive trees and cyprus trees punctuating the stone hills and the stone buildings. "On this sixth day of June 1967," Dayan said, "what a fantastic view!"

Narkiss nodded. Nineteen years ago the U.N. truce had come; for Narkiss, one day too soon. One more day of fighting, he was convinced, and his troops would have captured the ramparts and the Wall. Now once again there was danger that Jordan would ask for a cease-fire at the United Nations before his paratroopers could pierce the Old City wall.

Gur was suffering heavy losses. The Jordanian army was holding tight. Narkiss, although longing to rush into the Old City, decided, in order to save lives, to delay the attack until after dark.

As night fell, Gur moved his troops straight up the road to the hills around Augusta Victoria Hospital. One of his tanks went up in flames at once, as did a number of reconnaissance jeeps. Casualties were heavy.

Narkiss expected a Jordanian counterattack and alerted his commanding officers. At five o'clock on Wednesday morning, he received a telephone call from General Bar-Lev, Deputy Chief of Staff: "We are already being pressed [by the U.N.] for a cease-fire. . . . The Egyptians have been carved up. Don't let the Old City remain an enclave."

Was this to be a repetition of 1948? Narkiss telephoned Gur: "Time is running out. The sooner you complete your operation, the better it will be for the sake of Israel."

Later, Gur told a group of us: "I didn't want to take Jerusalem as fast as possible. I had had enough losses. I wanted to take it the classic way—the way the Romans took it, from the eastern hills of Mount Scopus. My plan was the same, to take the eastern part of the hills and then come into the Old City through the Lion's Gate. But now I had to prepare three plans.

"We decided to implement all three plans at the same time.

One regiment was to go to Mount Scopus to capture the Augusta Victoria Hospital and its heights. Another regiment was to make a frontal attack near the Old City wall. The third was to move around the wall from Herod's Gate to St. Stephen's Gate and break through the gate to the Wailing Wall."

The first regiment of tanks and men moved up to Mount Scopus. There on the eastern hills, the Old City on one side, the Dead Sea on the other, stood the old Hadassah Hospital and the Hebrew University, unused since 1948 when seventy-seven doctors and nurses, en route in buses, had been massacred by the Arabs. The buildings were an enclave of Israeli territory, but the road that led to them was in Jordan's hands.

The troops and paratroopers blazed their way up the once forbidden road and captured the old Hadassah Hospital and the university buildings. Working in the new Hadassah Hospital, the doctors and nurses heard over the radio that Mount Scopus had been liberated. A cry of joy rang out. World-famous professors danced with porters. Medical students from Africa who had refused to go home in the days of tension danced with the doctors who had survived the concentration camps. The men who had worked on Mount Scopus wept.

Gur, sitting in a half-track, was leading the second regiment in a frontal attack. He pushed the enemy until his column stood in the square outside the Turkish walls of the Old City.

From there Gur could see the holy places of his boyhood. "The Temple Mount was before us, with its gold and silver cupolas and all the New City beyond. . . . At this point I ordered my brigade to attack the Old City. We swept the old wall and not a shot was directed at or hit the holy places."

The heaviest casualties again were among the commanders. They were racing to see who would get into the Old City first. No one could stop the impetus now. The Israelis were on their way to the Wall.

Gur told his bearded driver, Ben-Tsur, to race ahead. They saw a car in flames outside the gate. The gate was half-opened. Ben-Tsur flung it wide open and, heedless of grenades and snipers, he sped on toward the third gate, the last before the Mount of the

Temple. A motorcycle barred the road. Was it a booby trap? Gur was somehow certain it was an Israeli cycle. It was not. They sped right over it.

Gur had promised a red-haired Orthodox kibbutznik, Zamush, that he would take him along to the Wall. Now he called Zamush on the radio. "Zamush, leave your company and rush to the Temple Mount." Within minutes, Zamush was there with a group of boys and a flag.

But they could not find the Wall. Houses had been built all around it and they got lost in the narrow streets that wound into blind alleys. The paratroopers raced against the sides of the deserted houses and the shuttered kiosks, knowing snipers lurked everywhere. They knocked at doors. No one answered. Finally an old Arab opened his door. He looked at them—unshaven, filthy, their eyes bloodshot—and trembled. "Don't kill me. Please, don't kill me."

"We don't want to kill you," a young second lieutenant from Kfar Blum pleaded. "We need you. Help us find the Wall."

The Arab repeated, "Don't kill me."

One of the boys had coffee in a canteen. He poured a cup for the old man, who drank it and grew calm. He took the paratroopers by the hand and led them to the Wall. Motta Gur and Zamush followed. Then all the battalion came in. The soldiers and the officers stood at the Wall and wept.

The flag of Israel was hoisted over the Western Wall. Chief Rabbi Shlomo Goren blew the shofar (the ram's horn), and the eerie notes Te-Kee-Ya pierced the ears of the soldiers. Soon after noon something took place that the world has never seen. All the generals and all the commanders who had fought for Jerusalem—Dayan, Rabin, Narkiss, Motta Gur—and hundreds of their soldiers came together at the Wall. The dreamers and the fighters stood there. It was as if Solomon looked down on them from the City of David. Two thousand years of agony had helped them win this battle that now they might stand before the Wall of Jewish history. Six million Jews had helped them win the battle, and each man, silently or aloud, uttered his own prayer—the "Shehechi-yanu," the thanks to God that he had been sustained to live to see this day.

Prime Minister Eshkol came. Teddy Kollek, the mayor of Jerusalem, who had spent sleepless nights dashing about his city lifting the spirits of the people, came. Later, at Ben-Gurion's request, a soldier cut down the Arab plaque bearing the name the Arabs had given the Wall—Al-Buraq, the name of Mohammed's horse that had flown him to heaven. Soldiers who had carried their prayer shawls with them into battle put them on their shoulders and prayed. In the old tradition, Dayan scribbled a note on a piece of paper and pressed it into one of the little openings in the Wall.

All day and through the night the paratroopers, dirty, tired, their uniforms dusty and bloodstained, kept coming to the Wall, touching it, caressing it, kissing it, weeping. The Wall and their tears came together.

On Mount Zion, the commander of a paratroop unit stopped his half-track on the little plaza in front of the Roses' house. "We're going in to the Old City," the commander told Mrs. Rose. "We've been selected. We're to put the flag of Israel on the Tower of David. But we haven't got a flag."

Pauline Rose climbed the stairs to her bedroom, pulled a sheet out of her cupboard, opened a tube of blue paint, and painted a Star of David on the sheet. Then she hurried down to her garden, found a long stick, and attached the sheet to it.

The paratroopers drove off waving her flag. At the Tower and Citadel of David, they scaled the stone rampart and raised the blue and white flag of Israel.

Returning from the mystery of the Wall, the paratroopers lined up on the garden stairs of Albert and Pauline Rose's house. They wanted the two most precious things in this strange war: water and a telephone. Pauline gave them water and Turkish coffee and they drank it as if they had not drunk for days, and indeed they had not.

On the telephone a young paratrooper could not convince his wife that he was alive; she had already begun the seven days of mourning. She had been told that he was killed in Sinai.

Another soldier telephoned his father. "Abba [Papa], I've found your house in the Old City."

Another showed Pauline the keys he had been carrying in his pockets for twenty years. "I'm going home," he said.

Just before sunset on Friday, the ninth of June, to usher in the Seventh Day, as they had done each week before this week of turbulence and fire, Pauline and Albert Rose with a tiny band of soldiers walked past the Bergen Belsen monument to the Tomb of David. But now they did not stop at their little synagogue on the roof. They continued, stumbling over the rubble and ruin of the war, past the Church of the Dormition—whose roof had been burned by an Arab shell. The soldiers guided them around the mines and booby traps. At last they reached the Dung Gate and entered the Old City.

The sun was almost setting as they reached the Temple Mount, then the Wall. They touched the bleached and gnarled and weather-beaten stones, on which sun and mountain winds and winter rains and snow had left their mark. The soldiers joined hands with Pauline and Albert and wept and danced in front of the Wall.

> O come, my friend, to meet the bride,
> O come and welcome the Sabbath queen.

8

War in the North

Aᴛ ᴅᴜsᴋ on Sunday, June 4, Major Mottel, a reservist army officer and farmer, ordered the children of Dan, a kibbutz situated below the Syrian Heights, into the air raid shelters. They were not to come above ground until further notice.

In Kfar Blum, a kibbutz just south of Dan, Ruthie Criden, who had left America before the War of Independence, tucked her little granddaughter Ilana into her crib in the underground bunker. Ruthie's husband and son were somewhere at the front.

In Kiryat Shmona, picturesquely built on a mountain overlooking the drained and now green Hula Valley, Avram Yehezkiel, the deputy mayor, who had come with the great exodus from Iraq in the early 1950's, gathered his wife and their ten children around him. He was going out on patrol with the border police. "If shelling from Syria begins, you are to stay away from the windows. Remember."

In the mountains, Brigadier General David Elazar sat in his half-track field headquarters with detailed maps of the Syrian and Lebanese borders and the northern sector of the West Bank of the Jordan spread before him. These were his areas of command.

Dark-haired, slim, with the grace and style of a Kennedy, Elazar talked to his aides. Syria was the wildcat; the Syrians had been harassing and shelling the kibbutzim and the immigrant villages on and off for twenty years, stepping up the infiltration and sabotage after the leftist victory in their country in 1966. Even the blasting the Syrians took from the Israeli air force in April, when the Syrians attacked Gadot, did not stop the daily harassment.

Elazar, known as "Dado," the underground name he had taken in the Palmach to get the British off his scent as he brought "illegals" into Israel, once again went over the problems of the Syrian Heights. As G.O.C., General Officer commanding the Northern Command, Dado had the dual assignment of defending the kibbutzim and villages—his front line static defense—and keeping his troops, dug in behind the settlements, on constant alert, ready to move forward on counteroffensive maneuvers.

For Gavish in the south, the waiting had ended at dawn on Monday. For Narkiss, in the center of Israel, the waiting ended by 10:00 A.M. For Elazar, it ended in the early afternoon. Under Rabin's coordinated command, Dado took part of his northern army over Israel's borders to the West Bank, toward the city of Jenin.

"I joined the first attacking brigade," he told me afterward. He was in the first half-track, leading the forward command group. "We were outside Jenin when I gave the command to attack. When some of my forces penetrated Jenin, I decided to join them and enter the town right with them. I sent word to my boys, 'I'm advancing along a certain route . . .'

"Unfortunately there was a misunderstanding. The boys were waiting for me on another road. I was about eight hundred yards from the town when a Jordanian tank opened fire on my half-track. Thank God, it didn't hit!"

This was not Dado's first narrow escape. Born in Sarajevo in 1925, Dado had slipped out of Yugoslavia just ahead of the Germans; he was rescued by Youth Aliyah. In Israel, Youth Aliyah became his family and his home; he lived with a Youth Aliyah group in Kibbutz Shaar Ha'amakim near Haifa—a Jewish adolescent living in the Promised Land under British rule with Arab neighbors. In the battle for Jerusalem in 1948, he was, at the age of twenty-three, the youngest battalion commander in the army. Today, although married, with three children, he pooh-poohs all the big stories of bravery. "Heroism is very simple," he says, and blows rings of smoke in the air, "very simple—just to go and die."

MEDITERRANEAN SEA

LEBANON

SYRIA

Kiryat Shmona

Baniyas

Dan

TEL FAQ'R
TEL AZIZIYAT

Kfar Szold

Kfar Blum

Levahot

Habasham

HULA VALLEY

Gonen

Kuneitra

Ashmara

Gadot

Migdal Ha-Emek

Kfar Hanassi

Safad

GALILEE

ISRAEL

GOLAN HEIGHTS

Acre (Akko)

Sea of Galilee (Lake Kinneret)

Tiberias

Ein Gev

Kinneret

Tel Katzir

Tawafik

JORDAN

0   5   10   15
Miles

GOLAN HEIGHTS

WEST BANK

Beit Shean

Jenin

Tubas

Tulkarm

Taybe

Nablus (Schechem)

Kalkilya

Tel Aviv

SAMARIA

Jordan River

Damia Bridge

Ramallah

Latrun

Jericho

Allenby Bridge

Jerusalem

ISRAEL

Bethlehem

Gush Etzion

Hebron

Fawwar Refugee Camp

Es Samu

JUDEA

Dead Sea

JORDAN

HILLS OF MOAB

Beit Shean

Jordan River

0   25
Miles

Yet he is constantly astounded by his soldiers' bravery. "In the war, you're too busy to know what each man is doing. It's only afterward, when you dig around, you find out. In the battle for Jenin, one of my boys, Lieutenant Gad Repen, was commanding a tank platoon. His tank was destroyed by fire from the enemy tanks. His face was burned. He lost one of his hands in the shooting. He was surrounded by enlisted men; he was the only officer. He wouldn't leave them. He got first aid, and continued to command and conduct the battle for two hours until reinforcements arrived. Only then, finally, would he leave for a field hospital."

Jenin was a major objective; here the Jordanians had long-range artillery from which they could menace the Israeli town of Afula, the immigrant town of Beit Shean, and the vital air base of Ramat David. The Arabs had 30 Patton tanks guarding Jenin, another 88 near the Damia Bridge on the Jordan River, and two battalions of the 40th Armored Brigade—nearly 120 tanks to Israel's 100.

The battle for Jenin persisted through the evening, with neither side taking prisoners. "We attacked them at night," Dado said, "and at night it is impossible to take prisoners." But the city surrendered before dawn, and Dado's forces swept on through Tubas toward Nablus, known in the Old Testament as Shechem—"a place," according to the ancient rabbis, "destined for evil. There Dina [Jacob's only daughter] was violated, there Joseph was sold, there the Kingdom of the House of David was divided."

Apparently the Jordanians expected the Israelis to attack Nablus by the conventional route, coming down the isosceles lines of the Big Triangle, from Jenin south to Tulkarm, then from the west to Nablus. Instead, the Israelis entered Nablus from the east.

The people of Nablus rushed into the streets, singing and applauding and cheering wildly. They thought the Israelis were a force of Iraqis on their way to assist the Arab Legion. Nablus surrendered with scarcely a shot being fired. For many Israelis this capture of Shechem, once destined for evil, had the same air of mystery, the same feeling of religious awe, that accompanied the capture of the Wall.

In forty-eight hours, the West Bank was cleared. With Mirage and Mystère jets and the light Fouga-Magister trainers pounding the Jordanians, Narkiss' forces had captured the southern part of the West Bank, Dado's the northern. Dado moved his forward command group north toward the Golan Heights.

Except for the normal barrage of shells they lobbed into the kibbutzim, the Syrians seemed rather quiet on Monday, the first day of the war. It was clear to the Israelis that the Syrians were getting news of glorious Arab battles from Nasser and Hussein—that Egypt had wiped out Tel Aviv, that the Israeli army was crumbling under Hussein's Arab Legion. All day and all night Monday the Syrians waited, until they too heard the news of Rabin's press conference, held at one thirty on Tuesday morning.

Shortly after 2:00 A.M. the patrols in Kibbutz Dan heard the noise of tanks and armored cars on the Syrian side of their border. About 4:00 A.M. the Syrians laid down a heavy artillery bombardment on the kibbutz.

From the northeast, columns of tanks moved down from the top of the mountain, heading for Dan. Another column of Syrian infantry and tanks descended from the Baniyas Heights, firing their cannon. The kibbutz returned the fire with mortar and artillery.

When the Syrian tanks (Soviet T-34's) approached the wadi, the dry river bed just below the kibbutz defense lines, the Israelis pinned them down with heavy fire. The Syrians reached within six hundred yards of the kibbutz, and then were repelled. Swiftly they reorganized and came on for another attack. One tank managed to get close to Dan's outermost fence; the Israelis blistered it with fire. Their engine still running, the Syrians clambered out and fled. The Israelis jumped in and brought the tank into the kibbutz. A second Soviet tank fell into the wadi.

Driven back, the Syrians changed their strategy from attack to defense, and an artillery duel began. The Syrians apparently wanted to determine two things: the range of Israel's artillery and the range of her tanks. Later, Elazar characterized the attack on Dan and the similar ones on Tel Dan and Shear Yashuv as "secondary feints intended to draw our forces to that area, and perhaps to effect small territorial gains so that the enemy would be able to boast they had captured one or two settlements."

This was the only place the Syrians fought on Israeli soil. Elazar sent in tank regiments, set up anti-tank emplacements, and spread an armored force across the north "to fire on the batteries of the enemy," and in the event of an attack, "to prevent the capture of any position or settlement." The kibbutzniks and the army drove the Syrians back.

From the fifth to the eighth of June the Syrians laid down an almost ceaseless blanket of artillery fire on the kibbutzim and towns in the range of their cannon. Two men were killed; sixteen wounded were rushed to the hospital in Safad. Throughout the north houses were demolished; chicken coops, barns, tractors, and cars were destroyed; livestock was killed; fruit orchards and fields of grain and cotton were burned. The northern villages knew the war as no other part of Israel knew it; for six full days they took its brunt.

A regular rhythm of life developed in the kibbutzim under the firing. The Syrians would fire for several hours, then there would be a lull. As soon as the first shell was heard, everyone above ground jumped into a trench and raced into an air raid shelter. During the lull, people would run from the dining hall through the trenches to the shelters carrying hot food. Women and children would climb out of the shelters to eat on the grass nearby. Some would dash to a house to take a shower. The lulls came at specific times, as if the Syrians too wanted to eat and have a siesta. Then the shelling would begin again, and life would go on underground.

Of all the Arabs who encircled Israel, the Syrians were the most vicious. Yet by Wednesday night—when it was clear that the enemies on the other fronts, routed and defeated, were ready to accept a U.N. cease-fire—it looked to the settlers in the Galilee as if the war would soon be over. Once again Syria, the hit-and-run killer for nineteen years, would be allowed to go on harassing, terrorizing, murdering at will.

The kibbutzim and settlements sent a delegation to Prime Minister Eshkol. The Cabinet met all night listening to the arguments: "We can no longer live the way we have lived for nineteen years. . . . We can no longer work in our fields and be shelled. . . . You can't abandon us now. . . . If you can't send the army up the Heights, we'll go up ourselves."

(Earlier that same day, watching Damascus television in command headquarters, a group of Israeli pilots saw, not the usual belly-dancers or Arab movies, but two captured Israeli pilots. While they watched, almost unbelieving, they saw the Syrians kill their comrades and mutilate their bodies for all the world to see. The pilots, in a bitter assault, fighting for the first time with hatred, attacked Syrian ground forces, Syrian artillery, and completed the demolition of the Syrian air force that they had begun on the sixth of June.)

Eshkol said he could promise nothing. Early Thursday morning the delegation drove home discouraged, tormented. Victory was on every front except theirs. "Many of us felt," General Rabin had said, "that the Syrians were the people who had brought about the war."

On Thursday, the Syrians accepted a U.N. cease-fire, to which Israel agreed. To the farmers in the north it was unthinkable that the Syrians would once again go unscathed and unpunished, just as they had in 1948 and 1956. "That night," General Elazar decided, "when I was told not to attack because of the cease-fire, was the worst moment of my life."

But the Syrians apparently could not break a habit. Scarcely an hour after the cease-fire, they threw heavy shells against Ha'on, Tel Katzir, Gadot, and Maagan, four kibbutzim in the lower Galilee.

At 4:00 A.M. Friday General Elazar climbed into his sleeping bag under a canvas stretched like an awning from his half-track to the earth. He had had almost no sleep since Monday when he entered Jenin. He fell into a deep sleep. The tarpaulin kept out the light as the sun rose over the Galilee mountains. All around him officers and men talked quietly or slept.

At 7:00 A.M. Elazar was awakened. General Dayan was on the phone. "Dado," the familiar voice said, "are you ready to attack?"

"Completely."

"Go ahead."

Elazar gave the command. From Kibbutz Dan and Kfar Blum and Kfar Szold, from Gonen and Notera, from Ashmara, from all the kibbutzim and settlements that had known the Syrian fire for nineteen terror-filled years, the army now moved with trucks and half-tracks and jeeps, with infantry and tanks, and with the Israeli air force.

They moved up the cliffs, some of which had never been scaled by men. Near the Hula Valley the precipices soared straight up from the valley floor below sea level to a thousand feet above sea level in little more than a mile. For months men had sat in the settlements along the Hula studying through binoculars where goats or sheep placed their hooves as they grazed their way up the perpendicular heights.

In Kibbutz Dan, Major Mottel, watching through binoculars, saw the first Israeli tanks burst into flames, blown apart by Syrian mines and anti-tank fire. The volunteers in tractors and heavy bulldozers, opening roads for the tanks, were killed one after another. The tanks followed crawling, some almost on their sides. The Israelis were still low enough on the slopes to make every tank an easy target. The Syrians blasted away.

Mottel saw men leap out of turrets to pull the wounded out of the burning tractors and tanks; he saw tanks shoving the dead vehicles out of the path into the mine fields. He watched as the men in the burning tanks continued to fire until they ran out of ammunition. Under searing fire, they leaped out and raced to climb into another vehicle. The tanks lumbered and boiled up the Heights like prehistoric monsters.

"Tanks," Lieutenant Colonel Joey Criden thought to himself (his job was to repair the tanks in the Galilee), "tanks are engineering monstrosities, mechanical abortions." The Shermans, obsolete since 1945, could not have climbed the Heights had not the Israelis put in giant, new 750-horsepower engines.

Heading straight up one hill, a lead battalion of thirty-five Shermans moved in a column single file, absorbing ten tons a minute of Syrian 122 mm. and 130 mm. shells. Still the Shermans pushed on, crawling over barbed wire, knocking down pillboxes, jumping trenches, running over or mowing down Syrian soldiers. The men in the kibbutzim below the cliffs saw the slaughter. Each time a tank exploded, they knew three men were trapped in it.

The Shermans had to cross three lines that ran like fortified ribbons on the steep face of the mountain. The commanding officer, Colonel Arie, was wounded. The second in command, Major Rafi, jumped out of his tank into the turret of the lead tank and was killed. The Israelis, with less than half their original thirty-five tanks, captured Sir-a-Dib, above an underground oil pipeline, and pushed on to Kallah, a Syrian town heavily defended with Russian arms. The new commander, the third, was Lieutenant Naty. His radio was knocked out when a shell hit his tank turret. He rushed out of his tank, entered another, and continued directing his forces. A bullet nicked his skull, and the blood flowing down his chest short-circuited his microphone, so that this radio went dead too. He stood up in the tank turret, using his hands to lead the other tanks. He had only three Shermans to lead; the rest had been blown up. With three tanks he captured Kallah.

Shortly after the war General Elazar explained his over-all attack to me. "You can penetrate such an organized defense in different ways. I chose a narrow frontal attack. It's the most risky, and it may well not succeed. But its advantage is that if you do succeed, you soon have your troops in the enemy's rear. This is very important when you're fighting the Arabs. Psychologically, they break easily; they give up when you're behind them.

"So first we went in with the narrow frontal attack. Second, we wanted to give them the impression of a wide frontal attack, moving up on several fronts. This way you paralyze the enemy. He can't move because of the uncertainty. He doesn't know where to counterattack. We made the impression of a wide attack along thirty or forty miles by sending small groups up, but really we attacked along only one mile."

The target of this narrow frontal attack was perhaps the strongest of all the Syrian fortifications, Tel Faq'r. Here the Syrians had dug into three hills, a large one and two smaller ones. Elazar's plan was to have one unit attack one of the small hills while another unit attacked the largest hill. When his forces had almost reached the center of the large hill, a third unit would begin the attack on the final hill.

Leading the first unit up the first small hill was Lieutenant Colonel Moshe Klein, an infantry battalion commander who had come from Hungary. The Syrians destroyed his half-track; Colonel

Klein escaped from his burning vehicle and with his soldiers climbed the rest of the hill on foot—running, crouching, taking cover wherever he could find it.

He saw two groups of his soldiers moving up separately and, fearing that they might not recognize each other and shoot at each other, he stood up to coordinate the two groups. The Syrians killed him.

Behind him, his deputy, Major Zohar, who had also left the half-track, took over, organizing the men for another assault. A Syrian bullet pierced Zohar's neck; the medics carried him down the hill past the troops racing forward. Thirty-year-old Major Alexander Krinsky, who had come with Youth Aliyah from Poland fourteen years before, was rushed in; he organized the men for a new assault, led them up to the top of the hill, and there was killed.

Without officers, even without orders, the soldiers continued to advance. "Everyone, knowing his mission, carried it out," Elazar told me. "This is what is important. Of course the officers were always first, but when the officers died, the men knew what they had to do."

The largest of the three hills was blocked by a fence of barbed wire protecting the Syrian trenches. A young Jewish soldier from an Arab land, David Shirazi, threw himself on the barbed wire. He shouted to his comrades, "Step on me, because there are mines on both sides of me." Fourteen soldiers in his unit walked on Shirazi's body and entered the Syrian trenches. Shirazi stood up bleeding and followed his friends. He was killed in the trenches.

In a command headquarters on level ground below the Heights, a thirty-five-year-old officer using binoculars and radio directed part of the battle. "Twenty-three," he tuned his short-wave radio, calling a young sergeant battling on the slopes, "what resistance are you meeting?"

"They're shooting everything at us. We're completely cut off."

The officer turned the dial. "Sixty-two, I want you to change position."

A voice came over the radio: "Twenty-six. Twenty-six." It was the sergeant's voice, frightened, calling command headquarters. "This is Moshe. The platoon commander has been killed. What should I do?"

The officer turned back to the sergeant's frequency. When he spoke his voice was changed. He became teacher, father, counselor. "Moshe, this is your boss, yes?"

"Yes."

"Moshe, remember when you were at school, how you found out where the gunfire was coming from?"

"Yes, I remember."

"All right, now find out where the fire is coming from. I'll call you back in two minutes."

He turned the dial. "Captain, I want you to take your tanks and reach the sergeant now. You will take orders from him."

Back again to the sergeant. "Moshe. You will have help in a few minutes. You will be backed by the captain. You are in full command. You will take the objective."

Later, with Moshe in control of his sector, the officer radioed another unit to push its way up the hill. There was no answer. He called still another group. Again there was no answer. He turned the radio over to his chief of staff, and went out himself to take part in the battle.

Elazar sent reinforcements up the big hill for a final assault. The fresh troops joined the surviving soldiers who had continued climbing even as one by one their officers fell. Tel Faq'r soon surrendered. The battle had lasted three hours. Thirty-four Israelis and sixty Syrians were dead.

"In the first stages of the Battle of Tel Faq'r, the Syrian soldiers fought quite well," Elazar told me. "The soldiers in their concrete bunkers stood up and really battled. But the Syrian command was not a good one. The officers were not in the trenches. They were behind. They had command posts in more secure places, like villages. Therefore they didn't feel the battle. They didn't realize what they were doing. They couldn't react very fast.

"War to a certain extent is like a game. On the Jordan front, when I did something, I felt somebody react. But on the Syrian front, I didn't feel there was a player opposite. I had a big army, and I felt a lot of their soldiers fighting. But they did not have a good command with flexible minds and fast reactions. Their main disadvantage was their officers."

After Tel Faq'r the next objective was Tel Azaziyat, known as

"The Monster" to the farmers who had plowed their land under its deadly guns. The Syrians had fortified it heavily, ignoring the United Nations armistice line, which ran through Tel Azaziyat and which was supposed to make half of it a demilitarized zone.

As the battle opened, the Syrians from their concrete bunkers blasted every vehicle the Israelis sent up. But again the Israelis climbed on in the face of fire, and when the only vehicle to reach Tel Azaziyat was Lieutenant Colonel Benny's half-track with five soldiers in it, the Syrians surrendered. Their officers had fled, and the morale of the remaining Syrian soldiers crumbled against this army climbing into open fire.

All Friday afternoon the Israelis fought on, scaling the Heights, racing down roads, encircling camps and villages. The Heights and the Valley were blazing with smoke and fire. By evening they had climbed the Heights to Bakala, taken Tel Faq'r, Tel Azaziyat, Bourj Bravil, and had broken through at Darbashiyeh. They now controlled two bridgeheads on the Heights. They used the night to regroup their forces. And men from the kibbutzim ran out to bring back the wounded and the dead.

At dawn on Saturday, with heavy air support, the Golani Brigade, made up of crack infantry, pushed on toward Tel Tamra and then burst into the village of Baniyas, the fortified area where the Syrians had sought to divert the Baniyas River and the headwaters of the Jordan.

The tanks and troops were moving in fast for the final blow. An armored force that had helped take Baniyas mopped up the Syrian-Lebanese frontier. Another force raced over tough mountain terrain, knocked out anti-tank emplacements, and pushed on toward a major objective—the heavily fortified city of Kuneitra, the largest city on the Golan Plateau. Other forces joined them to mop up inside the town. The Syrian army was collapsing, retreating as fast as it could to Damascus some forty-five miles away.

A jeep driver speeding toward Kuneitra said to his companion, "The Syrians asked for war, and Kuneitra is where they're going to get it." But as they entered the town they learned that Damascus Radio had announced the surrender of Kuneitra three hours before it actually occurred; its inhabitants had fled.

Under Brigadier General El'ad Peled, an infantry force climbed the cliffs of Tawafik, an armored force pushed up on terrain un-prepared for tanks, and paratroopers brought in by helicopters cut the enemy's rear paths of retreat. The southern town of Butmiyeh fell to the Israelis. One day and three hours after the first break-through into the Syrian border, the battle for the Golan Heights was over.

General Elazar attributed the success of this "very bitter and hard battle" to three things: "The first was the efficient action conducted by our air force; the second was our initial impetus which threw the enemy off balance; the third was the fact that the commanding officers of the glorious Syrian army were the first to turn tail—which is the reason why among hundreds of prisoners in our hands there were so few officers."

The casualties were heavy: 115 Israelis killed and 30 wounded; 1,000 Syrians dead—no one knew how many wounded—and 600 taken prisoner. Some 80,000 soldiers and civilians had fled.

The Syrian army was not totally destroyed, but it was tempo-rarily ruined as a fighting force. It lost more than one-third of its three hundred tanks—forty were ridden off the battlefield by the Israelis. It lost 50 per cent of its artillery, and its infantry and tank brigades were severely hurt.

But most important of all, the Syrians lost the cliffs from which they had harassed and killed for nineteen years.

On Saturday afternoon, silence fell on the kibbutzim. The children climbed out of the shelters and were blinded by the sunlight. To Mottel in Kibbutz Dan the silence was that of a roaring ocean that had suddenly grown still.

On Saturday night islands of light glittered in all the hills and valleys of the north. The people were told, "Turn on your lights—even your searchlights. The Heights of Golan are ours."

The children slept in their own beds that night. It was their seventh day.

9

The Battle for Peace

THE SOVIET UNION, a kind of father-image to the Egyptians and the Syrians, was embarrassed by its protégés' poor scholarship, by their inadequate and often shoddy performance, and by their wasteful destruction of expensive tools and toys. But this was an understanding, forgiving, and affluent father. Although the war, except for sporadic border clashes, was over and the Arabs had been soundly defeated, he would try again.

He would try first in the United Nations. In that international forum, with the ears of all countries listening, the Soviet Union and the Arab states would attempt to regain through lies and false accusations what even they realized had been lost on the battlefield. The Soviets knew well that rearming the Arabs did not point the way to peace in the Middle East. So instead of negotiation and accommodation, an avalanche of gifts of war to the Arabs. Instead of conciliation and compromise, invective and propaganda in the U.N. It was clear from the beginning of the seventh day that even the peace, if it was ever to come, would be a battle.

It was 8:10 in the morning on Saturday, the tenth of June, when Hans Tabor, the patrician ambassador from Denmark, called the thirteen-hundred-and-fifty-fifth meeting of the Security Council to order in New York. In the rotating presidency of the Council, Tabor, president for the month of June, had evinced such diplomatic skill that overnight he became a television celebrity.

116

He opened the early morning meeting, as he had done each of the previous sessions, by setting the stage. "I shall now, with the consent of the Council, invite the representatives of Israel, the United Arab Republic, the Syrian Arab Republic, and Jordan to take places at the Council table; and the representatives of Lebanon, Iraq, Morocco, Saudi Arabia, Kuwait, Tunisia, and Libya to take the places reserved for them at the side of the Council Chamber, in order to participate without vote in the discussion."

The geography and politics of the Middle East were translated into human figures in the Council Chamber. Israel and the three Arab states that had fought her and that shared borders with her on the map sat at both ends of the semicircular table; seven other Arab states sat in a box at the side of the room; looming large at the middle of the table sat the Soviet Union, the United States, Great Britain, and France—the four powers that had played a major role in Israel's birth and history. The other nations of the fifteen-member Security Council filled out the table.

The early morning session opened on its usual note of acrimony. Ambassador Nikolai Trofimovich Fedorenko of the U.S.S.R., in the role of defense counsel for the Arab states, declared the evidence was now "irrefutable" that "Israeli aircraft have repeatedly bombed Damascus.* Thus the circle is complete. The perpetuation of the crime is proved." His anger was vented against Ambassador Arthur Goldberg of the United States. "We are forced to reject the attempt of the representative of the United States to confuse a clear situation. We cannot attribute objectivity to him. . . . This is one more piece of evidence of the lack of elementary conscientiousness on the part of the United States representative."

The next speaker on Tabor's list was Ambassador Gideon Rafael of Israel, who had decided that this Sabbath morning was the time to counter the insults of the Soviet and Bulgarian ambassadors. "To the best of my knowledge," Rafael said, "the United Nations is an organization based on the sovereign equality of States. Nothing in its Charter provides for prosecution and judges, and even less for all in one and the same person. Neither does it have

---

* Actually Israeli aircraft bombed, not the city of Damascus, but the Syrian airfields, and destroyed the Syrian air force.

defendants. I am the representative of a sovereign State and I act upon instructions from my Government only.

"The representative of Bulgaria [Milko Tarabanov] has alluded to my war record. I wish to set his mind at peace. During the war I was in charge of operations which included the dispatch of Israel personnel to aid the heroic Bulgarian resistance against the Nazis."

Each member of the Security Council had his own style. Rafael's style was different from that of his foreign minister, Abba Eban. Where Eban spoke with brilliant oratory, Rafael spoke with emotion. Eban's accent was of Cambridge; Rafael's of Germany, where he was born. Fedorenko's style was unique. His speeches were a mixture of Chinese proverbs and Soviet abusiveness. Whenever he came to the end of a speech, he would lift his right index finger and snap it into his palm. Immediately Tarabanov would catch the signal and raise his right hand, asking to speak.

Now, on this early Saturday morning, Ambassador George J. Tomeh of the Syrian Arab Republic, who looked and sounded like a college professor, lectured the United States and Great Britain. "I wish on this occasion to remind those Western Powers, friends, protectors, and spokesmen for Israel, that by their blind one-sided support of Israel they have encouraged the conquerors of Arab Palestine to become not only professional international criminals, but also pampered criminals. Those friends themselves are the ones who are sapping the roots of Israel!"

He articulated the distinction the Arabs drew between Jews and Zionists. One heard it throughout the Middle East—"We don't hate the Jews, we hate the Zionists."

It is "the Zionists who have spoiled Judaism," he said. The plight of the Arab refugees "falls within the criminal, neurotic, Zionist-Nazi complex. It is part of what the Zionists describe as the 'final solution of the Arab problem' to deport, expel, expropriate, kill, and annihilate. We still await the reaction of the American conscience to this tragedy."

The debate proceeded. Fedorenko: "The United States is revealed as a direct champion of the aggressor. . . . No hypocritical words can help American diplomacy to whitewash the dangerous policy pursued by Washington."

Goldberg: "I have no alternative, in light of the very provoca-

David Ben-Gurion, the Old Man of the desert. *(Morris Warman)*

Above, the Bergen Belsen monument on Mount Zion in Jerusalem, a replica of the wooden monument erected by the survivors of the German concentration camp. *(World Federation of Bergen Belsen Associations)*

The people of the *Exodus 1947* unfurl a huge black banner: England's Union Jack above a swastika. *(Ruth Gruber)*

Any Jew from any country in the world is free to come to Israel to live —whether he is blind or sighted, strong or maimed, rich or poor. A blind man waits in Casablanca's Jewish cemetery for the voyage to Israel. (*Ruth Gruber*)

There is no war without refugees and there are no refugees without war. The 600,000 Arabs who fled from Palestine during the War of Independence in 1948 were matched in number by 600,000 Jews who subsequently fled to Israel from Arab lands. Women from the exotic island of Djerba, off the coast of Tunisia, arrive in Haifa. (*Ruth Gruber*)

Pauline and Albert Rose, on the terrace of the house they rebuilt on Mount Zion. *(Ruth Gruber)*

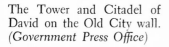

The Mosque of Omar on the Temple Mount inside the Old City of Jerusalem. *(Hadassah Magazine)*

The Tower and Citadel of David on the Old City wall. *(Government Press Office)*

Left, Chief Rabbi Shlomo Goren blows the Shofar (the ram's horn) at the Western Wall. (*Government Press Office*)

Right, all day and through the night the soldiers came to touch the Wall and pray. (*Government Press Office*)

Abba Eban, Israel's Foreign Minister, presents Israel's case at the United Nations. (*United Nations*)

Soviet Premier Aleksei N. Kosygin defends the Arabs at the U.N. Behind Kosygin, his face partially concealed, sits Foreign Minister Andrei Gromyko, and behind Gromyko is Soviet Ambassador Nikolai Trofimovich Fedorenko. (*United Nations*)

New immigrant children entering the clinic at Kiryat Shmona, a development town in the Galilee. (*David Rubinger*)

Dimona, a development town in the Negev near the Dead Sea, with its town plaza, the center of community life. (*Israel Education Fund*)

Jewish refugee children from Arab lands play outside their two-room apartments in Migdal Ha-Emek, a town of new immigrants in the North. *(Israel Education Fund)*

A painting of Nasser in a girl's school in Khan Yunis, the Gaza Strip's second city. Nasser, painted in baby-blue, holds a dove of peace while a Soviet rocket blasts off. *(Ruth Gruber)*

The two faces of refugeeism: above, in Israel; below, on West Bank.

At first Israel housed the Jewish refugees in camps and transit villages. Realizing that people deteriorate in camps, Israel built new homes, seen in the background, and tore down the old shacks or converted them into tool sheds. (*United Jewish Appeal*)

The Fawwar Arab Refugee Camp (below), near Hebron, where refugees continue to live. The concrete one-family houses were built by local Arab contractors and paid for by UNRWA (United Nations Relief and Works Agency). (*UNRWA*)

Officials of UNRWA: Khalil Labadi, Arab assistant to the Area Registration Officer in Hebron, standing with Mohammed Ibrahim Azzeh, Arab Camp Leader of the Fawwar Refugee Camp. (*Ruth Gruber*)

The Mukhtar, or Chief, of the Fawwar Refugee Camp. (*Philip H. Michaels*)

Israel reunifies Rafiah. Col. Aviv Barzilai, then military governor of Gaza Strip, at Arab feast with Mayor Abdul Hamid Gishton and another member of village committee. (*Philip H. Michaels*)

Arab refugee children in the Fawwar Camp, smiling, friendly, crying out newly-learned Hebrew words. (*Ruth Gruber*)

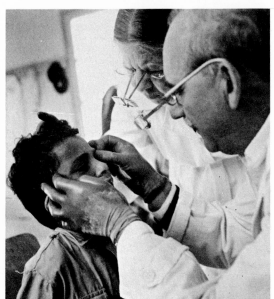

Professor Isaac C. Michaelson and Dr. Batya Maythar, both of the Hadassah-Hebrew University Medical Center, examine a Bedouin Arab school child for trachoma, dread eye disease of the desert. Israel has established schools and clinics in the desert for these nomadic people. (*Ruth Gruber*)

Arab home-owner in Gaza admitting a team of Israeli census-takers. (*Government Press Office*)

A young Arab woman with her children in Jerusalem. (*Government Press Office*)

Census-taking in Gaza; an Arab-speaking Israeli interviews Arabs. (*Government Press Office*)

Yaël Dayan and friends at her wedding. (*Philip H. Michaels*)

The generals and the soldiers, the dreamers and the builders came together at the Wall. *(Government Press Office)*

tive and inflammatory and unjustified statement just made by the representative of the Soviet Union, but to exercise my right of reply. . . .

"The United States sought by every means at its disposal, in the Security Council and outside the Security Council, to avoid this conflict, and, when the conflict broke out, to bring it to an end. I should again like to recall that when we urged that a meeting of the Council be convened several days ago, before any conflict was in the air, we were told that we were dramatizing the situation."

This was indeed one of the ironic touches of the debate. Before the shooting started, the Soviets had dragged their feet at the United Nations, pooh-poohing any sense of urgency. Once the war began, they could not call enough sessions. They asked for meetings at midnight and even before dawn. Millions of Americans became television addicts watching the drama of the Middle East being played before them. There were moments when I felt the Russians were using the techniques of the Moscow Trials on the American people, waking us at three in the morning when the darkness in our bedrooms was dispelled only by the bright light of the television screen, like the unshaded bulbs in the Moscow prison. The inquisitor bombarded us with epithets and scorn. Useless for work the next day, we could do nothing but sit again in front of the little box and fume or applaud.

As in all good drama, there was even a moment of comedy when Goldberg asked for a few minutes' recess. Fedorenko fought the recess as though he suspected Goldberg was about to corral the whole Security Council in behind-the-scenes shenanigans. Goldberg, explaining delicately that he only wanted to leave the room, withdrew his request.

The battle in the United Nations was for big stakes—global stakes. Goldberg, whose forensic techniques had been tooled in Chicago as a labor arbitrator and lawyer, seemed determined to prevent the Russians and the Arabs from swamping the Security Council. He became impassioned as he answered Ambassador Tomeh in defense of the United States. "The representative of Syria made a statement in reference to a remark of mine. I will recall the circumstances of that remark. The remark was made in the context of a malicious and false accusation that the United

States aircraft from carriers had participated in an attack. And I said, with respect to that remark, that people ought to put up some evidence that such an accusation was true. There has been no evidence offered. There can be no evidence offered of that because there is no basis for that accusation. That accusation was a false and malicious and scandalous one."

Tomeh: "I confirm categorically that the United States has helped Israel in its invasion of the United Arab Republic and Jordan and is to be held responsible for whatever destruction and killing have taken place in the United Arab Republic and Jordan and are taking place right now in my own country, Syria. If anything is scandalous it is the policy of the United States, which has been shameful for the last twenty years vis-à-vis the Arab world and vis-à-vis the Arab nations . . . the giving to Israel of all the tools of mass killing and massacre; the giving to Israel of billions in order to be able to devastate the Arab world."

President Nasser answered Tomeh's charges, better than anyone at the United Nations could have done, in an interview printed in the March 19, 1968, issue of Look magazine. Nasser admitted that he had indeed talked on the telephone with King Hussein on June 6 (see page 74), when they concocted the story that American and British airplanes had helped Israel defeat the Arabs. It was all a misunderstanding, Nasser declared. As for Tomeh's charges that the United States had given Israel billions to devastate the Arab world, Nasser acknowledged that from 1957 to 1967, the United Arab Republic had received more than a billion dollars from the United States, while Israel had received less than half a billion. "It's not just a question of dollars," Nasser said. "Friendship consists of other things too. Also, you [the United States] suddenly stopped wheat shipments last year . . ." It sounded like a replay of the old joke, "What have you done for me lately?"

At the U.N., Ambassador Goldberg chose not to answer the Syrian Ambassador's charges: "Ambassador Tomeh's personal comments, which are in violation of every type of diplomatic usage, are beneath contempt. . . ."

The meeting ended at 11:15 A.M.

When the thirteen-hundred-and-fifty-sixth meeting was called that same Saturday at 9:15 P.M. New York time, it was already

Sunday morning in Israel and the guns were silent in the Middle East. But in the United Nations the battle of words still raged. Mr. Fedorenko, fully aware now that the Arabs had suffered military disaster, fought to prevent a diplomatic disaster. "It is to be condemned," he said, "that there are great protectors of the lying representatives of Tel Aviv, and they are sitting at our table here. The Council cannot be associated with the maniacs of the war who cannot with open eyes see the light but can only see through a black patch."

The day before, Fedorenko had accused the Israelis of Nazi tactics: "They take their arguments from the same garbage heap of history and from the arsenal of the most famous criminals in history. They follow the bloody footsteps of Hitler's executioners who always accused the victims of their aggression."

The Soviet Union's insults and vituperations were matched, Rafael noted, in the annals of the United Nations only by the Arabs. "Ambassador Fedorenko," Rafael went on to say, "reached the heights of his crescendo today, when he compared Israel's fight for its existence to Hitler's aggression. This is unheard of. It appears that Mr. Fedorenko believes that, representing a powerful country, he has the right to trample on the honor of a small State and a people which suffered more from Hitlerite aggression than any other nation, a people one-third of which was exterminated by Hitler."

Rafael reminded the world that it was the Soviet Union that had become Hitler's bedfellow, that "neither Israel nor the Jewish people concluded a pact with Hitler's Germany, a pact which encouraged Nazi Germany to unleash its aggression against the world. . . . The representative of the Soviet Union spoke of a war psychosis. Who enflamed that war psychosis in the Arab nations? Who excited the Arab passions? Who supplied them with the arms to wage war against Israel? The record speaks for itself."

The Soviets and Arabs, working behind the scenes, realized they could not garner the nine affirmative votes of the total fifteen to pass their resolution that Israel pull back. The Security Council thus rejected placing blame or suggesting action. Its most valuable role was in issuing its calls for the cease-fires, which eventually brought the Six Day War to an end.

On the fourteenth of June the Council adopted a well-meaning and harmless humanitarian resolution on which everyone, Great Powers and little powers, could agree.

Considering the need to spare "additional sufferings," to make sure that "human rights should be respected even during the vicissitudes of war," and that prisoners of war should be treated according to the Geneva Convention of 12 August, 1949, the Council's Resolution 237 called upon Israel "to ensure the safety, welfare and security" of the people caught in the war's perimeter and to "facilitate the return of those inhabitants who have fled the areas since the outbreak of hostilities."

The war of words soon moved to the battlefield of the General Assembly, called into emergency special session at the request of the Soviet Union. Soviet Premier Aleksei Kosygin himself, with a sixty-six man delegation, flew to New York to continue the job of face-saving. He mounted the rostrum and denounced not only Israel, but its "imperialist backers"—the United States and Britain—for "unprecedented perfidy."

"The Israelis," he argued, were "guilty of unleashing the war," even as they were "spreading profuse assurances of peaceful intentions." Repeating Fedorenko's charges, Kosygin said he was reminded by Israel's "atrocities and violence" of "the heinous crimes perpetrated by the Fascists during World War Two." Repeating the Arab charges, the Soviet Premier said Israeli troops had burned Arab villages, destroyed hospitals, killed prisoners of war—"even women and children."

Kosygin called upon the General Assembly to act on the Soviet resolution to condemn Israel's aggression, make her retreat to her old borders, return all the Soviet hardware she had captured and "restitute" the Arabs "in full."

Ambassador Goldberg summed up Kosygin's speech. Kosygin wanted, Goldberg said, "to run the film backwards."

Israel's foreign minister answered Kosygin (who left in the middle of Eban's address) by accusing Russia of helping to ignite the war, afflicting the Middle East for fourteen years with a "headlong armaments race," paralyzing the United Nations as "an instrument of security," and of blind "identification with those who threaten peace against those who defend it."

Israel's choice, Eban said, was "to live or perish, to defend the national existence or to forfeit it for all time." He placed the start of the Six Day War on Nasser's "blatant decision" to close the Straits of Tiran. "There is no difference . . . between murdering a man by slow strangulation or killing him by a shot in the head."

"You come here in our eyes," Eban turned to the Soviets, "not as a judge or as a prosecutor but rather as a legitimate object of international criticism. To the charge of aggression I answer that Israel's resistance at the lowest ebb of its fortunes will resound across history, together with the uprising of our battered remnants in the Warsaw Ghetto, as a triumphant assertion of human freedom."

Eban called for direct negotiations with the Arabs, who "have come face to face with us in conflict; let them now come face to face with us in peace." Our watchword, he said, "is not backward to belligerency—but forward to peace." And President Johnson, watching the debate from Washington, suggested a plan, through Ambassador Goldberg, that would do two things: guarantee Israel's security and ease some of the refugee tensions.

Since Kosygin had come as head of state to participate in the United Nations rather than by invitation from the White House, touchy protocol dictated that the President could not go to New York to see Kosygin, and Kosygin could not go to Washington to see the President. A halfway spot was selected—the little college town of Glassboro, New Jersey.

Overnight, Holly Bush, the home of Dr. Thomas Robinson, President of Glassboro State College, was transformed. Fifteen air conditioners were hammered into windows, twelve phone cables including the Washington-Moscow hot line were installed, along with a stove, a refrigerator, a dishwasher, a long new dining table, and some favorite White House furniture.

Before, during, and after a U.S.–Soviet luncheon of roast beef and rice pilaf, the two leaders talked, for a total of five hours and twenty minutes, covering the spectrum of war and peace from the Middle East to Vietnam and the bomb.

Keeping the channels of communication open, the President and the Premier separated for a few days, and then resumed their talks in a second meeting. On a hot Sunday afternoon, as Glassboro citizens cheered and millions watched on television, Kosygin stopped his car to talk to the people. "I can assure you," he told them, "we want nothing but peace with the American people."

Kosygin seemed to sense America's determination to stand by its commitments; and there is no doubt that the meeting of the two leaders averted more immediate Soviet intervention in the Middle East. Yet a few hours later, appearing in a television interview program, Kosygin abandoned his role of peace-seeker and resumed the more familiar stance of defense counsel for the Arabs.

The fifth emergency special session of the General Assembly adjourned on the twenty-first of July without accepting any of Kosygin's demands. The sole Arab-Soviet achievement was a resolution critical of Israel's action in unifying and integrating Jerusalem. Like the Security Council, the Assembly adopted a mild, watered-down, face-saving resolution of "humanitarian assistance." It singled out the Commissioner General of UNRWA (United Nations Relief and Works Agency for Palestine Refugees in the Near East) Dr. Laurence Michelmore for his efforts in helping the refugees of the war.

There is no war without refugees and there are no refugees without war. This is a political fact of life and the Six Day War was no exception. In Israel I spent weeks visiting the Arab refugees (see Chapter 13), trying to understand what it meant to be an Arab refugee and what the chances were for ending refugeeism in the Middle East.

The battle for peace at the United Nations, like the battles in the Middle East, ended with a cease-fire. There were still scrimmages and clashes but the big guns were silent. Kosygin flew home.

The search for peace continued. On June 19, 1967, President Johnson committed the United States to a peace based on five principles:

"First, the recognized right of national life. Second, justice for the refugees. Third, innocent maritime passage. Fourth, limits on the wasteful and destructive arms race. And fifth, political independence, and territorial integrity for all.

"This is not a time for malice but for magnanimity," the President said, "not for propaganda but for patience; not for vituperation but for vision. On the basis of peace, we offer our help to the people of the Middle East. That land that's known to us since childhood as the birthplace of the great religions and learning can flourish once again in our time. And we here in the United States shall do all in our power to help make it so."

Border clashes continued; Arab terrorists infiltrated and killed; Israel retaliated and blew up homes where suspected saboteurs and guns were harbored. The Security Council met again, and on November 22, 1967, after long weeks of deliberation, with patient spadework by the British delegate Lord Caradon, unanimously adopted a major political resolution. In moderate tone it suggested that "a just and lasting peace" should include "withdrawal of Israeli armed forces from territories occupied in the recent conflict," as well as "respect for . . . the sovereignty, territorial integrity, and political independence of every State in the area and their right to live in peace within secure and recognized boundaries free from threats or acts of force." It also called for guaranteed "freedom of navigation through international waterways" and a just settlement of the refugee problem. It empowered the Secretary General to "designate a Special Representative" to proceed to the Middle East to "establish and maintain contacts with the States concerned" in the hope of achieving "a peaceful and accepted settlement."

The complexities of the political maneuvering—crucial, passionate, and often amusing—were revealed after the debate when each member of the Security Council explained his vote. The word *the* became an instrument of high politics and intrigue. The English text of the resolution suggested withdrawal "from territories occupied in the recent conflict." The French text read withdrawal "from *the* territories." To the delegates it was obvious that *the* territories could mean every inch of real estate; withdrawal "from territories" might boil down to minor border rectifications.

Within a few weeks U Thant appointed Dr. Gunnar V. Jarring of Sweden, who traveled to the capitals in the Middle East, arranged prisoner exchanges, and discussed such problems as refugees, borders, shipping on the Suez Canal, and the possibility of peace.

To win back his weary people, Nasser began blowing new

trumpets of war. At a worker's rally at the industrial town of
Helwan fifteen miles south of Cairo on March 3, 1968, he announced that the Israeli-occupied territory "should be liberated
regardless of what legal description it may be given.

"We swear from this place that we shall liberate this land inch
by inch regardless of the cost or sacrifice. We shall be one front,
the army and people, for the sake of the struggle for the liberation
of occupied territory.

"Israel shall know that this decision shall cost her a lot. Israel is
committing a fatal mistake if she imagines that the Arab national
front is weak."

The Soviets continued their role of backing the Arabs in the
United Nations and the Middle East. In the *Look* article, Nasser
revealed, "I begged the Soviets to send officers in to help retrain
our Army after Sinai. . . . We lost all our Air Force in June. . . .
We have a duty to liberate our own territory. If it can't be done
peacefully, we have to fight. Of course, we are rebuilding the
Army—we lost 80 per cent of our Army in June." The Russian
motive in helping Egypt, Nasser said, was pure anti-American:
"To reduce Western influence and domination in the Middle
East."

The Soviet role in the Six Day War intrigued everyone. Rumors
had circulated that Israel had captured seven Soviet MIG's at El
Arish on the first day of the war. Iraqi pilots, the story went,
unaware that Israel was already in control of the airport at El
Arish, had talked to the tower. An Israeli, answering in perfect
Arabic, directed the planes to land two at a time. Israeli ground
crews wheeled them off the airstrip and arrested the pilots. A few
weeks later, it was said, Israel sent three of the MIG's to the
United States. Israel denied the story. "The only MIG we have,"
Moshe Bitan, Deputy Director General of the Foreign Office, told
me, "is the one in which an Iraqi pilot defected. And that one is
still here."

Another rumor was that Israel had captured several Soviet
advisors. To prevent a military confrontation with the U.S.S.R.,
Israel had spirited the Russians off on a ship and sent them home.
Bitan denied this story too, though he admitted that three Polish

mining engineers had been caught with the Egyptian army in Sinai and sent back to Poland.

"Also," he later told me, "we found pictures of Russian technicians and of Soviet training maps when we entered Kuneitra on the Syrian Heights. We monitored the Soviet wireless networks they had set up in Syria; there were three of them, Sukhoi 9, 10, and 15. Frequently we heard the wireless operators—three men and a woman—broadcasting, sometimes in code, sometimes in Russian. During the battle in the Golan Heights, we overheard one of the Russian operators describing the fighting: 'I see the blacks running. The Jews are coming.'"

But it is needless to document the degree and variousness of the Soviet involvement in the war. The Russians by their own admission and for their own very good reasons were deeply committed to the Arabs. The defeat of Israel would have brought all the states of the Middle East, except Israel, under the United Arab Republic, which means, under Soviet hegemony. An Arab victory would have brought the Soviet Union's dream of a warm-water port in the Mediterranean closer to fulfillment. With victory for the Arab states, the U.S.S.R. would have advanced its objective of winning control of the whole area. The war in June postponed if it did not end the global nightmare of open war between East and West in the Mediterranean.

The rearming of the Middle East nations began almost before the ink on the cease-fire resolutions was dry. It was apparent, as Israel entered the era of the seventh day, that the Soviet Union wanted brinkmanship if not all-out war. The Russians replenished Nasser's arsenal with swifter MIG's, deadlier tanks, and better rifles than he had owned before the debacle in June. Scarcely seven months after the war, one thousand Soviet tanks once again threatened Israel on her southern front; another thousand faced her across the Syrian and Jordanian borders; five hundred Soviet planes waited in concealed or underground hangars in Egypt for the fourth round.

Israeli Intelligence reported that three thousand Soviet technicians had joined the Egyptian army, from top-ranking commanders all the way down to the commanders of brigades, battalions, and platoons. Soviet pilots were flying the MIG's and training the Egyptians. The Russians held the trigger on Egypt's missiles and rockets aimed at Israel.

It has been charged that the United Nations failed to solve the crisis in the Middle East. If the U.N. failed, it was because its member nations willed it to fail. By the very nature of its charter, the U.N. is the slave of the Great Powers and the little powers, not their master.

The U.N., it is true, made many mistakes. One of the most serious was pulling the UNEF out of Sinai and Sharm el Sheikh without giving the Security Council or the General Assembly time to debate and maneuver. It is true that U Thant made a last-minute flight to Cairo to dissuade Nasser from blocking the Straits of Tiran and barring Israeli shipping from free and innocent passage in international waters. But he was too late. Yet these were not fatal errors in the political drama of the Middle East.

Success or failure at the United Nations depended on its capacity to enlist the self-interest of the nations, especially the Great Powers, in the common cause of peace. In 1947 and 1948, the self-interest of the U.S. and the U.S.S.R. converged in the Middle East; in 1967, the two powers were poles apart. The British and the French were finished in the Mediterranean; now the U.S. and the U.S.S.R. confronted only each other, their armadas filling the sea and the sky.

At the U.N., as in the Middle East, the U.S.S.R. made it clear it was one hundred per cent behind the Arabs, while the U.S. sought to divide its friendship in terms of arms and planes, economic aid, and political votes between the Arabs and Israel. The U.N. was a reflection of the differences in the U.S. and the U.S.S.R. commitments.

The question should be, not whether the U.N. failed in 1967, but what the world would have been like in 1967 without the U.N. With all its errors and failings, the U.N. is still an effective outlet for pressures, a platform that can produce debates like those of Fedorenko and Goldberg, or of Kosygin and Eban, even if the debates are more diatribe than rational discourse. The U.N. is still a world arena where the Great Powers meet a strange foe—little nations that have no veto power but do have an equal voice and an equal vote. It is still a peace-keeping and a peace-searching body that can initiate cease-fires and produce resolutions like that of November 22, 1967, which may not bring permanent peace in themselves but help keep even uneasy truces in operation. The U.N. can still inspire man's hope.

As 1968 dawned, Israel appointed a new ambassador to the U.N., Yosef Tekoah, who is Russian-born, Harvard-educated, and a former ambassador to the Soviet Union. I asked him what he thought the prospects were for peace.

"Peace in the near future? No," he said. "Peace in our lifetime? Yes. The basic, simple problem is how to bring an end to this twenty-year war. There is no way except by contractual peace treaties.

"In the light of our past experience, we know there can be no compromise between peace and war—no twilight zone. There is either peace, spelling out in detail the relationship between Israel and the Arab states, or there must be war.

"The Arabs and the Soviets say, 'Israel should be more flexible.' But we cannot compromise. Either we will have war, or we will have peace. If the present conditions continue, there remains the danger of renewed hostility, and the greater danger that a conflagration might bring about a confrontation between the East and West."

The fumes of the sorcerer's apprentice fill the air over the Middle East. The potent brew of Arab hatred of Israel is being stirred anew by the U.S.S.R. and by left-wing radicals in Egypt and Syria. The Soviet Union may believe it can control the apprentice or, at best, manage and divert him. But Israel is prepared to take no risks, convinced the Arabs can be contained only by military capability and Israel's fierce determination to survive.

10

The Beat and Rhythm
of a Development Town

After the war in June, I journeyed throughout the land, north to the Golan Heights, east to the Jordan River, west to the Gaza Strip, and through the pre-June borders from the Galilee to the Negev to see and understand the aftermath of the war and to discover the direction Israel would travel after her stunning victory.

War and race—survival and integration—these are the two great problems in the world today. In the United States, they are defense against the bomb and the uplifting of Negroes. In Israel, they are defense against the Arabs and blending the Jews from Arab lands with the Jews from the Western World.

Integration is the word in America. Absorption is the word in Israel. The Six Day War multiplied the problems of absorption. Added to the burden of absorbing Jews from Arab lands, Israel now had the problem of what to do with the Arabs from Arab lands.

The unabsorbed Jews live in little frontier development towns; the unabsorbed Arabs live in refugee camps. These locales are not worlds apart—as they might seem; both are refugee centers, new villages born of the aftermath of the first Arab-Israel war in 1948. Without that war, there would have been no Arab refugees fleeing Palestine and no Jews fleeing Arab lands to a Jewish state.

There is almost a mirror-image even in their numbers: 600,000 Arabs fled Palestine; 600,000 Jews from Arab lands fled to Israel. After the Six Day War Israel found she had 1,000,000 new Arabs inside her new borders; and in the nineteen years before the Six Day War, Israel had taken in 1,400,000 Jews.*

To understand what it meant to be a refugee—Jewish or Arab— I knew I would have to live like a refugee. I knew the Jews in the frontier towns would let me live among them. I decided to move into the development towns to experience the meaning of Jewish absorption as it was after the war. Then I would visit the Arab refugee camps, and by talking with Arab leaders and refugees and UNRWA officials I would try to understand what it meant to be an Arab refugee.

Once again, as I had done each year since 1963, I went to live among the new immigrants, breaking bread and drinking tea with them in their tiny flats, sleeping on Jewish Agency immigrant cots, prowling the streets from dawn to midnight, visiting schoolrooms and youth centers, factories and workshops, waiting in queues at the Labor Exchange and the health clinic and the Jewish Agency Absorption Department offices, traveling in buses with the immigrants as they came off the ships in Haifa and the planes at Lydda, spending the first days of excitement and bewilderment, confusion and hope, with them in towns whose names were strange and sometimes not even listed on the map, towns that had been flung up overnight on the sand dunes of the Negev or carved out of the mountains of the Galilee to absorb the tide of immigration.

The Six Day War had created new Jewish refugees from Arab lands. Nasser himself revealed in the *Look* article in March 1968 that he had "arrested about 300 [Jews] as suspected Israeli

---

* After the Six Day War Israel took a census and discovered that, of the 1,000,000 Arabs living in the new territories, 340,000 were refugees. This refugee figure was 288,000 less than the one on UNRWA rolls. The study also discovered 30,000 Arabs in Gaza and 60,000 on the West Bank who did not qualify as refugees but who were on UNRWA's relief rolls.

The census, conducted by Israel's Statistics Bureau, lists 600,000 residents on the West Bank, including 120,000 refugees; 356,000 residents in the Gaza Strip, including 220,000 refugees; 6,400 residents on the Golan Heights, none of them refugees; 3,000 residents in the northern Sinai, with nomadic Bedouins roaming the rest of the peninsula; and 67,000 Arabs in the former Jordanian sector of Jerusalem, who are now considered citizens of Israel.

agents." As soon as the war started, every Jewish male in Egypt from the age of sixteen to sixty-five was arrested. In the Knesset, Gideon Hausner (Chief Prosecutor in the Eichmann trial) revealed that as late as December 1967 hundreds of Egyptian Jews were still imprisoned in the Abu Zabel prison in Cairo and the El-Berga prison in Alexandria, "at the mercy of sadistic jailers trained by German Nazis in the most cruel methods of torture."

Those who were freed from jail fled to Paris, Israel, and the United States. In New York an Egyptian Jew broke down as he tried to describe the terror in Egypt. He had been arrested as he left his apartment for work. The police would not allow him to call his family. Could he put his car in a garage? The policeman said, "You no longer have a car." "In the jail," the Jew said, "aged men were forced to strip and run about the camp while soldiers beat them. . . . A ten-year-old boy fell on his knees begging an Egyptian officer not to molest him."

In Morocco, despite the friendliness of young King Hassan, panic and terror started a new exodus of ten thousand middle-class Jews. In Tunisia, Arab mobs burned and gutted the chief synagogue and destroyed over a hundred Jewish establishments. President Bourguiba finally stopped the rioting.

From Libya, almost every member of the Jewish population—some forty-five hundred people—whose culture and language were Italian, fled to Italy. Some are still there, others have migrated to Israel. Most of their businesses were destroyed by fire.

Though the migration has slowed down considerably in the last few years, there are constant surprises behind the Iron Curtain. Soviet Jewry is still silent and trapped; but other countries, showing their independence from the U.S.S.R., occasionally unplug their borders and allow Jews to leave. The new postwar immigrants from North Africa and Europe come, as always, by ship and plane to Israel. The moment they put foot on the holy soil they are citizens of Israel.

To meet an immigrant ship at Haifa or a plane at Lydda Airport, to watch Israel's young army girls run up the gangway to help carry babies in their arms or guide the faltering steps of the old or the blind, to watch families being reunited, to watch men and women break down and sob as they see parents they have not seen for ten years or more, to know that the running is over—this is still for many the essence of Israel.

On the docks one night I approached a handsome woman traveling with her husband and two children. They had come from a country behind the Iron Curtain. We talked a while; she told me she was a pediatrician, her husband a doctor. I admired her two children and told her that they were almost the same ages as mine.

A bus labeled "Upper Nazareth" pulled up on the dock and all the immigrants bound for the new development town high in the Nazareth hills climbed aboard. I stayed on the dock watching and occasionally photographing the joyous reunions of families.

Suddenly I felt someone pull at my sleeve. It was the woman doctor. "Who are you?" she demanded hysterically. "Why were you asking me questions? What do you want from me? Why do you want to know all about where I came from? You must be a journalist."

"I am a journalist," I said. "But I am not going to publish your name. I know how dangerous it could be."

"I don't believe you. You are going to print my name in the newspaper. If you do, I will never see my family again."

"Please believe me, I don't want to harm you."

"You told me you are a mother of two children. As a mother, you can know what it would mean not to have your child, not to have your mother. If you write what country I came from, I am liable never to see my mother again. They do that."

The bus was about to leave for the frontier town. I followed her into the bus, and as we drove through the mountains toward Nazareth I tried to convince her that I was not the enemy.

At last her hysteria subsided. "You must forgive me," she said. "All our lives we lived in fear. And I am still afraid. You do not know what our life is like. They used to shoot us. Now they kill us piece by piece. They kill us by separation—separating us from our loved ones. Do you think I will ever see my mother?"

I lived in Upper Nazareth for a time and there met another woman immigrant—Suzy—whose experiences may be taken as typical. Suzy had short black hair, and she usually wore a gay cotton blouse, a skirt, and bedroom slippers. Her first day in

Upper Nazareth went like this: She met Shmuel, the Absorption Man . . .

"You are—how many people?" Shmuel asked.

"Thank God, we are three."

"Then you get three beds. You get three plates, three forks, three spoons, three knives, a table, and two stools."

"Where does the third one sit?" Suzy asked.

"He stands. He serves. He sits on the bed. Two stools get three people. Three stools get four people. Four stools get five people. You get two stools."

"Fine, I will stand. I will sit on the bed. In the Jewish land, I can sit on a bed and eat. Every day will be like *Pesach* [Passover]."

"Blankets—you got?" Shmuel asked.

"Yes, last night, and we needed them. The air here is so fresh. And it's free. It's free air. That's why I wanted to come. Jews must have a little freedom."

"Here you'll have freedom. This we got wholesale."

"Are you here long?" Suzy wanted to know.

"Five years. You should have seen Nazareth when I came—full of mud, full of stones. Not like today—a city."

"There must be millions of stones here."

"Me, I'm a big Zionist of stones. Every stone is like gold. Every stone is like money. From stones we build houses."

"We have no money," Suzy shrugged.

"Who has money? The whole country is in debt."

"I don't want to go in debt," Suzy said. "I want to work. Hitler left me eight fingers. With my eight fingers I can sew—at home or in a factory. Chaim will work. I will work. Avrum will go to school. I want to work and save money. The first thing I want to do is see the land. I want to see what the Jews have built on the Jewish land."

In the next days Suzy's husband went to the Labor Exchange to find work and her son went to school. At thirteen her boy was in the eighth grade, with thirty-five other students, who had come from thirty-five lands, speaking thirty-five languages, knowing thirty-five cultures. His early training had prepared him better than most of the students in science and math, but even so, science and math were taught in Hebrew here. In Hebrew he was illiterate.

One morning in Upper Nazareth I sat for several hours with the Absorption Man while dozens of petitioners came into his office. He listened to each one's problems, gave each a check to be cashed at the bank, and wrote the amounts in their little immigration booklets. A family of five that had received about ten dollars on the ship in Haifa when they arrived a few days before, now received another check for seventeen dollars to keep them in food until the father found work. A Moroccan woman with six children wept that her husband had run off. She was directed to the Rabbinical Court in Tiberias where the rabbis could decide how much money her husband was to give her for support after the police found him.

In the Absorption office of every town there is at least one young woman, called a *madricha* (a young instructor), who shows the immigrant woman how to cook on the little one-burner kerosene stove, how to set up the iron legs of the cots, perhaps even how to diaper the baby. She takes the family by the hand through the bewildering maze of Israel's institutions; she takes the father to the Labor Exchange to register for a job; she takes the whole family to the Kupat Holim clinic to register for medical care; she takes the school-age children to school, and the preschool children to the nurseries run by the volunteer women's organization. If a child is to be sent to a Youth Aliyah center or a kibbutz school, she arranges the appointments. If there are social cases in the family, she takes them to the Jewish Agency Social Work Department and the Ministry of Social Welfare.

There are seventy-five of these *madrichot* in Israel, and Israel could easily use three hundred and seventy-five. The ones I met— like Rachel Ouzan in Shderot, thirty years old, born in Tunis— were soft-spoken, dedicated, compassionate young women who had never been trained for their jobs, but who were almost instinctively skilled in making each newcomer feel wanted and at home in Israel. They do not speak the languages of all the newcomers, but most of them speak a language deeper than words—a language they carve out of compassion.

I found that Israel in peace as in war was a fantastic success story—a story of dynamic creativity, of boundless hope, and promise fulfilled; a land of new cities, new industries, new roads, new ports, new books, new plays, new museums—a twenty-year-old country soaring into orbit.

But it would be impossible to suppose that any country which had taken in over a million new immigrants could in so short a time have solved all its problems. As the shooting died down and Israel began to pick up the pieces of its life, Louis Pincus, the head of the Jewish Agency, which had assumed a social welfare role after Israel became a state, disclosed that there are still three hundred thousand immigrants who need public assistance. These are the unemployed and the unemployable, the unskilled, the maimed and the sick, the blind and the weak, the despondent and the alienated—people who have not yet put down roots, who eat the bread of poverty, who wear the clothes of poverty, and whose faces are scarred with the sicknesses of poverty.

You enter a two-room house in the little development town of Shderot near the Gaza Strip. You note that the ten children in the family sleep two and three together on narrow cots. You see chunks of bread on every bed, and you know this is a home of poverty.

"What do you eat besides this bread?" you ask the exhausted, overburdened mother holding one baby in her arms while three more hide shyly behind her skirts.

"We eat bread and tea and margarine."

"Nothing else?"

"Sometimes onions, if a neighbor shares them; sometimes a little cooked jelly; and once a week, for Shabbat, a chicken."

In the mental hospitals there are some people with the symptoms of schizophrenia. They isolate themselves, don't relate to others, have no interest in their surroundings, and show a total loss of energy. The symptoms disappear when the people are fed and cared for.

There is a peculiar Israeli syndrome called "Yemenite Grandmother Schizophrenia." Why grandmother? Why does only the grandmother lose her balance between reality and unreality? The answer is simple. In most families the father goes out to work and takes the time to get some food and something to drink. The mother may work as a maid; she gets fed in the household where she cleans and cooks. The children go to school and perhaps get a hot meal at lunch. The grandfather may be dead. But grandma is home alone all day and eats nothing.

The Ministry of Social Welfare provides some form of public assistance. "Each person in a family," Dr. Moshe Kurz, Director General of the Ministry of Social Welfare, told me, "receives about six to seven dollars per month. When we have surplus vegetables and fruit, we give them to these families for very little."

Opposed to the dole for the most part, Israel gives unskilled men relief work, called *dahak*. The men plant trees, build secondary roads, sweep the town square, or work as unskilled labor in neighboring kibbutzim. The number of days they work depends on the size of their family. "I can work," one man told me, "but how can I feed my wife and six children on fifty-seven dollars a month?"

It is a cycle of poverty that began hundreds of years ago in hostile lands and migrated to the development towns. The new countries of the world are watching Israel's experiments in trying to break the cycle. Here a community of new immigrants is absorbing still newer immigrants, reclaiming a people and reclaiming a land.

The story of the development towns built by new immigrants to absorb other new immigrants has never really been told. They are new faces in Israel. These little towns are saddled with all the problems of big cities and are gifted neither with the money nor manpower nor know-how to cope with their problems. Everything is new—the houses, the roads, the shopping centers, the gardens, the trees. The character of each town is molded by the people and their ethnic background. Here in microcosm is the whole story of absorption in Israel, its successes, its frustrations, and its dangers—all spread out as though on a laboratory table.

Some of these towns are spectacularly successful—towns such as Beersheba, Kiryat Gat, Dimona, and Elath. Why? In basic terms, they have work; they have schools; they have houses—even if these are not always adequate. One could almost make a simple formula: $J + E + H = A$ (Jobs plus Education plus Housing equals Absorption). But there are other towns which responsible officials consider "weak" towns or even "sick" ones. In these towns there are serious pockets of unemployment, the unemployment of the unskilled. There are inadequate social welfare facilities. There are few secondary schools. And there is poverty.

In the trials and errors of absorption, Israel's planners came to the conclusion that the pressure-cooker technique of putting Poles and Iraqis, Tunisians and Moroccans in one village did not work. Even Moroccans from the big cities did not intermix with Moroccans from the Atlas Mountains. The technique worked out by Israel's sociologists and psychologists is to keep people from one area together in a separate village, as in the Lachish Plan in the northern Negev. The villages there are homogeneous satellites with a heterogeneous center. In the central city, Kiryat Gat, there is a regional center for the schools, the industries, and the community facilities, where the people of all the surrounding villages can meet. Absorption in Israel is now taking on a neighborhood pattern for daily living, and a regional pattern for the integration of cultures.

Shderot, about fifteen miles south of Ashkelon near the Gaza Strip, is a pretty town of pink and white and gray cottages tiered on gently rising hills, with rambling streets, new apartment houses, a handsome split-level plaza, a municipal building, a bank, some restaurants, a movie, little shops, and the Sam Rubin Cultural Center with its Old People's Club. The center of town looks like Israel, but the side streets are Morocco transplanted. Many of the old men wear the white robes that one sees in the Atlas Mountains; most of the women wear gay colorful scarves around their heads and some still dye their hands and bare feet with henna, a symbol of fertility.

The Europeans in Shderot live for the most part in their own neighborhoods, the Moroccans are interspersed throughout the town, and the elite of the community—the professionals, the three new immigrant doctors, the dentist who works privately, the community organizer, the engineers in the Heletz oil fields—all live in the attractive three-story apartment houses facing the plaza.

As in all the development towns, Shderot has a democratically elected council. The Mayor of Shderot is Jonathan Ifrak, born in

Morocco, who came to Israel in 1950. Ifrak, over six feet tall, handsome, a former kibbutznik, a captain in the army reserve, the former secretary of the Histadrut in Shderot, is one of the leaders of Israel's Moroccan community.

"We have sixty-five hundred people here," he told me in his office in the Municipal Building on the plaza. "Eighty-five per cent of our population are from North Africa; of that number ninety-eight per cent are from Morocco, the rest from other countries in North Africa. The other fifteen per cent come from Germany, eastern Europe, South America, India, France, etc.

"Our two main problems are economic and social—jobs and education. We need more industries and we need more schools. We need things to keep our young people off the streets—a swimming pool, a sports gymnasium, youth clubs."

Shderot has fourteen factories and small industries, including a factory for prefabricated houses (where, significantly, new immigrants are building houses so that more immigrants can be housed as soon as they enter the country), a vegetable canning factory, a small shoe factory, a thermometer factory (built by an English non-Jew whose daughter has now married a Moroccan Jew), a cooperative bakery, and a large plant for making wires and cables.

Shderot is considered a "weak" town but not a "sick" one. The statistics are good. According to the figures given me by Herb Smith (formerly of Pittsburgh), Director of the Manpower Planning Authority in the Ministry of Labor, there are some twelve hundred in Shderot's labor force. About a hundred persons are now on emergency relief work.

One evening I sat in Shderot's main restaurant talking with a group of seven young men. They were in their early twenties— handsome, clean-cut, well-dressed, articulate. They had all served in the army, had been retired from active duty, and had been called up again for the Six Day War. In the army they had learned some skills. Now they had returned to Shderot where they were living in two- or three-room cottages with six or eight younger sisters and brothers, their parents, and sometimes their grandparents.

They all faced the same soul-searching question: Can we go back to our little towns and our big families, we who have faced the enemy and have taken the salute from the Prime Minister? Some in Israel have answered, "We can never go back." For them the sense of alienation is greater than for almost any group in Israel.

But these seven young men had come home. This was their town. All of them had jobs. One of the boys who worked in the local gas company told me, "I think we can understand Shderot. We understand its problems: nothing to do after dark, no place to go at night, no night school, no courses where we could improve ourselves. We can only sit here in the restaurant. We can't take girls out; in a Moroccan family you have to promise the parents you'll marry the girl the first time you take her out, and when you know you can't possibly get an apartment for at least two years, you think twice before you get married."

"Why did you come back?" I asked.

"Because we understand these problems. And this is home. But in five or six years, if some of these problems aren't solved, you'll have an explosion."

Explosion. *Explosion and Wadi Salib.* These are the words one heard constantly before the Six Day War.

On July 9, 1959, some of the North African immigrants broke out of the slums of the quarter called Wadi Salib in Haifa, took rocks and beer bottles and marched through the city, breaking the windows of government buildings and private homes, wounding thirteen policemen.

Wadi Salib threw the country into temporary shock. The Knesset held a debate; Moshe Dayan was dispatched to calm the people; a committee was appointed to study the problems of absorbing the Oriental Jews; and the leader of the riot, David Ben-Haroush, a new immigrant from Morocco, was sentenced to two years in prison. But after two months he was released and became a candidate for the Knesset.

The committee's report was issued on August 17, 1959. It found, as indeed most people have found, that there is no deliberate discrimination in Israel against the Oriental Jews, that "in many cases there is genuine desire, and a clear tendency, to give special care and priority to the Oriental immigrants in an effort to integrate them in all spheres of life in Israel."

It is perhaps Israel's destiny that, as in the great days of the Second Commonwealth, she is to be a crucible of world problems. The gap between affluent nations and developing nations, co-existence with hostile nations, the confrontation between the East and the West—all the problems exploding in the world are mirrored in this tiny land. Even the names given the new immigrants are East and West—*Oriental* Jews from North Africa and the Middle East and *Western* Jews from Europe, South Africa, and the Americas.

Absorption is the process of integrating the two groups of Jews. Absorption is transformation and acculturation. Absorption is breaking down the walled ghettos between cultures. Absorption is diminishing the educational and cultural differences. Absorption is helping the have-nots become haves.

Like integration, absorption is strength. The strength to overcome deprivation and sickness and apathy and defeat. The strength to know that the promise can be fulfilled, the dream made reality. Absorption means accepting Israel and being accepted by Israel. It means accepting each human being whether he is an aged peddler from the *mellah* of Casablanca or a biochemist from Warsaw. It means guarding the worth of each human being—neither violating nor destroying his own self-image. It means that no culture is denigrated and no people are denied the dignity and heritage of their own past.

"Why don't they talk of us as we are; not as people with such a terrible background?" Jacqueline Kahanoff, a beautiful Jewish writer from Egypt asked me a few years ago in despair. "The words they use—primitive, uncultured, inferior—these words come back to us and destroy us. We *have* a culture. In Egypt, it was an old and great culture; it goes back to Bible days. In Morocco, it was the culture of the extended family. People don't know about our culture."

Absorption means equality. It means teaching a child that he *does* have equal opportunities; that because he was born an Oriental he is not *ipso facto* inferior. It means putting down roots. It means becoming an Israeli. For people who have fled from countries of persecution to Israel, absorption, in its deepest connotation, means "Coming Home." In the development towns like Shderot absorption means survival. Without absorption the new little towns could become ghost villages and die.

Shderot's name is a lovely one. It means "boulevard" and it conjures up a wide, tree-lined passage. Shderot *is* a passage—a passage to Israel. For many of her sixty-five hundred persons life is good. There are weddings. Babies are born and old people die. Men go to work each morning in the factories and the neighboring kibbutzim. Children go to school and study and laugh and sing. Women shop for food in the outdoor market and take a little time to gossip. Mothers sit on the floor teaching their pretty young daughters to bake Moroccan bread. The neighborhood *shochet* (slaughterer) in his long white butcher's coat slaughters the chickens. Fish swim around in tanks waiting to be bought and boiled.

Shabbat is the day of rest; while Western children and parents in Tel Aviv go swimming or play soccer, the boys in Shderot and their fathers read the Holy Book. The fathers are determined to retain the ethics and moral standards of the teachers and prophets of Israel and to pass on the ethics to their sons.

The Jewish holidays are celebrated with joy. During the Sukkoth holiday (the harvest festival), hundreds of houses have little *sukkahs* (booths such as the children of Israel built in the desert as they fled from Egypt). Families eat their meals by candlelight under thatched roofs hung with fruit. In a *sukkah* in Eytan, one of the villages in Lachish, where I visited old friends from the Tunisian island of Djerba, I saw a kitchen chair, painted blue to ward off the Evil Eye, hanging from the thatched roof. The chair was for Eliahu Ha-Navi, Elijah the Prophet, so he could rest for a while during his descent from outer space and eat some fruit and sip a little wine in the *sukkah* to recharge himself before he continued orbiting around the world.

The job of absorption is far from over. The Israelis experimented. They took daring steps forward and agonizing steps backward. But as they struggled with the problems their own attitudes changed. When the big migrations from North Africa started there were many who said, "They are lost, this generation—this desert generation." They compared the newcomers with the people of the Exodus. "Moses kept them in the desert for forty years, so that all those who knew slavery would die off. We cannot help this generation. We will help the children and let the parents die off."

But as the migration continued, Israel realized she could not afford a desert generation. She realized that broken parents mean broken children. Fail-parents mean fail-children. Abandoned parents lead to abandoned morality. Deserted and despised parents mean a desertion of law and a hatred of order. The parents needed help, and the children needed help.

The answer lay in education.

11

Breaking the Cycle of Illiteracy

Until the War of Independence in 1948, there had been virtually no Jewish illiterates in Israel. The young pioneers who came out of Russia and Poland at the turn of the century to reclaim the desert were intellectuals. Possessing little more than the clothes on their backs, they loaded their knapsacks with beloved books. The religious people who came to the Holy Land to die arrived holding the sacred books of the Bible like precious children. There were some illiterate women who came with their religious husbands, but their children were immediately taught to read and write, and their sons were cast in the mold of the *yeshiva bocher*, the protected scholar who spent his whole day in the synagogue studying.

Hitler changed all of this. A whole generation of Jewish youth grew up in the forests and the caves, in the slave labor camps and the concentration camps of Hitler's Europe. When the survivors came to Israel, many were already beyond school age. Israel had no free secondary schools and too few teachers to fill the vacuum Hitler had created.

It is part of Jewish mythology that every single Jewish boy learns to read at least the Bible. But there were many villages in the Atlas Mountains of Morocco, isolated villages in Iran, and cave-dwellers' settlements in Libya which teachers could not reach and where schools did not exist. In the tiny synagogues, those who could read, read for those who were illiterate.

Thus it comes as a shock to many people that Jews, the People of the Book, should be illiterate. Israel has a quarter of a million illiterate and semiliterate adults, according to Itzhak Navon, the former director of the Anti-Illiteracy Program, whose Moroccan mother learned to read at the age of sixty. But one should caution against developing a new stereotype: not all the illiterates are Orientals. In fact, one-fifth of them are from Europe and some are native-born Israelis.

Nearly 50 per cent of the flood tide of recent immigrants are children under seventeen, children who need schools and teachers, doctors and nurses—the whole structure of support which a nation rightfully owes its children.

This is a country of children. Walk along the streets of any development town and you see hundreds and hundreds of children. Some are well-dressed. Some sing as they walk home from school. Some ride their bicycles. But others are unguarded and uncared for.

A woman running after me on the dirt street in a slum area of Shderot, cried, "You are a mother. As a mother, you know how it feels to see your children on the streets all day. Help us. You must help us. Build more schools for our children. Keep them off the streets. The streets are evil."

The picture must be put into perspective. Seven hundred thousand children go to school in Israel. In the development towns, secondary schools are now free, but in the rest of the country they are not free, as they are not free in most countries of the world where there are not enough resources to build high schools and staff them.

When you enter a development town, you can almost tell from the faces of the teenagers whether there is a high school. In Kiryat Shmona in the Galilee, the coming of the high school changed the lives of many of the young people. I talked with some of the seniors in the high school. Judith Benolul from Spanish Morocco, a lovely graceful girl, told me she wanted to go to the Hebrew University in Jerusalem and study to become an architect. Sarah Sakagu, recently from Europe, was studying to become an English teacher. While we drank tea and ate delicious homemade cake, her mother told me, "I have one child left out of four. Hitler killed the others. I want Sarah to study, so she can live the life we couldn't live."

A few miles from Kiryat Shmona is Hazor, another development town. Both Kiryat Shmona and Hazor overlook the magnificent Hula Valley, but in the teenagers' faces in Hazor you see apathy and hopelessness—no high school in their town.

In Shderot, where there was no high school until 1968, there was Rachel, a girl so gifted that the municipality gave her a scholarship of $166 to attend the high school in Beit Berl and prepare for the University. At Beit Berl, she found she would need $100 more. But there was no money in anyone's budget. Her father needed every penny to put bread in the mouths of her family. The girl came home. She never matriculated. She just gave up, defeated, doomed.

On the other hand, there was Yakov Maaman in Kiryat Shmona, a handsome boy with piercing eyes, black hair, and a neat moustache, who was born in Meknes in Morocco and whose mother and father are both illiterate. "When I finish high school," he said, "I am going to the Hebrew University and the Weizmann Institute. I am going to become a nuclear physicist."

Education is free and compulsory for nine years, from kindergarten through the eighth grade. But the gap between the children of the West and the children of the Orient grows as the children go up the educational ladder. The proportion of Oriental children who enter elementary school is 63.2 per cent. In the eighth grade, it is 53.6 per cent. The gap is narrowing here; scarcely five years ago, only 30 per cent finished the eighth grade.

The proportion of Oriental children now entering secondary school is 45.3 per cent; it was 21 per cent five years ago. But by the time the students finish high school—even now—the figure plummets to 18.9 per cent. Five years ago, it was even a steeper descent, to 12 per cent. In the universities, the percentage of Oriental undergraduates is now 12.6 per cent, and among graduate students it is 7.8 per cent. Five years ago, at the Hebrew University, the number was less than 5 per cent; there were more Arab students at the Hebrew University than there were Jews who had come from Arab lands.

The glaring dropout area lies between the ninth and twelfth

grades, right in the heart of Israel's school system. Too often, many of the Oriental children who enter high school spend a year or two in some basic trade training and then drop out to take low-paying jobs—a pattern that can only perpetuate the inequities between Israel's European Jews and her Jews from Arab lands.

Preferential treatment for deprived children is firm governmental policy. Hanoch Rinot, former Director General of the Ministry of Education, told me, "We have developed a whole new network of approaches to the problem of what is best for each child. Our philosophy is no longer equalitarian. It is based on the fact that there are different needs and different starting points. But there is one goal.

"There may be social and cultural problems at home. There may be no books, no libraries, no place at home for a child to study. But there are no ethnic limits. There are no objective limits to the heights any child can reach.

"We have lengthened the school year to ten and a half months for ten thousand children. A few years ago we instituted the 'long day' where children can stay in school several hours after their classes and get special teaching, do their homework, or have organized play. We are reinforcing the children of Oriental extraction to help prepare them for their matriculation in college. We are trying constantly to increase the number of scholarships to secondary schools."

There are striking similarities in absorbing new immigrants into Israel and integrating new migrants from Puerto Rico and the rural South into New York and other Northern cities.

To begin with, there is the difficulty of language. In Israel, Hebrew may be as strange to a child who has come from Algeria or Romania as English is to a child from Puerto Rico. Both places must teach the language of the land as a second language; and often the children have to teach their parents to speak and read and write the strange tongue.

Next, in the gray slum areas of Israel and New York large families live on the thin edge of poverty. The parents, overburdened and illiterate, are unable to motivate their children. The child of poverty too often knows only the frustration of failure.

In both places, but especially in Israel, there is leaderlessness among the poor. The Jews from the Islamic countries are for the most part unskilled. There are a number who come with skills—doctors and technicians from Iraq, teachers and rabbis from Morocco—but often, as in the Algerian migration, those with professions or training go to France, while the poor and unskilled, with their many children, migrate to Israel—without community leaders.

In both Israel and New York, there are the culture and habit-patterns of the deprived, who have their own mores and their own goals, rooted as deeply as middle-class mores and middle-class goals. In both places, the children of illiterate parents often grow up in a silent world. There are few words and fewer ideas. The vocabulary of illiteracy is largely monosyllabic and frequently punitive. Communication is strangled in superstitition and fear.

But in Israel the problems of absorption and integration are less complicated than in New York, for in Israel Jews are absorbing Jews, not whites absorbing Puerto Ricans and Negroes; the problems do not derive so much from differences of race or color—although such differences exist—as they do from disparities of geography and cultural history.

One of the weakest links in Israel's educational system is the teacher. At one end of the spectrum is the older teacher who came thirty or forty years ago from Europe, and who brought not only European methodology and ideology, but European prejudices; at the other end is the young, untrained, uncertified teacher. A young army girl, full of compassion but with perhaps only one month of teacher training, stands before a class of forty or fifty children from Morocco, Tunisia, Romania, Poland, Iraq, and Iran. She may have come out of a comfortable middle-class home in Tel Aviv or Jerusalem, surrounded by books and paintings. The children facing her are as foreign and strange as if they had come out of the interior of Africa—and some of them have. She has had no time and no opportunity to learn anything about their background, their mores, their values, their culture. Quite probably she cannot even visualize the poverty in which her charges may be living in Israel. I heard of one such young teacher who in utter innocence asked a little girl, "Why don't you ask your mother to help you with your reading?" The child burst into tears. "My mother is an idiot. My mother does not know how to read or write."

Before the war in June, the folk hero was the sabra, born of this land, descendant of the Second Aliyah—Israel's "Mayflower stock," who came from Russia and Poland after 1900. This folk hero was the son of "Ashkenazi" Jews—the term applied to Jews from northern Europe—in contradistinction to the "Sephardic" Jews from Spain and the lands that once made up the Turkish Empire.

One of the most poignant stories I heard a few years ago was of the little Sephardic boy from a Moslem land who was asked what he wanted to be when he grew up. "I want to be an Ashkenazi," he said. A character in a novel written by a young Iraqi says bitterly, "In Israel there is a feeling that even God is an Ashkenazi." But the Six Day War welded the Ashkenazi and the Sephardic Jews. They fought together and died together; bullets and the enemy made them one.

Absorption was speeded up. The folk hero was no longer the Ashkenazi sabra. He was anyone who had helped save the Jewish people from extinction. There was even an added aura if the hero was a newcomer from an Arab land.

The Oriental Jew began to lose some of his sense of inferiority. He now felt entitled to equality. Equality of education. Equality of opportunity. No longer did he need to protest that he was denied equality; the country recognized it belonged to him on the basis of his own achievement.

Oriental fathers changed their attitudes toward the role of education. Patriarchal men who only a few years ago complained, "Why should my son go to school? Back where we came from he would have gone to work like our Arab neighbors by the time he was six or seven," were now eager to send their children to school.

The uniqueness of Israel is that the thin top layer of highly skilled, highly educated, highly committed people is reaching out to pull up the thick bottom layer of the unskilled and uneducated. Educators and social workers in Israel, understanding the dangers inherent in the alienation of a whole segment of society, have begun a massive program to break the cycle of deprivation and illiteracy. They are seeking especially to get at some of the basic causes of the drop-out problem—parent illiteracy and, particularly, early childhood neglect. The aim is to eliminate illiteracy in one generation. Like almost everything in Israel, the drive against illiteracy is child-motivated and child-centered. Israel also believes however that the education of the parent is a necessary step in the education of the child.

The illiterates are taught by regular teachers, by volunteer women, and by army girls. Even a few fashionable ladies who formerly spent their mornings at the beachfront cafés of Tel Aviv, sipping coffee with floating ice cream, have changed their cultural pattern. Now they sit in the two-room apartments of immigrant women, teaching them to read Hebrew from right to left.

How does one find the illiterates? In a city they can remain invisible. Many of them are reached by volunteers in a street-by-street, door-to-door campaign. Over tea or coffee or orange pop, the volunteers discuss the program gently and delicately. No woman they meet is ever illiterate; but she knows everybody else in the building who is—the janitor who sweeps the halls, the old man who loads the garbage onto the sanitation trucks, the neighbor with ten children upstairs. After a while, the woman would drop her defenses.

"I never went to school," one woman told us. "Now my son writes me letters from the army and I can't read them. Could I go to school?"

The volunteer takes such persons to the school building, where grown men and women sit in the graduated chairs of elementary schoolchildren, learning basic reading, writing, and arithmetic from four in the afternoon until six thirty, five days a week.

In the development towns, some of the women, fresh from Moslem lands, are too shy to go to school and sit with men. So the teachers go to their homes to teach them. In the factories, classes are held after the four o'clock shift for workers who hold down jobs but cannot read.

The picture in Tel Aviv is paradoxical. The city has nearly fifty thousand illiterates and semiliterates, yet Tel Aviv has fourteen public branch libraries and more bookstores than drugstores. The slums, the worst in the country, are a short bus ride away from a galaxy of art museums, skyscrapers, two universities, and a music conservatory. Immigrants dressed in the medieval robes of Yemen and Morocco thread their way through traffic jams as hectic as the rush hour in Times Square; in their hands they carry special newspapers printed in basic Hebrew.

Very few programs in Israel are the province of one agency alone. Thus the literacy campaign is multibudgeted; and though it is run by the Ministry of Education and Culture, it has the co-operation of other organizations, such as the municipalities, the Jewish Agency, the Histadrut, which years ago started the program to end adult illiteracy, and the army.

To this day the army is the greatest educating and integrating force in the country for adults. This intensive use of an army as a conscious force in integration is unique.

The army program began out of necessity. In 1948, young men fresh from Auschwitz and Cyprus stepped off the immigrant ships into the War of Independence. Many knew no Hebrew; others were totally illiterate. There were tragedies; a few were killed simply because they did not understand combat orders. Even Mickey Marcus, the West Point general who helped Israel build the "Burma Road," was tragically killed the night before the first truce because he could not remember the Hebrew password. He himself had given instructions to kill anyone who did not know it.

A kind of instant school for soldiers had to be created in the middle of the war. Books had to be written. Courses had to be set up. At the very hour Israel was fighting seven Arab states for her right to exist she had to teach thousands of immigrants not only how to use a gun but to read and write.

The first Chief Education Officer of the army was Colonel Aharon Ze'ev, a white-haired poet known simply as Ze'ev. Ze'ev set up the first army program of education and wrote many of the books himself. Like Robert Frost or Carl Sandburg, Ze'ev has a face that is a mixture of strength and softness, of wisdom and suffering. He speaks in a hoarse whisper, as though he were reading folk tales to children. And he does. He writes lyrical poems for children and epic prose for adults. Education is his life. On a trip to South America, a general in the Argentine army asked him, "How did you defeat the Egyptians so fast?" Ze'ev answered,

"Every army is trained to run. Our army ran *toward* the front. The Egyptian army ran *away* from the front. The difference is education."

In 1962 Ze'ev retired and turned the job over to his protégé Colonel Mordechai Bar-on, a historian and educator whom I had first met when he was a student at Columbia University. On a warm August evening, with Bar-on's wife leading us, we went through the new art galleries of Jaffa, then climbed up and down the cliffs of Biblical Joppa, where Jonah, fleeing from a new assignment in Nineveh, had shipped off to Tarshish and landed in the belly of a whale. We finally sat down at Janet's, a restaurant on the seacoast, and chose our own fish to be broiled, while we talked of this army, which, rejecting no one, taught its soldiers to read and write as well as defeat four enemies forty times its size.

Bar-on, tall and soft-spoken, is a kind of Commissioner of Education, responsible for fourteen schools: the Mickey Marcus central elementary school, five Hebrew schools where mainly immigrant soldiers study, two schools for leadership training, three central high schools, and three other high schools based in army camps.

Of all the army schools, the one most typical of Israel—of her flexibility—is the Mickey Marcus school in Haifa, a collection of makeshift barracks in a fashionable neighborhood across the road from the posh Dan Carmel Hotel. The Marcus school is compulsory. Any Israeli soldier who is illiterate or who has not completed elementary school must attend that school at the end of his tour of duty. There, in a three-month crash program, studying from early morning until late at night, each soldier is given the equivalent of eight years of elementary school, and a diploma.

The high school program is not compulsory, but any soldier can now take a crash high school program and in four months do the equivalent of two years of high school. The soldiers start this high school program after they finish their army stint and still receive army pay and rations.

In the Marcus elementary school the faces of the two Israels merge through education. The teachers and the pupils are all twenty years old. The teachers, all girl soldiers, are high school graduates; the soldiers, all unlettered, or unschooled, are a living roll call of the towns from which the Jews have fled—Baghdad, Casablanca, Tunis, Sana, and cities behind the Iron Curtain.

Through rough experience the army had learned that the soldiers would not accept the Marcus school at the beginning of their army service. The first attempts were disastrous. There were knifings, fights, and deserters. But by the end of their army service, the soldiers were motivated. "They are doing soul searching," one of the early commanders of the Marcus school, Lieutenant Colonel Avraham Tsivion, had explained to me one year. "After two years in the army, sharing the same tents with boys who have education, they ask themselves what they want to do and where they want to go. By now, instead of rebelling against the army, they are trying to find themselves. Some are tough and rough; some are aggressive; in every session we have two or three who cut their arms to draw attention. But suddenly it takes. Something happens; it's a rebirth."

After the war in June, the new commander of the school, Lieutenant Colonel Itzhak Ziv, led us around the grounds and through the classrooms. We were joined by an attractive young second lieutenant, Daphna Terkel, dean of the school. In the high school classes, we asked the boys what they had done during the Six Day War. Gabarel, a Yemenite, had fought on the Jordan front; Itzhak from Rabat, Morocco, had fought in the Sinai desert; Menashe from Greece was a toolmaker in the air force. The others, with no units to join, had stayed at the school, studying. Israel Galaim, whose family came from Stanislav in Poland, had fought the war driving for the Israeli commander at Sharm el Sheikh.

"What happens to a boy like Israel Galaim, who has been driver for the Commander of Sharm el Sheikh, when he returns here to go to high school, and then must go home to a little frontier town like Shderot?" I asked Colonel Ziv. "Can he adjust to that life? Can he move back to the two tiny rooms in which his family may be living?"

"It's not easy. The government has a whole series of ways to help him. If he wants to study, the government will give him about two dollars a day while he is in training. It helps him find a job. If he marries, he is given a house in a development town and his rent is a few dollars a month. But the important thing is, he knows he must help himself."

Midway between Beersheba and the Dead Sea lies Dimona. A handful of pioneers and new immigrants founded Dimona in the desert about ten years ago. Now it is a bustling town of twenty-two thousand people, a conglomerate of unskilled workers and semi-literates living side by side with engineers from the Dead Sea Works and nuclear scientists from the Dimona nuclear reactor.

Seven months before the Six Day War, I had journeyed to Dimona for the opening of the Edith Lehman High School, an Israel Education Fund comprehensive school built by funds raised by the Women's Division of the United Jewish Appeal of Greater New York. Four hundred and fifty pupils whose ages ranged from fourteen to eighteen, and whose families had come from around the world, would now study together in the same classrooms.

I returned to Dimona after the war. The Vice-Mayor, Jacques Amir, a former kibbutznik, drove us to the Dimona high school, "a blessed school," he called it. High schools in the development towns, though they are free, are not compulsory. Only elementary school education is compulsory.

"At the end of the last graduating year," Amir said, "Mayor Gabi Sabag and I went to the elementary school. We told the graduates how important education was. We knew that some of their fathers still didn't believe high school was important. We said, 'Look, any of you who want to go on to the Edith Lehman school, and whose parents say No, you should go to work, write us personally. We will talk to your parents.'

"Eight children wrote us. Gabi Sabag and I went to the homes of the eight children and talked to their parents and all of them agreed and let their children go to school."

Educational psychologists, worried about alienating children, might raise their brows at such tactics. But the mayor took pride in the fact that "ninety-five per cent of the elementary school children of Dimona have gone on to our Edith Lehman school. We have the highest percentage in the country, and maybe even," he smiled expansively, "in the world."

What had happened to Dimona's students in the war? "Every boy and girl who graduated from our school is in the army. It is the highest proportion in the country. One of our first graduates became a frogman and was killed.

"Many want to go on to college. But it is a great problem because they need scholarships. Some want to become doctors, teachers, and lawyers and return to Dimona to live."

"Can they readjust to life in Dimona?" I asked Jacques Amir the question I had asked Colonel Ziv in the Marcus school. We had been joined now by the Director of Education, Avner Shitreet, a lawyer who had left a lucrative career to work in Dimona, and Avigdar Schachar, Director of the high school, who had written several books and even a song about Dimona.

"The boys who come back from the army are the first ones to get the jobs," Amir said. "They also get the first openings in public works. We have industries here—a textile industry that employs two thousand people. We're on the brink of success, but we need more factories to become a real success. If unemployment increases, and if the public works projects which employ thirty per cent of our men should end, we face a serious crisis. It's interesting that the boys from our high school who came back from the army are less bitter about the scarcity of jobs and the tiny apartments than their parents are. They can see hope. With education and their experience in the army, they have something in their hands."

Ten boys from Dimona had died in the Six Day War and many were wounded. One of the wounded was twenty-four-year-old Jean-Claude Melamed who had come from Tunisia. An ironworker at the Dead Sea Works, Jean-Claude had fought as a reservist under General Sharon in Sinai. His tank was hit by a shell; his two companions, the driver and gunner, were killed. Jean-Claude took over the cannon and knocked out four Egyptian tanks. Once again his tank was hit. His leg was smashed. He continued pouring fire from his machine guns until he had no bullets left. In the midst of enemy fire, he began to climb out of the tank.

Just at that moment a tank of an Israeli commander was hit. There was an exchange of officers. One of the officers, surfacing from his tank, spotted Jean-Claude and rescued him. A few seconds later, Jean-Claude's tank exploded in flames. Inside the officer's tank, he tied a tourniquet on his own leg and survived. In the Lehman High School the children talked of Jean-Claude as if he were already a legend.

The heroism of the Jews from Arab lands wrought its change on the climate of the little development towns. The problems were still there. The cycles of poverty and illiteracy still needed to be broken. But there was no despair. Absorption was working. The Jewish refugees from Arab lands were climbing the long road out of poverty, sickness, and misery. The gap was being closed.

Step by step, the newcomers had entered into the landscape of Israel. Israel had room for them, had goals for them, had need of them.

It was time now for us to cross the old borders into the Arab towns and the refugee camps to see the other face of absorption.

12

The Gaza Strip

Now, on the seventh day, the people of Shderot had crossed the no-longer existing border into the Gaza Strip. They looked quietly into the eyes of the Arabs who had vowed death to the Jews a week earlier.

Could these merchants in long, striped nightgowns, selling *pitta* (Arab bread) and *felafel* (a delicacy of vegetable paste fried in fat) and soda pop, these eager eight-year-old salesmen in pajamas pushing flowered pencils from Red China, these men smoking hookahs in cafés from which Oriental music screamed—could these be the fierce warriors who had shouted they would drive every Jew into the sea?

Gaza Town was open at last—open for the Arabs to exit, and the Jews to enter. For nineteen years, except for the brief interval right after the Sinai Campaign in 1956, Gaza and the Strip had been shut tight. Nasser had kept the Arab refugees in the eight camps in the Strip like prisoners in a concentration camp, and even the local Arabs, who were not refugees, needed passports to go from the Strip to Egypt.

Now they were free to travel eastward, through Israel to Jerusalem, to the West Bank, or—if they wanted—to leave Israel, cross the Allenby Bridge, and live under King Hussein in Jordan. And the people of Shderot and the kibbutzim on the Gaza Strip were free to travel to Gaza.

We drove down the Gaza Strip, fifty miles south from Tel Aviv, on the coastal road from Ashdod to Ashkelon. For years I had looked at the Strip from the fields of Nahal Oz and Nirim, from the air raid shelters of Kisufim and Ein Hashlosha, from the freshly dug trenches at Kfar Aza, unable to cross over. Everywhere the road had been marked with signs: DANGER: FRONTIER. Now the signs are gone.

The hot sun beats down on the villages and camps in the Strip, which is twenty-five miles long and five miles wide, between the Mediterranean and the Negev desert. Cotton and wheat and corn tremble in the intense light. Arab women bend low in the fields, their long skirts pinned up on the side, shawls protecting their heads from the sun and the stinging flies. Old women walk like dancers, balancing on their heads heavy sacks of harvest in wicker trays. Girls slip by noiselessly, balancing jugs of water.

In open-air coffeehouses along the road, the men sit in long Arab robes, their heads draped in white *keffiyehs* (Arab head kerchiefs), smoking hookahs and talking. Boys walk lazily, dressed in sleeping pajamas. The women barely look at us, but the men stare—hostile, sullen, bitter.

It seems to me that I have known Gaza and the Strip forever. Here Delilah had beckoned the Philistines to come and shave Samson's head for eleven hundred pieces of silver. Here the Philistines gouged out Samson's eyes and chained him to two pillars supporting the roof of a Philistine lord's house; gathered on the roof were three thousand men and women, watching merrily. Samson, eyeless, in one last act of strength, pulled the pillars and the house down on top of himself, and in his dying killed more Philistines than in his life. For its sins Gaza was punished by the Lord. "I will send a fire on the wall of Gaza," Amos the Prophet quoted the Lord, "which shall devour the palaces thereof."

Before the war in June, Gaza had known many fires: Canaanite, Philistine, Hebrew, Greek, Roman, Turkish, French, British, Arab, Israeli. Napoleon conquered it only to lose it again. The British liberated it from the Turkish army in the First World War. In 1948 the Arabs of Palestine fled to Gaza. They were led by the Mufti of Jerusalem, who promised them they would soon return to Israel with a victorious army. But they never did. The Egyptians imprisoned them within the borders of the Strip, where they were housed and fed by the United Nations Relief and Works Agency. Gaza Town was the administrative center of the Strip. From here the Egyptians ruled the three cities Gaza Town, Khan Yunis, and Rafiah (called Rafa in Egypt) and controlled the camps. From here Gaza exported the main crop of the Strip—oranges—worth about ten million dollars a year. Wealthy Arabs owned the citrus groves and the fishing industry along the Strip, as well as the shops in Gaza Town, and lived in elegant villas right near the dilapidated shacks of the native populace.

After the Six Day War Gaza Town was booming. Everyone from Israel—from Ashkelon, Beersheba, Tel Aviv, the kibbutzim, the valleys beneath the Syrian Heights—seemed to be going there to look and to buy. And indeed Gaza had everything—transparent nylon nighties hanging suggestively on little racks right on the street, underwear, fancy slips, perfumes. The faces of pretty Chinese girls smiled from cans of talcum powder. There were goodies to buy from the Soviet Union and most of its satellites.

At four one afternoon, I dropped into the well-laden shop marked "Anan Brothers," to talk to Motee Anan, one of the richest men in Gaza.

"I've been robbed three times," he said, explaining why a team of young Arab men in white shirt-sleeves was busy clearing radios and vacuum cleaners, record players and hair dryers off the shelves, "mostly by local Arabs, though a few things were taken during the war by Israeli soldiers. So every afternoon we lock everything away in our warehouse." Someone told me that in a recent robbery, Motee had lost $300,000. It seemed like a fortune until I learned that Motee Anan was the agent for General Electric, Procter and Gamble, and a score of German, Japanese, and American firms.

Motee spoke English and looked like a Westerner. Born in Jaffa, he had come to Gaza in 1948 as a refugee; but he left four years later to study at the University of Illinois. He became an American citizen, returned to Gaza in 1960, married, and was now the father of five children.

"How had the local population lived under Egyptian rule before the war in June?" I asked him, trying to visualize the life of the free Arabs—not the refugees in the camps.

Motee looked at the boys pulling electrical luxuries from the shelves. "We had the same restrictions as the refugees. The curfew affected us all. For twenty years we had a curfew not only in Gaza Town but in the whole Strip. It lasted from midnight until four A.M. Nobody could walk on the streets unless he had special permission."

Motee of course owned a car, but if he wanted to drive his car at night, he had to go to the police station and get a pass. "Nobody could go from Gaza to Egypt unless he had a visa. If they blacklisted somebody, say they considered somebody dangerous—maybe he was a member of the Moslem Brotherhood [extremists] or a smuggler—he would never be allowed to leave the Strip to go even to Egypt.

"But after 1956, Egypt wanted to make Gaza prosperous—not for the people in the camps, but for the local people. They wanted to make them happy. So anyone who wanted to open a store here could open one, and he could import things from anywhere he wanted. Egypt restricted imports into Egypt, but we could import from any country in the world. The Egyptian people could come here and buy anything they wanted. There were always big Egyptian officials coming here to buy. You can't find in Cairo what I have in my shop.

"The other good thing Egypt did was let the local people go to the university in Egypt free. Very few went, it's true, but they could go if they wanted to.

"What was bad was that the top administrative personnel in Gaza were all Egyptians. The Governor, the Finance Director, the Welfare and Customs men—all the key positions were with the Egyptians. Not one of us could get any government jobs with the Egyptians."

"Do you have hope for a peaceful solution?"

"I hoped we might reach one because we are tired. We suffered three wars. All the people hope they will be compensated for what was taken from them. The people who weren't compensated want to go back and live in Israel. Some of them feel Gaza and the West Bank should form a Palestinian government and have a Federation with Israel.

"But the most important thing is that we should also have

access to Arab countries. The refugees whose condition is worse than before, they want to go back. Those who live better in the camps than they did before, they want to stay. We want peace," he finished, "which restores our dignity."

At the western end of the Strip lay Gaza's third city, Rafiah, a divided town, a miniature Berlin or Jerusalem. Half of Rafiah was Gaza Strip; half was Egypt. A customs house inside the town marked the division, like the Berlin Wall or the Mandelbaum Gate. Not only could the people of the Strip not leave; the people of Rafiah could not go freely from one side of their little town to the other. They needed passports and special papers.

After the war in June, Israel decided it was time for unification.

One warm morning we joined a bus-load of journalists, television cameramen, and movie crewmen bound for Rafiah. We were going to observe the festival that would mark this day in history. One of the world's divided towns was going to be made whole again.

After our ride down the Strip, we reached the shattered houses on the outskirts of Rafiah and entered the town. Its streets are typical of desert towns—men in front of coffeehouses, young boys in sleeping pajamas, and no women. We drove past fine villas and flimsy shacks until we arrived at the beach and the Mediterranean. Here we stopped. Tables were set under a makeshift wooden canopy, over which flew three blue-and-white flags of Israel.

An honor guard of Arab policemen—crisp and military in their khaki shirts, khaki pants, white belts, and arm bands reading "Police" in Arabic and Hebrew—waited in formation. Each of them carried a gun. Israel had reappointed Arab policemen and civil servants to keep the local machinery of government functioning. It was one of the first signs of confidence in the local population.

Two Arab sheiks, one in a long black robe, the other in a brown robe, drove up in a limousine. They shook hands with some of the Israeli army officers who were already waiting. A mukhtar from Khan Yunis, with a startlingly red moustache, Abdul Hamid Gishton, was to become Mayor of unified Rafiah. He wore a spot-

less white keffiyeh and a beige cotton *gallabeah* (Arab gown) over
an aqua cotton gown. He was short and looked like a tough labor
boss, more like a Cossack than an Arab.

Now the two Israeli army leaders arrived: Colonel Barzilai, who
would relinquish his post as Military Governor of the Gaza area,
and Colonel Alpeleg, Governor of Rafiah, who was to return in a
few days to his civilian job of running a chemical factory in Tel
Aviv.

The honor guard saluted; an Arab on a camel dashed down the
beach waving a large flag of Israel; the officers shook hands with
the Arab leaders; and then everyone was invited to sit down. The
tables burgeoned with Arab food rushed out to us by Arab
waiters—white rice, yellow rice, chick-peas, mutton, watermelon,
grapes, coffee, miniature apples. We were asked discreetly not to
eat until the speeches were over.

Colonel Alpeleg, who had short-cropped reddish hair and a
sharp bony face, put down his pipe. The speeches began. He spoke
in Hebrew and Israeli officers translated his words into Arabic.
"We want a future in which we can raise our children knowing
that tomorrow will be without fear. I know that not you made the
war, but that you pay the price of the war—because I meet here
the widows and the orphans of the war. Israel is determined to
have peace. We will make peace." The Arabs listened to the translation, and applauded quietly.

Now Barzilai spoke. He was a regular army man, heavy-set,
bulky, with green eyes set in a sun-tanned face. "War is something
that is very easy to begin," he said. "But it's very hard and takes
very long to repair the damages. We in the Military Government
have done and we will do everything in our power to make life
easier for the population and their families. The Military Government will not take the place of the local leaders and the civil
committees in supplying the necessary services. What we want to
do is create conditions under which life can become normal again.

"Except at night, when there is still a curfew, everyone here can
go freely and without papers to Gaza and to El Arish. El Arish,
which was Egyptian and was closed to most of the people of
Rafiah, is now open to everyone.

"We are ready to give a lot of money to create employment for those who want to work. I hope the new committee will know how to use this money and the means we give them to avoid starvation and unemployment. We are a democratic state. Everyone can think and wish anything he likes. We ask the people only to obey the law and keep the peace. I wish success to the committee. Life will be comfortable here, and the people will like to stay. I hope soon it will be hard to believe there was a war here."

He was answered by the red-moustached mayor. "In the name of God, and with thanks to our master, Mohammed, we thank the Governor for what he has done for us and the way he treated the population here. And we thank Colonel Alpeleg and his people for their efforts. *Shalom Aleichem.*"

Colonel Alpeleg gave each Arab on the committee a paper document signifying his membership in the village committee. Alpeleg and Barzilai shook each one's hand, cameras recorded the handshakes, the officers said *"Betay'avon"* (good appetite), and everyone started to eat.

Hassan Ibrahim Aduan, who had been a teacher of Arabic in the Rafiah Preparatory School for students thirteen to sixteen years old, spoke English fluently. With his eyeglasses, a thick black moustache, and serious mien, he looked like a teacher. He wore a white burnoose over his gray jacket and blue trousers, and a white keffiyeh. He told me he had learned English in the school in Khan Yunis.

"I am an Arab refugee from the Varga village near Yavneh in the center of Israel. In 1948 I came to Rafa [he used the Arab name for his town] and I am now thirty-three years old. I lived in Palestine Rafa and I was free to travel only from Rafa to Gaza. I could not go to the Egyptian Rafa unless I had a pass.

"Peace is good now. There is no killing now. Everything is good now. We can go freely to the West Bank of Jordan. I have relatives in Nablus, whom I have already seen."

We were speaking easily, freely, like guests at a private dinner party, when I asked him what might have happened if Egypt had won the war.

He shook his head. "If Egypt had won the war, nothing would have happened. We were under the rule of Egypt for nineteen years. We were living in peace; we had good standards."

"If Egypt had gotten as far as Tel Aviv . . . ?"

"I think they would be kind to the Jews. I have heard that Egypt would like to give Palestine back to her owners, but I never heard them say they would drive every Jew into the sea. If you heard them say that, it was only propaganda. They don't mean what they are saying."

Twenty years of hatred spewed on the air—and now he was saying they didn't mean it!

(When we visited the girls' school in Khan Yunis—the Strip's second city—we saw hanging on the walls the paintings made by the students and their teachers. There were pictures of Egyptian soldiers with huge knives, lunging at Jewish soldiers who lay terrorized and dying. In what was supposedly a kibbutz, though it looked like a dark village out of *Ivanhoe*, Egyptian soldiers fired guns and burned the buildings, while the Jews lay in the courtyard covered with blood. An Egyptian woman held a baby with a bullet hole in its stomach. My favorite was of Nasser, painted in baby-blue, wearing a Roman toga, with a halo around his head. In one hand, he held an olive branch, in the other a dove, while a Soviet rocket blasted off above the dove of peace.)

The warmth of the afternoon began to fall away. The sand dunes grew golden yellow and the Mediterranean seemed cool and blue-green. Hassan Ibrahim, teacher, member of the village committee, went on talking.

"I don't know the truth. Egypt says Israel started the war. Israel says Egypt started the war. I'm not a soldier. I don't know the truth. I have heard my friends telling that the Arabs live good in Israel. I don't know the truth. In the village committee we hope we will make things good for all the people of Rafa—to find work, to help the poor people who have lost their men in the war."

"Of the thirty-five thousand who are refugees living in the camps near Rafiah, and the five thousand local people," I asked, "how many do you think would be willing to leave?"

He answered slowly. "If Israel told all the refugees they were going back to their homes, seventy per cent would go back. But if they cannot go back to their old homes, maybe twenty per cent would be willing to go to the West Bank or Jordan. The others would all stay here."

The feast had ended. The Arab sheiks and mukhtars climbed back into their automobiles and were driven away. Colonel Alpeleg walked toward his car. He had been Military Governor of Gaza in 1956. "The situation is much more difficult today," he said. "They have had hostile education for eleven full years. On the other hand, they were expecting us to punish them severely. They are astonished now. They look like a child who expects punishment from his parents and therefore doesn't trust them even when they smile at him."

We drove to the customs house to see where Rafiah had been separated and where the Egyptian border had begun. There were no streets, only sand. Even the main road was sand. Hundreds of children ran after us, but the men, dressed in robes and wearing Japanese beach slippers, watched us sullenly.

Outside of Rafiah our bus broke down. Its rear axle had snapped. The men in the bus flagged down a command car and loaded three of us on it. The driver was a young major in Intelligence.

"I'm carrying ammunition," he said, "I'm not allowed to take you. But you are a woman, and there is a problem. We don't want you sleeping out there in the desert."

"I'd be perfectly safe," I protested.

"You would be safe. But no need to take any risks. We know what the Arabs would have done if they had won. The Germans killed us with gas. The Arabs would have killed us with knives. But we will have to learn to live together."

13

Taybe Revisited . . . and the Fawwar Refugee Camp

HALF AN HOUR east of Tel Aviv in the Plains of Sharon, where orange groves, vineyards, and gardens thrive on precious irrigation water, lies the Arab village of Taybe. I wanted to know what had happened to my friends in Taybe during the war in June, what especially had happened to Hassan Baransi, whom we had first met in 1956 and who owned the biggest house—indeed the first house—in the village.

So, early one morning, Nissim Gabbai, a jovial Iraqi, drove my husband and me to see our friend. When we arrived in Taybe, we had difficulty in finding Baransi's house; it was no longer the first one in the village. All around it, new houses had sprung up. No longer was it the biggest house; there were villas larger and more beautiful, painted in lovely pastel blues and yellows. And suddenly there it was, set back from the road, with an outside porch and a garden. We drove up and knocked at the door.

A young woman appeared. Nissim told her in Arabic that we were looking for Mr. Hassan Baransi.

"He died five months ago," she answered in English. "Please come in. I am Sameih, his daughter."

The living room was just as we remembered it—immaculate, cool, with chairs lining all the walls. Sameih waved us to seats and sat down smiling. "Of course I remember you," she said. "But

166

those days I couldn't come into the living room because you had your husband with you." She chuckled. "I peeked anyhow."

I liked her at first sight. She was a radiant girl of eighteen, with naturally glowing olive skin, intelligent brown eyes, and black hair caught in a ponytail which was tied with a green ribbon. She wore a purple cotton housedress and purple sandals.

She understood why we had had trouble finding her house. "So much has changed since you were here. It used to be the best house, but now my brother has a bigger house than this. And so many new houses—they cost a lot of money, maybe two hundred thousand Israeli pounds."

That was nearly seventy thousand dollars—a fortune for anyone. Were the Arabs in Taybe really so rich?

"Not everyone is rich, but many are," she said. "Everybody works. The men work in the factories, in construction. They own land and farms. We own a big *pardess*"—she used the Hebrew for "orange grove" as naturally as a sabra—"and we have five tractors."

She spoke easily, unself-consciously, without boasting. "I've come back from school in Nazareth," she said. "Everything's different now. When you were here before, our father never allowed us to go outside Taybe to study. We had to be home every night before dark. Now we go to Haifa, to Natanya, to Tel Aviv, and Jerusalem—anywhere we want—to study. My friends are studying to be nurses, teachers, social workers—even doctors."

She was the new young Arab woman in Israel, at ease with herself, unrestrained by anxieties or doubts. I had the feeling she could achieve anything she wanted. Her English was fine; her Hebrew was excellent; her Arabic of course was flawless. In addition she had learned French in Nazareth. She had broken completely with the harem tradition, but not in rebellion or disorder. She was quiet and well-mannered and was now running the large household for her mother, who came to sit with us.

Mrs. Baransi, round and large, wore a turquoise gown over her pajama trousers, and a white shawl fluttered on her head. She sat like a matriarch. She had given birth to six sons and four daughters and had known the highest status an Arab woman of her generation could achieve. Sameih translated everything we said for her mother.

Lutfieh, the seventeen-year-old daughter, entered the living room. She was dressed like Sameih and had the same black hair and olive skin. She was studying to become a teacher at the Teacher's Seminary in Haifa.

Were they frightened during the war, we asked, with the Jordanians right on their border?

"Not at all," Sameih said. "We were sure Israel would win."

Lutfieh nodded.

"We live in Israel," Sameih went on. "We were born here. We went to school here. We want Israel to survive."

The girls had been visiting Arab villages on the West Bank. "Many people over there would like to come and live in Israel," Sameih observed. "They want to live in Israel and be free. There is no freedom there. They can't do anything because of their king."

Lutfieh disagreed. "Your answer is not right," she told her older sister. "The people there are free also."

"But not free like us."

The girls gave their mother a running translation. Mrs. Baransi left the living room and returned later with a relative. The girls introduced him; he was Saleh Baransi, a cousin, and we soon learned that he was the town's dissident.

Only three men in the whole town of ten thousand people had been picked up when the war began in June. Saleh was one of the three. Why had he been placed under custody?

He shrugged his shoulders. "I cannot answer. In two wars, in 1956, and now in this one, the Arabs of Israel proved they are faithful. It was recognized by Ben-Gurion; and now it's recognized by Eshkol. There was not a single action of an Arab against Israel in this war."

Most of the quarter of a million Arab citizens of Israel had indeed been loyal. Only a handful in the whole country had been arrested as potential saboteurs. Later we learned that Saleh was part of a small underground. Israel knew them all; she gave them no chance in June to act as a Fifth Column.

Sameih wanted to let us know that her cousin Saleh was the exception in Taybe's loyalty. "In all of Taybe, only one man ran away to Jordan," she said.

"Why should I run?" Saleh said. "This is my fatherland. I was a teacher, and I was discharged in 1961."

"Why do you think you were discharged from your teaching job?"

Again he shrugged his shoulders. "I'm trying to live with them in peace."

It was the phrase we heard constantly in the refugee camps. What did it mean? Saleh would not define it. "Just that—to live in peace."

The girls moved uncomfortably away from him in the living room. Mrs. Baransi sat with her hands folded in her ample lap. Then I realized what was being played out in this Arab living room: the gap between the generations—the mother still living in the past; the cousin openly fighting the present; and the two young women, going to school, coming to terms with being Arabs in Israel. Here was one kind of fate for the Arabs, a fate which held some promise for the future. Another fate—which was a dead end of stagnation and lack of promise—lay in Gaza and the West Bank, in the refugee camps.

Every autumn, as predictable as the falling leaves, the Arab refugee problem is placed on the agenda of the General Assembly of the United Nations to be X-rayed and examined, discussed and debated. It is like a political cancer resisting surgery.

After the war in June, the refugees who had lived on the West Bank under Hussein and in the Gaza Strip under Nasser found themselves under Israel. Until the war the refugees had been political pawns; now, for the first time, they were in a "host" country that wanted, and indeed needed, to help them.

The simple truth is that there are Arab refugees today because the Arabs made war on Israel in 1948 and were defeated. If there had been no war there would be no refugees.

The Arab leaders knew exactly what they were doing. Back in 1947 they had announced to the world that they would defy the United Nations and launch a holy war. The Secretary General of the Arab League declared: "This will be a war of extermination and a momentous massacre which will be spoken of like the Mongolian massacre and the Crusades."

It is now almost universally acknowledged that the Arab refugees were the victims of their leaders' propaganda in 1948. They were told to flee the country; then the invading Arab countries would drive every Jew into the Mediterranean, and the Arabs would return in the wake of their victorious armies.

The British in Palestine, much friendlier then to the Arabs than to the Jews, informed the Foreign Office in London that Arabs were fleeing Haifa in small boats to go to Lebanon and Syria, and that the Jews of Haifa, who had long lived peacefully with the Arabs in their city, were going down to the boats begging the Arabs to stay.

The British Superintendent of Police in Palestine, A. J. Bidmead, wrote his government in a confidential document: "Every effort is being made by the Jews to persuade the Arab populace to stay . . . [but] Arab leaders reiterated their determination to evacuate the entire Arab population."

The war that the Arabs began in 1948 and continued in 1967 was paid for with precious lives, Arab and Jewish; and the war created the refugees. Yet the Arab refugees are by no means unique. Since the Second World War over forty million people have become refugees: Hungarians, Germans, Chinese, Indians, Pakistanis, Algerians, Tibetans, Angolans—the list could go on.

These refugees have almost all been resettled. In the Hungarian refugee resettlement—the swiftest in history—two hundred thousand Hungarians, who had fled from Hungary to Vienna in 1956, were absorbed by countries around the world in five months. In twenty years, the Arabs have still not been resettled. I know of no other instance in history where a world organization—the United Nations—fed, housed, schooled, and healed people with such compassion and love; but by keeping them in camps, the U.N. helped put off the day when they would have to face the realities of their existence. Their host countries, instead of making attempts to absorb them, used the refugees as tools and blundered into a war with Israel.

Laurence Michelmore told me in his office at the U.N. building in New York that since 1948 only five thousand Arab refugees have left the camps for countries outside the Middle East. Dr. Michelmore, Commissioner General of UNRWA, which began work in May 1950, is a tall, soft-spoken, blue-eyed American, an experienced civil servant who had served under Harry Hopkins in the W.P.A. in California. Most of his time is spent in UNRWA's headquarters in Beirut, Lebanon, where he administers the four field offices of Jerusalem, Damascus, Gaza Town, and Beirut. Through him, the world community has been spending $37 million each year, all on the Arab refugees.

"Ours is a unique operation,' he told me. "Actually the U.N. has two distinct refugee organizations: the U.N. High Commissioner for Refugees, who has responsibility for all refugees in the world except the Arabs; and UNRWA which has responsibility just for the Arabs. We get our funds through voluntary contributions from governments, individuals, and organizations."

"Who is an Arab refugee? How does the world define him?" I asked Michelmore.

"Our definition is a person who lived for two years or more in Palestine immediately before the conflict in 1948, who lost his home and his livelihood as a result of the hostilities, and who is in need. It includes people who may have been born outside of Israel—for instance, in Lebanon—or persons who had other nationalities. And it includes the children born after the hostilities." Some refugees now have grandchildren and even great grandchildren.*

I can think of few tragedies in the world greater than the tragedy of uprooted people. I had known and lived with uprooted people in the Oswego camp in America, in the D.P. camps of Germany, and the prison camps of Cyprus. But I had never seen the Arab refugee camps. Arab lands had been barred to me since 1948.

After the war in June, I spent weeks visiting camps in Jericho and Nablus and Hebron on the West Bank, and the camps in the

* Until the war in 1967, the refugees lived in four host countries: Jordan, Egypt (in the Gaza Strip), Syria, and Lebanon. The majority were in Jordan. According to UNRWA's relief rolls in January 1966, there were 697,000 in Jordan on both the East and the West Banks; 301,000 in the Gaza Strip; 162,000 in Lebanon; and 138,000 in Syria. Thus before June 5, 1967, there were nearly 1,300,000 registered refugees, of whom 873,000 received all types of UNRWA aid, while the rest received partial assistance. About half of the original 1948 refugees have left the camps and have been absorbed by their host countries.

Gaza Strip, talking with the mayors of the towns, political leaders, religious *kadis*, teachers, and the refugees themselves.

One million Arabs had suddenly become part of Israel after the lightning war. Not all were refugees in camps; some were local Arabs living in the Arab villages and towns; some were refugees who had moved out of the camps and lived freely wherever they chose, even in Jerusalem, but who remained on UNRWA relief rolls, fed and supported by world philanthropy. But it was the refugees in the camps that most concerned me.

Early one morning, my friend Sylvia Horwitz drove my husband and me to one of the largest camps on the West Bank, the Fawwar Camp outside Hebron, an hour's drive south of Jerusalem through Bethlehem and the Plain of Moab which once Naomi and Ruth had crossed.

Along the road we passed hundreds of Arabs in white keffiyehs and white cotton pantaloons doing road work, using primitive picks to break up the stones. Machines could have done in a few hours the work these labor crews were doing in weeks. But Israel, knowing the Arabs needed to have food, gave them, not dole, but the same relief work she gave the new immigrant Jews. The Arabs received the same pay, approximately $1.50 a day; but they were allowed to work as many days as they wanted, unlike the Jews whose days of employment depended on the size of their families.

The white stone houses of Hebron lay in the hills before us. Here Abraham had pitched his tents and buried his beloved Sarah in the cave of Machpela. Here Abraham himself was buried, and after him, his son Isaac, then Jacob who had been brought home from Egypt, Jacob's wives Rebecca and Leah, and finally Jacob's statesman son, Joseph.

Along the main road, past modern Arab villas and coffee shops, at the outskirts of Hebron we found the area office of UNRWA. The round shield of the U.N., painted blue and white, hung on a tall closed door. In English and Arabic, the legend ran around the shield: UNRWA AREA OFFICE.

We entered a courtyard and climbed a long flight of stairs that reminded me of an old-tenement fire escape. On the upper floor of an old Arab building were the simple offices of the education and registration divisions of UNRWA. We were looking for the area director of all the camps in the Hebron district, Ismail Ali Tahboub. But Ismail Ali Tahboub had fled to Amman in June.

In his absence we were welcomed by Khalil Labadi, the assistant to the Area Registration officer. All the UNRWA area offices were headed and staffed only by Palestinian refugees. Khalil Labadi was no exception. Good-looking, with a black moustache and balding head, Labadi, originally from Ara near Haifa, lived in East Jerusalem with his wife and five children, and traveled by bus to his UNRWA job in Hebron each morning.

His was a key position. It was he who determined who was an Arab refugee. He was the keeper of the records. He knew the vital statistics of births and deaths.

"I was a teacher in UNRWA from 1954 to 1955," Labadi told me. "I taught geography, mathematics, Arabic, and sometimes English. Then I was selected to join a course in health education—to work among the refugees to raise their standard of health. I did this for three years; then I was transferred to the welfare section. From there I was promoted to this registration section."

"Where were you on the fifth of June?"

"I had left my home in Jerusalem and come here early in the morning. When I heard about the shooting, I tried to get back to Jerusalem. I reached Bethlehem and walked on foot to a village in the suburbs of Jerusalem. I stayed there with my brother for two days. On the third day people came from Jerusalem and spread propaganda—the Jews are killing Arabs, raping women, murdering children, burning houses. So I was afraid. My brother and his sons and me, we walked to Jericho. There I stayed fifteen days. I couldn't reach Jerusalem. There was no transport. My wife and five children were in Jerusalem. They didn't know where I was. I decided to go to Jerusalem on foot. I walked up into Bethany.

" 'Where did you come from?' the soldiers asked me.

" 'Jericho.'

" 'Where are you going?'

" 'Jerusalem.'

"At first they said there was no transport to Jerusalem. I said, 'I know, but I haven't seen my wife and children for eighteen days.'

"After two days transport was available, so I went to Jerusalem.

I found that my children and my wife are well. I was very happy."

"Was any of the propaganda true?" I asked him.

"No. There were no atrocities. There were some women and children killed, but they may have been killed by stray shots."

"Were any of the refugee camps in your area shelled or bombed?"

"None."

"Why then did some of the refugees run from these camps across the Allenby Bridge to the East Bank?"

"They were afraid of the bombs. They were afraid the Jews would slaughter them."

"Do they still believe that?"

"No. Now that the Jews have not killed any, the people realize they were mistaken. To some extent the people even believe that some of the things they heard before were untrue. But the people tell me they still do not feel they are safe. This is the result of any war."

Sitting at Labadi's side was a young fair-haired man, dressed like Labadi in a white, tieless shirt. He was Abdel Kadir Saleh, whose work classification on the UNRWA payroll was "interviewer." His job was to interview the refugees who came for ration cards and who had special problems to discuss. He decided to interview me. He wanted to know who I was, whom I represented, and what I thought about the whole refugee problem. Prepared for such an emergency, I had brought along the Arab edition of a book I had written on Puerto Rico, which was printed in Cairo. The two young men leafed through the book; they could of course read it; I could not. They were particularly fascinated by a photograph of an Arab in a black robe with a white keffiyeh standing with a beautiful young Indian woman in a silken sari at the Puerto Nuevo Steam Power Plant in San Juan. My credentials were evidently satisfactory. Abdel Kadir Saleh permitted me to interview him.

He was nine years old, he said, when his family fled to Jordan from Faluja near Kiryat Gat in the northern Negev. "After the war in June, I went back to Faluja. I saw the trees. It was beautiful. I was sad, because this is my land. I met many of the Jews there. We discussed this problem. They told me, 'We will compensate the refugees.' But it is not enough. I might get compensated for my land. Here I earn only my salary."

Every refugee we met talked of the land he had owned, even though he might have been an infant when his parents left.

"You were a child then. Why did your family leave?"

"Because it was war. Everybody was afraid. If the Jews had a means of escape, the Jews would escape too. They have the sea behind them and the Arab states before them. They have no escape. But we had places to run to . . ."

We descended the outer stairs to drive to the Fawwar Camp with Labadi as our guide and interpreter. On the way he told us that some 500,000 refugees had occupied the West Bank before June 5. (The Israel census taken right after the Six Day War found 120,000 refugees on the West Bank; 100,000 had crossed to the East Bank.) There were twenty camps on the West Bank, four of them with 95,964 refugees under the jurisdiction of the Hebron Area Office.

We drove four miles through the barren hills to the Fawwar Camp, stopping at its outskirts in front of a small white concrete building. On it was the U.N. shield, inscribed in English and Arabic: UNRWA CAMP LEADERS' OFFICE.

We entered the little building and met Mohammed Ibrahim Azzeh, the camp leader, a large man with graying hair, a thin graying moustache, and small light eyes that squinted as he talked—probably from having spent long years in the sun. He had been appointed by UNRWA fifteen years ago.

Azzeh looked like a leader. Instead of desert clothing, he wore a green shirt with an open collar. He could have been an Israeli boss on a big works project.

"Before June fifth, we had about five thousand people in Fawwar Camp," he said. "About one thousand have left. Some left because they were afraid of the war. Others were on the East Jordan Bank working in the harvest, because the dry rations we give them are not enough. About five hundred were over there before the war; the other five hundred left after the war."

"What made the Arab refugees run again? For some, this is the second time. Did they learn nothing the first time they ran?"

"There is the fear of death, the love of life," he said. "I tried to convince some of my relatives to stay. But I failed."

"Why did you stay this time?"

"In 1948 when the first war happened, most of the people left their homes. I lived in Beit Jebrin; we're a large family. We lived in many of the villages in the Hebron area between Hebron and Beersheba. I saw what happens when the refugees leave their homes. They suffer a lot. In their refugee status they lead a very bad life. Help from UNRWA is just to keep them in bread and water. So if I have the influence, I try to stop them. I know Israel has become a state. I'm not afraid of what the people are afraid. I know Israel is a member of the United Nations and Israel would not do any harm. The Israel government has been very correct in my camp. I don't know about the other camps, but in my camp I don't notice that the Israel government interferes with the refugees. The military authorities haven't harmed anybody."

Over an old wardrobe in his office hung a sign:

NEVER PROMISE
unless sure

On another wall, a huge blackboard marked "UNRWA" told the story of the camp:

UNRWA

huts: 980   tents: nothing

	families	persons
off. residents	840	4,648
unoff. residents	41	278

The blackboard listed headings for the services provided: Administration, Health, Education, Sanitation, Supplementary Feeding, Welfare. Under Welfare was the heading Community Center for Men and under that Library, Atheletic Group, Illiteracy. "Seventy per cent of the men can read and write," the camp leader told us, "but most of the older women are illiterate."

Azzeh described the food rations distributed to the people. Once a month, each family head comes to the distribution center to pick up his family's ration of dry foods. Every person listed on the ration card receives a daily diet of 1,500 calories in summer and 1,600 in winter.* *The people are not required to live in a refugee camp to draw these free U.N. rations.* They can live in towns, villages, even in the Holy City of Jerusalem. All they need is to be listed on a ration card; and most cards contain the names of at least ten persons.

Misuse of the ration cards had become a major scandal. Dr. Michelmore had told me that "merchants in Jordan managed to get whole families' ration cards. The merchants came themselves to present the cards each month. They picked up the rations, and sold them for their own profit. It was widespread and significant, and we regarded it as a very bad practice. But we couldn't control it, until after the war in June. Now we have clamped down on the merchants."

In the halls of the United Nations, it was widely known that since the early 1950's, 30 to 40 per cent of the free rations were going to people ineligible by UNRWA's own definition. Arabs who had never lived in Palestine, Arabs indigenous to the areas where the camps were set up registered with UNRWA to get ration cards. Apparently some of the staff members employed by UNRWA, refugees themselves, saw no harm in adding extra names to the U.N. relief rolls. Newborn babies were passed around, it was said, from family to family, to be registered on innumerable ration cards.

Why had UNRWA tolerated such a deception? "From the beginning," Michelmore said, "we attempted to apply our definition of a refugee. But there were a great many duplicate registrations in the early days. People died and their deaths were not reported. People left the area, and their departures were not reported. People got jobs, and their names were not taken off the ration cards. But we've been working on identifying ineligibilities and removing them from the rolls. In Lebanon, we've completed a recheck of each family. In Gaza, we were able to get access to the

---

* During the seven summer months, each eligible refugee receives 10 kilos (22 lb.) of flour, 600 grams (1.3 lb.) each of sugar and pulse (dried beans, peas, lentils, etc.), 500 grams (1.1 lb.) of rice, and 375 grams (13 oz.) of edible oil or fuel. In winter the daily diet is raised to 1,600 calories by the addition of 400 grams of flour and 300 grams of pulse. Woolen blankets and kerosene for heating and cooking are issued during the five winter months; and each refugee receives about 3 kilos (6.5 lb.) of clothes.

records of the people who left for Kuwait, and of those who were allowed to go to Cairo for higher education and then go abroad to work. We now have actual records of deaths; and we have line checks in Gaza, when they come for food, to make sure the heads of families are living there.

"Our greatest problem," he said, "was in Jordan. There, anything touching the relief rolls and the census was a major political issue."

Hussein had consistently refused to allow UNRWA to count the number of refugees in Jordan, estimated by UNRWA as 37 per cent of the population. Certainly, there was economic advantage in inflating the relief rolls. U.N. food was money, whether the food was sold by corrupt merchants or by the refugees themselves. Each name on a ration card, Dr. Michelmore told me, was worth $1.20 per month; a card with ten names was worth $12.00 every month. Multiplied hundreds of times, ration cards could make a man rich. An American State Department spokesman, quoted in The New York Times on June 14, 1966, estimated that "200,000 of the 450,000 refugee cards issued for Jordanian camps have fallen into the hands of merchants and other unauthorized users."

But the Arab refugees were a political threat to Hussein. They lived under the king but most of them loved Nasser. Hussein's excuse to UNRWA for refusing to allow a census was that it would have an "adverse reaction on public order."

Of all the abuses of the ration cards, the most shocking was uncovered after the war in June, when it was learned that the Arabs had sold their cards for money to buy arms and guns for the Palestine Liberation Army to defeat Israel. It was a perversion of world philanthropy. Food sent to keep Arab children alive was converted into guns to kill Israeli children across the borders.

Shukairy's Palestine Liberation Army, conscripting all young Arab men in the Gaza Strip born between 1937 and 1944, fed them with UNRWA rations, and, Dr. Michelmore told me, "in the last days of May and June, even established their fortified positions for their attack on Israel close to UNRWA camps."

UNRWA food thus became an economic, political, and in the end, a military weapon in the war against Israel. But for the children in Fawwar Camp, the food meant extra milk and a decent hot lunch six days a week. At seven in the morning, Azzeh told us, eight hundred and fifty children are given milk to supplement the regular breakfast their mothers fix for them. At noon, they all trot off to the camp's feeding center where, along with pregnant women, nursing mothers, and old people, they have a fine lunch of meat, seasoned with garlic and cooking fat, potatoes, vegetables, *pitta*, and a hot drink with sugar.

The refugee camps, like the development towns in Israel, have a beat and rhythm and their own set of priorities. Food is first, then shelter, then schools.

In the British prison camps on Cyprus, the children rescued from Hitler went to school from six in the morning until twelve, when it was almost too hot to survive, and one saw sixteen-year-old boys and girls sitting in a classroom—a room built in the space between two quonset huts, with some potato sacking sewn together for a roof—sixteen-year-old boys and girls going to school for the first time, learning that one plus one equals two. They looked like no other schoolchildren in the world. There was a hunger for learning, and beneath the hunger a deep apathy and bitterness. One and one equals two. They were almost ripe for marriage and children of their own. One and one equals two.

In the Fawwar Camp, Azzeh told us, "school is not compulsory, but the majority of the children do go. We have one school for boys, and one for girls, through the ninth grade. We don't have a secondary school or a vocational school."

UNRWA ran the schools in cooperation with UNESCO. The United Nations built the schools, paid the teachers (all of whom were Arab refugees), paid the tuition for those children who went on to secondary schools run by the governments of the host countries, and bought the textbooks printed by the governments of Jordan, Egypt, Lebanon, and Syria.

In nineteen years, the schools in the refugee camps had molded a whole generation of refugees. What had they been taught?

"The usual things," Azzeh said, "history, arithmetic, Arabic."

Schools are a microcosm of the world children will live in when they grow up; here they learn their national purpose. What kind of textbooks had the United Nations bought for their wards from the printing presses of Cairo, Amman, and Damascus? Azzeh said, "Ordinary textbooks, the same kind all the children in Jordan use."

I had seen a few of the textbooks in the camps in the Gaza Strip and on the West Bank. Mithkal Natour, a young Arab teacher with startlingly beautiful white teeth, who lived in the village of Kalansawa near Nablus, had shown me the math books from which he taught. Married three years and a father of three children, Mithkal had invited us into his home with a warm *Tfadal* (welcome) and shown us the books used in his school. He was busy deleting "the bad parts." Israel had discovered that in books like one of Mithkal's texts, called *Israel, the Stolen Land*, Arab children were being taught that the Jews had stolen their homes, and they must fight to regain them.

In the last chapter of a high school textbook titled *The Palestine Problem*, the students were exhorted: "You, the Arab student, are called upon to save your stolen homeland with all your strength and all your resources. Take Abd al-Rahim, who fell fighting for Palestine, as your example and idol."

Why did UNRWA countenance hate and propaganda against a member of the U.N. in schools run by a U.N. agency? Michelmore explained, "We followed the curriculum of the government in the area in which we worked, and we used all their textbooks. UNESCO said it was important since the students in our schools would have to take the same exams as the students took in the host country's schools. For refugee students to compete meant that they had to study the same literature, the same history, the same math that was taught in Cairo or Amman, Damascus or Beirut. That's why we had to buy the textbooks printed in the host countries, and follow their curriculum."

Sitting in Azzeh's office, I turned to Labadi, who had earlier been a teacher in the camps and who had struck me as a moderate Arab. "I gather," I said, "that in some of the schools new math was hate math."

"It's true," he said. "Anti-Jewish and anti-Israel propaganda was taught in every single school. These children believe their fathers have been kicked out of their homes and land. These fathers will die some day. It means the motherland will be forgotten. They want their children to understand what happened in the past. They want them to remember about their homes in Jaffa. They want their children to go back to their land, if not by peace, then by war."

We had paid our respects to Azzeh. Now he joined us in our car to drive under the blazing sun to the camp itself. For nearly twenty years I had pictured Arab refugee camps as hovels, with tents and muddy roads, weary men and listless women, and half-naked children. For most of us, Arab refugee camps conjured up the D.P. camps of Germany and Poland. My own image was of Bergen Belsen or the British prison camps in Cyprus, with their unbearably hot quonset huts, barbed wire, and people thirsting for water and freedom.

The Fawwar Camp resembled none of them. It looked like an urban-renewal housing project in a developing country. Nearly a thousand concrete one-family houses, painted in pastel yellow or gray, bordered the highway and ran, in narrow streets, up the hills. The houses reminded me of community projects in Puerto Rico, though the lush green trees of Puerto Rico were lacking.

The houses, Labadi told us, had all been built by a local Arab contractor, under U.N. specifications and paid for by the U.N. There were school buildings, a community center, and some tiny kiosks.

It looked like a modern Arab town of stone and adobe, but it had few of the vital organs of a town—grocery stores, butcher shops, vegetable markets, and clothing shops. Few were needed. The people were given everything free, unto the third and the fourth generation.

There were no tents, no quonset huts, no barbed wire; in fact, the Fawwar Camp looked more prosperous, sitting on the road, than many of the local Arab villages. In the villages, although many of the houses were of stone or concrete, some were little more than shacks; but even the poorest villages were green and shaded with flowers and trees, while the Fawwar Camp, with only a few trees and almost no flowers or vegetation, lay naked in the sun.

As in every camp I have visited anywhere in the world, hundreds of children flocked around us, smiling, friendly. Here they tossed

newly-learned Hebrew words at us. Labadi had given us a handsome UNRWA pamphlet which reported in 1965 that "some 40
to 50 per cent of the total [refugee population] was destitute or
almost destitute." These children did not look destitute. They had
none of the tell-tale signs of destitution and malnutrition—
trachoma, tinea, and T.B.—I had seen in other Arab lands. They
looked healthy and well fed.

The Arab refugee camps have kept Arab culture and customs
intact. Each camp, just as each village, has its own mukhtar, or
chief. Labadi and Azzeh took us directly to the Mukhtar of the
camp. It was a necessary courtesy that any visitor be ushered
directly into his home. The Mukhtar would then know who was
visiting and what his mission was. The Mukhtar was host and
spokesman for the entire camp population.

We were led inside a compound of concrete houses in which
the Mukhtar and his family lived behind a stone wall in complete
privacy. Azzeh introduced us to a good-looking young man dressed
in a white shirt. He was the Mukhtar's son. In excellent English,
he invited us into his father's house.

The Mukhtar, a virile-looking man with a large black moustache, dark eyes, wearing a wrinkled yellow robe and a yellow knit
stocking cap, bowed politely. We entered a one-room concrete
house, that looked, from the outside, like most of the pastel houses
we had seen along the highway. But inside, it was a single room,
with a huge table which dominated the whole house. There were
no couches or pillows as in some Arab homes; straight-backed
chairs were set around the table and against the walls.

The Mukhtar escorted me to the head of the table and sat close
by. Labadi acted as official interpreter, since the Mukhtar apparently spoke not one word of English.

Within moments, six or seven elders wearing white or checkered
keffiyehs entered silently, bowed, and took chairs around the table.
There was a rustle of noise, and the charming unending ballet of
Arab hospitality began. Tiny cups of delicious Turkish coffee were
set before us; bottles of orange soda were brought into the living-
room house, and we were urged to drink before any serious conversation could start.

I had told Labadi that I was particularly interested in the curriculum of the camp schools and the textbooks children studied from. While the coffee and soft drinks were served, Labadi introduced a fiery-looking young man, wearing a Western jacket, pants which matched, and no headdress. Labadi said, "He's the man here who knows everything about education."

Before I could speak, let alone ask a question, he said, in flawless English, "I refuse to talk to you." Then, in a kind of frozen smile, he qualified himself. "If you want to talk to me as a woman to a man, I will talk to you about such things."

The smile disappeared. "But nothing else. I must honor my obligation. I signed a paper not to give information to any journalist about my work or my politics."

For whom had he signed the paper, we asked. "I refuse to tell you," he said.

At last the coffee was drunk, the soda pop was nearly finished, and the Mukhtar turned to me. It was time for conversation. As the guest, I was asked to open the dialogue.

"We know how difficult it is to live the life of a refugee," I began. Labadi translated. The Mukhtar nodded; the elders were silent. "Do you foresee a day when you will no longer live as a refugee?"

"How do you want me to live?" the Mukhtar answered. "What do you want to change in my life?" Without waiting, he went on. "I want a place which I know is my home to work in. I want the kind of work which is a future for my children. I was a farmer in the Gaza area. I want to go back to my land."

I tried to tell him about the forty million people who had lost their land and their homes after World War Two.

He shook his head. He talked in Arabic with the other leaders, and with the fiery educator who would not talk with me. They all agreed that I was mistaken. Forty million people, indeed. "No," he said, "in the history, no people were ever driven from their land and their homes."

I did not press the point. Instead I said to the Mukhtar, "War does terrible things. But if other countries in the world offered to take in some of the refugees, would you go?"

The whole room seemed to grow cold. The educator bit his lips. The other leaders waited apprehensively. The Mukhtar spoke.

"Never. I will not accept any exchange of my land or my village. If I was asked to go to Australia or America, I would not go. If they gave me a house like this, all of gold, I would not accept it."

One of the elders said, "I lived in Jaffa. I owned much land there. I want to return to Jaffa."

Suddenly I had a feeling that everything was unreal. The word "Jaffa" touched it off. It seemed to me nearly every Arab I met had come from Jaffa, owned a villa in Jaffa, and was lord of uncounted acres of orange groves and fertile land, all within Jaffa's boundaries. If all of them told the truth, Jaffa must have been, not the truly beautiful (but also slum-ridden) Arab city I once knew curving like a scimitar on the Mediterranean south of Tel Aviv, but a lost continent greater than Atlantis.

The line between reality and dreams was lost in the Mukhtar's living-room. The great Arab philosopher Alghazali had written in *The Survival of Religious Studies*: "Know that a lie is not *haram* [wrong] in itself but only because of the evil conclusion to which it leads the hearer, making him believe something that is not really the case. . . . If a lie is the only way to reach a good result it is *halal* [permitted]."

The lie had been told for all these years, growing until it had grown into truth. It was a phenomenon of all refugees; the past, from which they had fled, voluntarily or involuntarily, grew more golden and idyllic as it receded. In the midst of the great German-Jewish migration to America, the joke grew that a Pekinese dog had been asked what he had done "back home in Germany." "In Germany," he answered, "I was a St. Bernard."

The lie had been part of the whole Six Day War. The lie in the telephone call Nasser and Hussein had made; the lie in the Arab claims that they had destroyed every single Israel airplane the first day of the war; the lie in the sudden kiss of brotherhood when Hussein journeyed to Cairo on May 30, though scarcely three months before, Nasser had called him in the hall of the Cairo University, "the adulterer of the Hashemite family."

I tried to bring our conversation back to a moment in history which I thought the Mukhtar could not deny. "In 1948 it was the Arabs who declared war. They would not accept the United

Nations' resolution. They walked out. I was in the hall of the U.N. when it happened. These camps are the result of that war. One cannot turn history back."

He brushed aside my reference to history.

"The Arab governments lost the war and they were defeated," he conceded. "But the Arab people feel that one day the people should reach their aims and declare their rights as individuals. We will not leave the camps until we return to Palestine, no matter how long it takes."

An air of waiting began to pervade the room. I had a sense of the waiting that had lasted twenty years, and perhaps could last another twenty. They had time, while they were waiting. Waiting for what? I tried to put my finger on it. Waiting for another war—for the fourth round? Waiting for Allah or God or Godot to turn the clock back twenty years? Meanwhile they lived in a Kafka-like world of unreality. Our conversation was like two trains running on different tracks.

I had come full of hope. Now that the war in June had exposed the camps to the eyes of foreign observers, perhaps we could end the stalemate, liberate the people who wanted liberation and freedom. I knew, from past experience, there is always a hard core who do not want to leave the easy secure life of a camp. UNRRA (United Nations Relief and Rehabilitation Agency), the wartime refugee agency in Europe, headed first by Fiorella La Guardia and later by Herbert Lehman, had simply shut down the D.P. camps a few years after World War Two ended. Even the hard-core D.P.'s were forced to make a decision to settle in a nearby town or travel abroad.

But UNRWA took the position that it could not resettle the Arab refugees without a mandate from the U.N. General Assembly. The U.N. was deadlocked on the questions of repatriation, compensation, and resettlement. In December 1948, the General Assembly adopted the now famous resolution, called simply "Resolution 194, Paragraph 11," in which the U.N. resolved "that the refugees wishing to return to their homes and live in peace with their neighbors should be permitted to do so at the earliest practicable date, and that compensation should be paid for the property of those choosing not to return and for loss of or damage to property which, under principles of international law or in equity, should be made good by the Governments or authorities responsible."

"Both the refugees and the Arab governments," Michelmore told me, "have taken the view that this is something the U.N. has promised. They are waiting until this promise is fulfilled. It's true Australia and other countries have offered to take in some of the refugees. But as long as Resolution 194 is introduced every year and reaffirmed by the Assembly, the refugees feel they should not migrate."

Israel has demonstrated its willingness to contribute to the solution of the refugee problem. In 1963 Israel declared its support for a United Nations draft resolution which invited both Israel and the Arab states to begin negotiations to solve the refugee problem. The Arabs bitterly refused. The Arabs claim it is the refugee problem which has eaten away the prospects for peace; the Israelis claim it is Arab belligerency which has made peace impossible and that the refugees are the victims of that belligerency.

Israel's Ambassador Michael Comay, speaking before the Special Political Committee of the United Nations on December 14, 1967, summarized Israel's position: "The Arab refugee *problem*, as such, remained frozen in Arab belligerence and became its political instrument. The integration which did take place was not admitted. Instead the refugee statistics swelled from year to year and the gap grew wider between myth and reality. We in Israel have now been able to observe at first hand that in most areas the distinction between refugees and non-refugees has become blurred."

Meanwhile, without publicity or fanfare, Israel has already paid compensation to some of the refugees of the war of 1948; and many families separated by the war have been reunited. On the Allenby Bridge, there is a constant flow of refugees from the war of 1967—some leaving for Amman, others returning to join their families and reclaim their homes.

It seems to me the solution of the Arab refugee problem lies in three areas—resettlement abroad, compensation, and repatriation. The United Nations has demonstrated, by its humanitarian and generous care for the Arab refugees, that the problem is not an Israeli-Arab problem alone. It is a United Nations and, therefore, a world problem. It is time now for the world to call a halt to this refugeeism. Israel should be asked to retain some of the refugees; the Arab states in the Middle East should all be asked to accept and integrate some of the refugees; and the rest of the world, especially the countries of immigration—Australia, Canada, Argentina, Brazil, the United States, and perhaps the Soviet Union—should open their doors. The figures for each country would need to be worked out by demographers rather than politicians.

The late President Herbert Hoover pointed out after the War of 1948 that Iraq, with its fertile and empty Tigris and Euphrates valleys, had once been the breadbasket of the Middle East. He recommended that Iraq take in a good number of the Arab refugees, since they speak the same language, practice the same religion, cherish the same culture, and are rooted in the same historic past as the Arabs of Iraq. The Palestinian Arabs, he argued, would not only end their own deterioration, but could once again make the Tigris and Euphrates fertile.

The late U.N. Secretary General Dag Hammarskjöld had a great dream for the Middle East. In 1958 he proposed a vast U.N. aid program for the "economic integration" of the Arab refugees. The nations of the world would spend two billion dollars in five years (instead of the thirty to forty million a year they were now spending) to create productive jobs for them. His hope was to end the deterioration of the human beings in the camps, make the first steps toward peace between the Arabs and Jews, and help bring prosperity through agriculture and industry to the Middle East.

In the breathtakingly beautiful mountain town of Sofar, Lebanon—where, traveling with UNSCOP in 1947, we listened to Arab testimony in the mornings and spent our afternoons and evenings like pashas dining and being entertained in palatial villas—the leaders of nine Arab states met in the summer of 1958 to discuss Hammarskjöld's proposal. They rejected it outright. It would mean, they said, settling the refugees permanently in the areas now sheltering them. Far better to let them live in camps. The refugees themselves, of course, had little or nothing to say. Their value in politics heavily outweighed two billion dollars. The refugees were condemned to further years of mass deterioration by political leaders, most of whom had no refugees in their own countries.

In nineteen years the world has spent three-quarters of a billion dollars to keep the refugees inside the camps. If the world were to adopt Hammarskjöld's plan, it could solve the problem forever. Now for the first time there is a host country that would accept the challenge, communicate it, and implement it.

The first requisite would be the liquidation of the camps. The second requisite would be to give the people opportunities to earn their own bread. They should be given jobs, land which they can own and farm, free transportation, and help for the first two years.

Israel has shown the world that she knows the techniques of absorption. Her experience in absorbing the Jews from Arab lands, her army's experience in educating illiterate and semiliterate soldiers, the agonizing trials and errors and ultimate success of turning a people into a nation—these are all lessons that Israel could apply in helping the Arabs integrate into the economic life of the region. And they are lessons that Israel could share with other lands.

I knew it was useless to suggest solutions to the Mukhtar. He was intransigent. In a sense his was an idyllic life. His oldest son was in Saudi Arabia working in the rich oil fields, but his family still drew food rations in his name. Babies were born, but no one "died" in a refugee camp. Farmers left to harvest the crops on the East Bank, some went to America or Canada, old age or illness finally overtook some of the people, but such departures were rarely, if ever, recorded.

He himself lived in a kind of miniature kingdom inside the camp. He led us through his compound. He, his wives, and all his children occupied five houses. One was the living-room house in which we had talked. Now he led us across the paved yard to another concrete house which he called his harem. One of his wives, with a white shawl on her head and a tattooed face, welcomed me shyly into the harem. It was a one-room house with mattresses and blankets stacked neatly from the floor almost to the ceiling. The harem was spotless. The three other houses were for the children who now crowded happily around us. Well-trained, they had not uttered a sound to disturb us during the long hours we talked in their father's house. Now their exuberance enveloped us as they hopped in front of our cameras, putting their faces inches away from the lens. The Mukhtar disappeared for a few minutes. When he returned he had changed his yellow stocking cap for a snow-white keffiyeh. Only then did he let us take his picture.

14

The General and the
North African Lady

Six weeks after the war had ended, there was a commotion in front of Moshe Dayan's house. A middle-aged woman approached the police guarding his home. "I must see the General."

"Is he expecting you?"

"No. But I must see him."

"It's impossible—unless you have an appointment."

"But I came to this country just to see him. I have been trying to see him for days. Nobody will let me near him."

The police guard shook his head. "Everybody wants to see Dayan . . ."

"I'm leaving Israel tomorrow morning. I cannot leave without seeing him."

Just then Dayan drove up dressed in old khaki clothes covered with dust. He had been out all day on an archaeological dig, his favorite avocation.

"What's going on here?" he asked.

The woman approached him. "General Dayan, I have come from North Africa just to see you. During the Six Day War, I made a vow that if Israel won, I would bring you four thousand dollars. I want you to give it to any school you choose, so they can train more officers like you and the ones who won the war."

Dayan said, "Please come in."

In the living room, he asked his father-in-law, Zvi Schwarz, a Jerusalem lawyer, to chat with the woman while he changed his clothes.

The Dayan household was in upheaval. Cooks, waiters, and waitresses were preparing mountains of food; workmen were putting the last touches on the hill they had bulldozed and leveled just above the Dayan garden. A huge many-tiered cake was wheeled out. Ruth Dayan, wife of the General, wearing gold sandals and a black silk dress, embroidered, she told me later in the evening, by an Arab friend in Bethlehem, raced in and out of the living room. Her mother, Rachel, a child-care expert, was carefully ironing a white wedding gown while Pauline Trigère, the French-American fashion designer, hovered over her.

Tonight there would be a double wedding in the Dayan family. Their twenty-eight-year-old daughter, Yaël, who is a novelist and a lieutenant in the army, and Asaf, their younger son, an actor, were both to be married.

Freshly shaved, wearing a white short-sleeved shirt and dark trousers, Dayan entered the living room. "Tell me about yourself," he said to the North African woman.

"I prefer not to tell you my name," she said, "nor the country I came from. It would be too dangerous for my family if the ruler of my country discovered what I was doing."

Dayan understood and did not press her.

The mysterious woman opened her purse and drew out $4,000. Dayan shook his head. "I cannot take any money."

The woman looked appalled. "You must take it. It is not for you. It is for Israel."

"But then we must know your name to give you a receipt."

"If the government must give a receipt, let them send it to my brother who works in Haifa. His name is different from mine, since I am married." She gave Dayan her brother's name.

Invited to stay for the wedding, she entered the garden with the first of the three thousand guests and slipped into the background.

What impressed me most about the garden that night was the lighting. Emerald spotlights played on desert shrubs, palm trees, ancient Greek and Roman columns, and on the Byzantine and Arabic treasures which Dayan had dug up. The garden was terraced on the side of a gently rolling hill. Tables had been set on different planes.

The aristocracy of Israel rubbed elbows with farmers; university presidents sat with kibbutzniks; heroes of the Six Day War greeted Druze friends wearing immaculate white turbans; Arab mayors chatted with Israeli Arabs wearing identical white keffiyehs. The obscure woman from North Africa watched them all.

Under a canopy on top of the hill, Chaplain of the Army Shlomo Goren married Yaël to Colonel Dov Sion, whom she had met in Sinai in the weeks of tension. The words were spoken, ancient words in an ancient language, while Dayan and Ruth, and David Ben-Gurion and Paula, gave the bride away. Colonel Sion crushed an empty wine glass under his shoes lest he forget, even in this moment of happiness, the destruction of the Second Temple.

The orchestra burst into an old Jewish melody from the *shtetl*, "*Hossen, Kallah, Mazel-tov*" ("Bridegroom, Bride, Congratulations"), and then into the anthem of the Six Day War, "*Yerushalayim Shel Zahav*" ("Jerusalem the Golden"). The people applauded, the wedding party returned to the house, and in a few moments Dayan reappeared with his son Asaf and Aharona, a willowy dark-haired university student.

They ascended the narrow path between the crowded guests until they stood under the canopy on the lighted hilltop. Yaël's wedding had been military; this one was not. The chief rabbi of Tel Aviv and the cantor, in a magnificent silver-and-white robe and a high white silk hat, recited the ancient words. Again a glass was broken, the band burst into the wedding song of the *shtetl* and the song of the war, and the guests ate from the tables laden with food.

Dayan stood in a small circle of friends talking about the woman from North Africa. One of his friends teasingly asked what school he would give the money to. Would he give it to the school he had attended, The Girls' Agricultural School, where he had been the only boy? (Dayan's parents, pioneers of Kibbutz Degania on the Sea of Galilee, had helped found the farming village of Nahalal, near Nazareth. Here they sent their young son Moshe, to the local high school, a girls' farming school established by WIZO [Women's International Zionist Organization]. At the

school he had met Ruth Schwarz, a pretty young Jerusalem girl
who had come to spend the summer.)

I kept searching the faces of the men around Dayan, trying to
find an answer to the question the nameless woman from North
Africa had raised. Perhaps if one could find that answer, one
would have the key to understanding how Israel had won the
war.

"Really," we tried to draw Dayan out, "how *do* you create the
kind of officers you have?"

Dayan smiled, a funny twisted smile. He was a different Dayan
tonight. The image was no longer that of the dashing, eye-patched
hero. Tonight he was the proud father and, even more, the doting
grandfather of Udi's two children. Udi, his oldest son, had tried to
rejoin the frogmen for the war, but he was rejected. Israel could ill
afford to have him captured. Furious, Udi, the most restrained of
the three Dayan children, had enlisted in the paratroopers.

Dayan evaded our question. "We really do have great commanders," he said expansively. He gave no precise formula for
winning the war, but there was an unmistakable force behind
everything he said—his own love of this land. He knew the country
in depth and breadth, foot by foot; he knew it walking, driving,
flying over it, digging deep into its Biblical and archaeological
past.

Sitting on a low chair in Dayan's living room, his long legs
stretched out on the rug, was General Ezer Weizman, married to
Ruth's younger sister, Reuma. Weizman calls Dayan "the Brother"
or "the Brother-in-law," but their style is totally different. Dayan
still carries the farm at Nahalal with him, lonely, earthy, immediate. Weizman, a city boy, born in Tel Aviv to President Chaim
Weizmann's older brother, was a pilot in the British R.A.F.
during World War Two. Tall, moustached, with light blue eyes,
Weizman was one of the chief architects of Israel's air force; he
trained its men and gave it its spirit.

Yet when the war broke out in June it was not Weizman but
his friend, General Mordechai Hod, who led the air force. Weizman had been promoted to Chief of the General Staff Branch.

"How did we win the war?" Weizman repeated my question.
"The air force won the war. We swept the skies. Once we denied

the enemy their air forces, we hit everything of theirs that showed up above the ground. The can was opened by the air force."

How had they created their commanders? "It depends on your teachers"—Weizman got up and paced the living room—"on your leadership, the example you give when you command. Don't let anybody kid you that we're an undisciplined army. Spit and polish aren't discipline. For us, discipline is complete knowledge of your weapons, knowledge of your terrain, knowledge of your enemy, and above all, knowledge of the men you command. God help a commander if he doesn't know his men."

In the Six Day War, Weizman had sat on one side of General Yitzhak Rabin, the Chief of Staff who later became Ambassador to the United States; Chaim Bar Lev, called home swiftly from Paris and later to succeed Rabin, sat on the other side. Rabin directed the army. Rabin had made the plans. Dayan had sent the morale of the country sky-rocketing and added changes in the strategy of surprise inherent in his own personality. But the over-all strategy of the war was Rabin's.

Shy, with a boyish grin, meticulous and careful and slow-speaking, Rabin, who had long ago won the affection of the officers and soldiers in his army, captured that of the civilians in a speech he made at Mount Scopus when he was given an honorary Ph.D. "This Army, which I had the privilege of commanding through these battles, came from the people and returns to the people, to a people which rises in its hour of crisis and overcomes all enemies by virtue of its moral values and its spiritual readiness in the hour of need."

The generals of Israel seem cast from the same mold. Most of them are forty-two or forty-three; only a few, like Dayan, who was born in 1915, are in their fifties. Most of them finished high school, and then broke off their studies to join the Haganah. They fought the Germans in the Second World War, the British in '46 and '47, the Arabs in '48 and '56 and again in '67. Six top generals were ex-Palmach—Rabin, Bar Lev, Hod, Gavish, Narkiss, and Elazar. The others, like Tal and Aharon Yariv, Chief of the Intelligence Branch, had fought with the Jewish Brigade in Europe. In their thirties and forties, hungry for education, they finally returned to universities in Israel or abroad to complete their studies.

The man they had trained under in the Palmach was Itzhak Sadeh, a writer, a perfectionist, and an arctic enthusiast. (On bitter cold winter days, when the Mediterranean could be freezing cold, Sadeh would invite his friends to join him in his early morning dip.) He cast Israel's future generals in his own mold. He was a man who knew no fear, a creative artist who gave the army a sense of destiny and soul.

The land itself had shaped the character of the generals. They were the inheritors—inheritors of the pioneers who had braved malaria and hostile Arabs to build the kibbutzim. From the moment of their birth or their arrival in Israel, they created the land and were created by it.

In May of 1967, the generals had watched the Arabs and the Soviet Union clutch at Israel's throat with fingers of fire and steel. They saw the world prepare to sit in mourning for the death of a gallant nineteen-year-old nation. The world shared the same horror, fascination, and inaction with which thirty-eight neighbors on a quiet street in New York watched a murderer attack and kill a helpless girl called Kitty Genovese.

But the Jews of Israel—soldiers, politicians, and ordinary citizens—had had many teachers; Adolf Hitler and Adolf Eichmann were only the most evil. Six million Jews were also teachers. For two thousand years Jews had been helpless, with no army to do the fighting and no land in which to fight. Now they had both.

The cohesion between the people and their army and their land had helped them win the war. The army was "flesh of the land." Knowing the populace was behind him gave every soldier the sense of belonging. Thus he could plunge forward in Sinai and pull dying men off a burning truck, even as he was dying; thus he could fling his body on barbed wire and urge his comrades to step over him; thus he could push his tank up the Syrian Heights when every tank before his was in flames.

In the midst of the war in Sinai, a soldier sat on his bunk, unable to go on. Combat fatigue and the deaths of his companions had crippled him.

Someone brought him a package with a letter from a school

child. "Dear Soldier, I am sending you this chewing gum, I am not afraid of bombs because I know you are out there protecting me and will not let anyone kill me."

The soldier stood up from his bunk and joined his comrades in the fighting. "I felt like a lion," he said.

They are all lions, I thought, watching them now at the wedding. The process of absorption had welded them together. Heterogeneous, from seventy-nine lands and seventy-nine cultures, they were now a nation eager to live, and willing to die, for each other.

Why had the Arabs not fought as they did? Egypt was homogeneous, with one land, one people, one culture, with no new immigrants to absorb. There had even been a "socialist revolution." Yet Nasser had not succeeded in welding a nation whose people had a sense of belonging and a willingness to die for their land.

The Syrians too, homogeneous, with a "leftist revolution," had failed to instill their people with a sense of national purpose. Officers had deserted soldiers, and all had fled before the Israeli army. The concrete bunkers gave them protection; but even in the bunkers there was a caste system; there was no solidarity, no sense of brotherhood, no ancient tie to the land of the Golan Heights.

Bravest of the Arabs, the Jordanians were divided in their loyalty to their own king and their government. Nasserism beguiled them; but Nasser offered them dreams of conquest, not of nationhood.

The sense of belonging had come with absorption; nowhere was the devotion of each soldier in the Israeli army to his fellow man more meaningful than in the evacuation of the wounded under fire. The Talmudic code, "He who saves a single life, it is as if he had saved the whole world," had infiltrated the very core of this army. And the dead were as precious as the living.

On the first day of the war, as Israel's pilots flew in combat over Egypt's heavily fortified positions in El Arish, a pilot was shot down in a Fouga Magister. His comrades knew he had died; there is no way of ejecting from the Fougas.

After the Israelis captured El Arish, they searched for the body of the dead pilot. It was futile. They could not imagine where the

Egyptians had buried him; it was obvious they would not have carried his body back to Egypt.

The Israelis finally decided to look among the Egyptian dead. Perhaps the Egyptians had buried him with their own soldiers. They dug up the bodies, and found him.

Their search was not lost on an Egyptian prisoner. A doctor from one of Cairo's aristocratic families, he had haughtily refused to cooperate with the Israelis; he had even refused to treat Egyptian wounded prisoners.

Now, as he watched the Israelis carry the dead pilot to head-quarters, to prepare him for the flight home, the doctor asked to see the Israeli commanding officer at El Arish.

"I want to apologize. I offer my services. I will do anything you ask; I will go anywhere you request. When I see what you do for a dead man, I understand why you won the war."

It was all here, I thought, as I stood beside the mysterious woman from North Africa . . . life and death, the importance of every single life, the obsession with survival.

As the generations of Israel milled through the garden, they seemed to tell the whole story of this land. Here were David Ben-Gurion and Chaim Gvati and Avraham Harzfeld, old pioneers, the founding fathers who had torn up the soil with their fingernails. Here was the middle generation—Moshe Dayan and Yigal Allon and Yigael Yadin, sons of the founders, who had fought all the wars—the wars against Hitler and the British and the three wars against the Arabs. And here were the grandchildren—Yaël's and Asaf's generation, more urbane than their parents and their grand-parents, more artistic, less kibbutznik, and of the three genera-tions, the most beautiful.

The faces of the Diaspora had blended and dissolved into this third generation face of Israel. They would carry on. The task of defense would be theirs. The task of absorption would be theirs.

"The Six Day War is over," Rabin had said, "but the Seventh Day, the day of rest, has not yet been gained."

15

Jerusalem on the Seventh Day

On the evening of Tish'a B'av, the ninth of Ab, the day of fasting in August when Jews mourn the destruction of the Second Temple in A.D. 70, we joined thousands of pilgrims to walk up to the Western Wall.

The people wound their way up Mount Zion, the sacred hill, past the Church of the Dormition with its newly damaged roof, through the Zion Gate arched in the Turkish stone rampart that Sultan Suleiman the Magnificent had built to wall in Jerusalem.

We climbed slowly in the moonlight. Above us and below us on the roads carved into the mountains were thousands of people moving upward, like pilgrims in a medieval painting, their faces lit by the moon in its ninth day of ascent.

There was no sadness in this Tish'a B'av. Hassidim with long curls and black caftans and sneakers danced up the winding hills. Youngsters laughed. Orthodox women, their arms and legs and heads covered, talked happily and busily.

Suddenly we were upon it—the Wall itself. Thousands and thousands of people were massed before it. Huge searchlights turned the golden yellow stone into pure white. Even the tufts of grass and weeds that had grown between the stones of the Wall seemed vibrant.

I joined the women at the right side of the Wall. Some were touching the Wall; some were reading out of prayer books; some were weeping. Some of the women lit Sabbath candles and sought

198

to place them in the Wall. A Moroccan woman who had come five years ago out of the Atlas Mountains gave me a candle and I lit it from her flame. I tried to set the candle into a niche in the Wall. It would not hold. No matter, the tallow had dripped patterns of white beauty on the stones.

For two months in Israel—living among the Jews, visiting the Arabs, retracing the steps of the army—I had tried to unravel the mystery of Jewish survival.

I stood with the women, and prayed silently. I prayed for my husband, for my children, for my mother. I prayed that there would be war no more. It was a very personal prayer; yet it seemed to come from three thousand years of Jewish history.

I walked toward my husband who was praying with the men. Here, the whole Diaspora of Jews was joined together. Men were praying in tiny groups as they had prayed in communities in Africa and Asia, in the little villages of Europe for hundreds of years. The Yemenites sat in a circle on the floor; they sang and swayed. In Yemen, they were not allowed to ride on camels; they had defied their oppressors by rocking back and forth on their dream camels.

The Hassidim shook and danced in ecstasy. A soldier with a stump for a leg leaned his crutch on the bridal-white Wall and prayed alone in silence. A group of soldiers draped their prayer shawls on their heads, and prayed together—thankful that they were whole.

People pushed little notes into the crevices of the Wall and wept. When this Wall was freed, everyone wept. The radio announcer of Kol Israel wept as he described its liberation. Atheists who were never Bar Mitzvah wept. Socialists, Marxists, dialectical materialists who had no patience for "these religious tales" wept. Sabras born after the Wall was denied them wept with men who did not dream they would see the Wall again in their lifetime.

I looked closely at the faces of the people—the German Jews, the Poles, the delicate-featured dark-skinned Jews of India and Yemen, the Moroccan women covering their heads with bandanas. I had never felt so close to them before. We were one.

I was an American and a Jew. What then was it that made me feel so close to these ear-locked graceful little men swaying on the floor, who had come out of a world hundreds of light-years away from my world in America? Why was my heart pounding, my eyes filling up as I traced the tallow of the Sabbath candles dripping everywhere on the Wall?

Standing now at the Wall, I knew that though I had been born a Jew—though I had felt a sense of becoming in years past—I had *still* needed to become a Jew. These months in Israel in the era of the seventh day were months of becoming . . . in a never-ending process.

Somehow, in front of the Wall, you confronted yourself as in a sacred mirror. You saw not alone what you were, but what you hoped to be. You saw, with tears, the errors you had made, wounds you had caused, and you prayed that here they might be forgiven. Once again, blindly, you touched the gnarled and pocked and sun-beaten stones, and a yearning to find the right way seemed to come through the stones and suffuse you.

The Wall embraced us all. We carried it with us in the lands of our Dispersion. Every Jew was a tiny stone in this Wall of Stone on a hill in a golden city. Suddenly I knew that this was the Wall of Survival.

Here at the Wall, the whole country came into focus. Israel lay below these mountains, spreading out to the desert and the sea. The years I had known this land seemed to roll in . . . the color of the Negev sand, like Sabbath loaves of bread . . . the snow-capped mountains in the north . . . the kibbutzniks and the children in the air raid shelters . . . the Hassidim in their gold silk caftans and fur hats . . . the new immigrants descending from the planes and the ships . . . the peace that begins to descend on Israel by Friday afternoon and lasts all through the Sabbath.

I had known a hundred Seventh Days in this land. There had been the Black Sabbath of Latrun in 1946 . . . the Sabbath in November 1947 when the nations of the world tore Palestine in half . . . the Sabbath eve of the birth of Israel . . . and the Sabbath end of the war in June.

It was evening and it was morning——

Chronology

1917

Nov. 2   The Balfour Declaration

1920

San Remo Conference—Britain given mandate for Palestine.

Jewish community of Palestine, made up mainly of farmers and workers, creates the Haganah (self-defense).

1922

League of Nations ratifies mandate.

1929

Jewish Agency is created in Palestine to represent the Jews; it becomes a shadow government.

Aug. 24   Sabbath slaughter of Jews in Hebron, Jerusalem, and Motza.

1933

Adolf Hitler becomes dictator of Germany.

1936

England sends Royal Commission under Lord Peel to Palestine.

1937

Peel Commission recommends partitioning of Palestine.

1939

May 17   Britain issues "White Paper" restricting Jewish immigration to Palestine to 1,500 a month for the next five years.

1939–1945

World War II. Six million Jews are murdered. Britain permits Jews of Palestine to fight Hitler in the Jewish Brigade. The Palestinian Jews fight against Rommel in the desert, against the Vichy French in Syria, and are dropped by Allied planes into Nazi-occupied Hungary, Yugoslavia, and Poland. The Arabs remain neutral or ally themselves with the Axis.

1941

Jews of Palestine create the Palmach, the striking force of the Haganah.

1944

President Franklin D. Roosevelt creates the War Refugee Board to help rescue "the victims of enemy oppression." The United States brings one thousand refugees from eighteen war-torn countries to a safe haven in Oswego, New York.

1946

Jan.   Britain and the United States set up Anglo-American Committee of Inquiry on Palestine.

April 30   Committee reports to President Truman and Foreign Minister Ernest Bevin that it has voted unanimously to allow 100,000 D.P.'s to enter Palestine.

June   Bevin scuttles the report. In Palestine Jews react with acts of sabotage and terror.

June 29   Black Saturday—British arrest thousands of Jews and imprison the leaders of the Jewish Agency in Latrun.

1947

May 15   United Nations Special Committee on Palestine (UNSCOP) is set up.

July 18   *Exodus 1947* is captured by British outside Haifa.

Sept. 1   UNSCOP recommends partitioning of Palestine, and creation of two new independent states, Jewish and Arab.

Nov. 29   United Nations General Assembly votes to partition Palestine.

1948

April 12   Arabs murder seventy-seven Jewish doctors, nurses, and students on the road to Hadassah Hospital on Mt. Scopus.

May   Massacre at Gush Etzion.

May 14   The birth of Israel. President Truman grants Israel *de facto* recognition.

May 15   Seven Arab states invade Israel. The War of Independence begins.

May 17   The U.S.S.R. recognizes Israel.

1949

Fifty thousand Yemenite Jews airlifted to Israel.

Jan. 29   Britain recognizes Israel.

Jan.–July   Dr. Ralph Bunche of the United Nations arranges armistice agreements between the Arabs and Israel on the island of Rhodes. Jordan is given most of Arab Palestine, and Egypt is given the Gaza Strip.

May 11   Israel admitted to the United Nations.

1950

May 25   France, Britain, and U.S. sign tri-partite declaration guaranteeing the borders of Middle Eastern nations.

1951

One hundred twenty thousand Jews airlifted from Iraq; thousands more flee from Arab states.

July 20   King Abdullah of Jordan is assassinated by a Moslem fanatic.

1952

July   Naguib and Nasser overthrow King Farouk of Egypt.

1954

April   Nasser overthrows Naguib.

1955

Nasser creates Fedayeen, terrorist groups under Egyptian army command.

Sept. 27   Egypt signs arms agreement with Soviet Union and Czechoslovakia—Egyptian cotton for Soviet guns.

Oct.   Egypt and Syria sign joint military command.

Dec.   Egypt obtains agreement from U.S. and Britain to finance Aswan Dam.

1956

May   Nasser establishes diplomatic relations with Red China.

July 19   John Foster Dulles announces U.S. no longer interested in financing Aswan Dam.

July 26   Nasser nationalizes Suez Canal in retaliation.

Oct. 29   War in Sinai. British, French, and Israelis plan co-ordinated attack against Egypt. Israeli armor enters Sinai and reaches Suez Canal in one hundred hours.

Nov. 2   Britain sends bombers to attack Egyptian airfields.

Nov. 3   Israeli troops take Gaza Town and Gaza Strip.

Nov. 5   English and French forces land on Egyptian soil after U.N. cease-fire is in operation. The Soviet Union recalls its ambassador from Tel Aviv.

1957

Jan.   Eisenhower Doctrine. President Eisenhower commits the United States to use its armed forces to protect Middle Eastern countries requesting help against "overt armed aggression from any nation controlled by international Communism."

March   Israel withdraws from Gaza Strip and Straits of Tiran after U.N. General Assembly enunciates doctrine of free and innocent passage through Straits and sends United Nations Emergency Force (UNEF) to take positions in Sinai, Gaza, and Sharm el Sheikh.

1958

Feb.   Syria and Egypt create United Arab Republic.

July   United States sends Marines to Lebanon, threatened by civil war.

1961

Sept.   Syria ends merger with Egypt; Egypt continues to call itself United Arab Republic.

1962

Sept.   Revolution in Yemen backed by Nasser. He sends Egyptian force of 40,000, later increased to 80,000.

Sept. 27   U.S. ends total embargo on arms to Israel.

1963

Israel begins work on the National Water Carrier, bringing water from the Sea of Galilee to the Negev.

March 28   Revolution in Syria. For eighth time in fourteen years, army overthrows civilian government.

May   President John F. Kennedy reaffirms U.S. support for territorial integrity of Israel and Arab states.

1964

Jan. Arabs meet in summit conference. Israel is the agenda.

Feb. Nasser proclaims: "It is we who will dictate the time. It is we who will dictate the place [for war with Israel]."

Nov. 7 Syrians send bulldozers to Baniyas opposite Kibbutz Dan to divert headwaters of the Jordan River.

Egypt helps form the Palestine Liberation Army, training refugees in the U.N. camps in Gaza and Jordan.

1966

Feb. Another revolution in Syria. Leftist extremists bring the leader of Syria's Communist party home from exile; relations with the Soviet Union and Nasser grow cordial. Syria begins constant sabotage and infiltration.

Aug. President Lyndon Johnson reaffirms U.S. promise to support territorial integrity of countries in the Middle East.

Nov. 4 Syria and United Arab Republic sign mutual defense pact. Soviet technicians teach Egyptians and Syrians use of the new Soviet hardware. Syria increases guerrilla warfare, infiltrating through Jordan.

Nov. 14 Israeli army raids Jordanian village of Es Samu.

1967

Feb. 23 Nasser, speaking at Cairo University, calls King Hussein, "the adulterer of the Hashemite family."

April 7 Syria attacks Kibbutz Gadot, Ein Gev, Tel Katzir, on Sea of Galilee. Israeli planes shoot down six Syrian MIG's. Egypt sends no help.

May Russia tells Egypt that Israel is preparing an invasion of Syria. Premier Levi Eshkol offers to send the Soviet Ambassador to the Syrian border to prove no troops are massing. Soviet Ambassador refuses to go.

May 15 Independence Day parade in Jerusalem. Eshkol learns that Egypt's army is massing at his border.

May 16 United Arab Republic proclaims state of emergency. Israel mobilizes.

May 18 U.A.R. asks U Thant to remove United Nations Emergency Force. Meanwhile, Nasser sends troops to Sharm el Sheikh before UNEF departs.

May 19   U Thant announces immediate withdrawal of UNEF. Seventy-three posts along Israel-Egypt border evacuated. Ahmed Shukairy's Palestine Liberation Army takes over the posts.

May 20   U.A.R. calls up reserves.

May 22   Nasser closes Gulf of Aqaba. Neither Israeli ships nor vessels carrying strategic materials to Israel allowed to sail through.

May 23   U.S.S.R. states unequivocal support for the Arabs.

May 26   Abba Eban sees President Johnson after talks in Paris and London. Johnson suggests a delay of ten days or more to work out a declaration by the maritime powers affirming the right of free passage. Johnson's plan fails. Nasser's 80,000 troops in Yemen brought home. They are sent deep into Sinai. Nasser writes in *Al-Ahram* he is "ready to undertake total war with Israel."

May 27   Algeria mobilizes.

May 28   In New York, 100,000 Jews and Christians march on Riverside Drive to demonstrate solidarity with Israel.

May 29   Morocco offers support to Nasser.

May 30   King Hussein journeys to Cairo, exchanges brotherly kisses and signs defense pact with Nasser. Egypt's General Riadh becomes commander of Hussein's Arab legionnaires. Egyptians are now in command of Jordan's army. Syria and Nasser close the circle on Israel's north. In the south Egyptian army shells Nahal Oz, a kibbutz near the Gaza Strip.

June 1   Iraqi troops and air force sent to Jordan. President Aref of Iraq gives his blessings: "My sons, this is the day of the battle and of revenge for your brothers who fell in 1948. We will meet in Tel Aviv and Haifa." Syria denounces Jordan as "the home of treason." In Israel General Moshe Dayan is brought into the Cabinet as Minister of Defense.

June 2   President de Gaulle, long a friend of Israel, declares that France will remain uncommitted and neutral in the Middle Eastern crisis. In the Gaza Strip Egyptians shell more kibbutzim, burning wheat fields, barns, and chicken houses.

June 4   Reinforcements—two Egyptian commando battalions and an Iraqi division—are sent to Jordan.

MONDAY, JUNE 5

The Six Day War begins.

7:45 A.M.   Four hundred Israeli planes bomb Egyptian airports and within eighty minutes the Egyptian air force is destroyed. Israeli armor penetrates Gaza Strip. Eshkol sends word to King Hussein through U.N. General Odd Bull: "We shall not initiate any action whatsoever against Jordan. However, should Jordan open hostilities we shall react with all our might. . . ."

10:00 A.M.   Jordan shells Jerusalem.

10:30 A.M.   Jordan's Arab Legion captures U.N. Government House on Hill of Evil Counsel.

11:00 A.M.   General Hod reports to Dayan: "I am certain there is not another bomber left in Egypt."

12:00 Noon   Syrians raid oil refinery at Haifa.

Afternoon   Jordan's air force drops bombs on Kfar Saba, 4 dead, 15 wounded.

Israeli air force attacks Damascus air base, Jordanian air fields and radar stations, and twenty-three Egyptian radar stations.

Israeli Northern Command attacks Jenin, northern apex of Big Triangle on West Bank.

3:00 P.M.   Khan Yunis and Rafiah in Gaza Strip captured.

3:50 P.M.   Israeli forces capture U.N. Government House.

5:30 P.M.   Battle for Jerusalem begins.

7:20 P.M.   Israelis capture Abdul Aziz Hill and Bet Iksa in Jerusalem.

7:30 P.M.   Jordanian long-range artillery shells Lydda, Natanya, Tel Baruch Beach, and Kfar Sirkin.

9:15 P.M.   Tel Aviv is shelled from the West Bank; direct hit on a house in Masaryk Square.

TUESDAY, JUNE 6

1:30 A.M.   Yitzhak Rabin holds press conference. Announces smashing victory in air and Sinai desert.

2:00 A.M.   Paratroopers begin campaign for Old City.

3:45 A.M.   Israelis capture Police School, UNRWA building.

4:00 A.M.   Syrians attack Kibbutz Dan, infantry and tanks penetrate within six hundred yards and are driven back.

Before dawn   Jenin on West Bank surrenders.

6:00 A.M.   Attack Sheikh Jarrah area, opening access to road to
and after   Mt. Scopus, on which seventy-seven doctors and nurses
had been massacred in 1948. Jordanians dig in on Mt.
Scopus and shell residential areas of Jerusalem.

Natanya bombed by Iraqi air force stationed in Jordan.

Nablus surrenders with scarcely a shot fired.

Gaza, encircled and captured. Egyptian and Palestine
Liberation Armies defending Gaza surrender.

El Arish and Abu Agheila fall.

Latrun, Ramallah, and Kalkilya captured.

In Galilee, ceaseless bombardment of kibbutzim and
villages by Syrians in the Golan Heights.

WEDNESDAY, JUNE 7

8:30 A.M.   Paratroopers penetrate walls of the Old City.

10:15 A.M.   Old City captured. Jordan's Arab Legion retreats in de-
and after   feat. Israel controls entire West Bank.

In Sinai columns reach Bir Gifgafa. Israeli Navy torpedo
boats reach Sharm el Sheikh. Sailors raise flag of Israel
over Straits of Tiran. Blockade is broken.

Syrians keep shelling villages in eastern upper Galilee.

THURSDAY, JUNE 8

U.S.S. *Liberty*, electronics intelligence ship, attacked by
Israel in Mediterranean.

Israel sends apology and declares she had mistaken
Liberty for Egyptian battleship. U.S. accepts apology.

FRIDAY, JUNE 9

2:00 A.M.   Israeli columns reach Suez Canal. Egypt accepts cease-
fire. War in Sinai over.

11:30 A.M.   Israeli Northern Command under General David Elazar
and after   storms Heights of Golan; captures Tel Faq'r, Tel Azaziyat.

SATURDAY, JUNE 10

Morning   Baniyas captured with heavy air support.

2:30 P.M.   Kuneitra surrenders.

7:30 P.M.   Syria accepts cease-fire. War ends.

INDEX

209